THE RAVEN'S SONG

A MEMOIR OF EARLY CHILDHOOD

by

LULA P. COOPER

CONTENTS

AUTOBIOGRAPHICAL SKETCHES

PART I: THE FAMILY

PART II: YEAR BEFORE MY BIRTH
MY BEGINNING YEARS

PART III: A TIME FOR SCHOOL
AND OTHER LEARNING

PHOTOGRAPHS

ACKNOWLEDGEMENTS

To my family, my heroes, John "Dick," Alicia, Ellen, Lynn, John, Jr.

To Willis C. Gravely, Lockland Wayne High School English teacher who encouraged my writing, my art, acting and singing

To Ethel Snyder, my best friend who insisted on my completing college which led to the writing of this work.

To Nancy Rogers, dearest friend and my "Buddy Reader-Editor."

To my maternal family for providing me with these stories.

To Geri Davis, Mae and Worth Mallory, the Sisterhood of Temple B'rith Shalom and the many others who encouraged me to publish this work.

To Nancy Owen Nelson, Ph.D, English Literature, Editor One Street Writers of Prescott, Arizona, Editorial Comments.

To John R. Carter, Sr. for his invaluable assistance in preparing this book for print.

PROLOGUE

When I embarked upon writing *The Raven's Song: a memoir of early childhood,* I began to write out of my feelings as a child and of the assessment of my home environment with maternal relatives as an emotional maelstrom. My story was to be of my growing and developing into an adult who overcame the adversities of such an environment. It was to show that I had become a person who had succeeded in helping to achieve gains in the Delaware and national civil rights movements of the 1960s, become a recipient of presidential and gubernatorial appointments, had established myself in the local arts and poetry communities and been a competent child care professional.

Ethel Snyder, my best friend for thirty-seven years, had from 1968 to 1979 tried to persuade me to complete my college education. She said to me, *"Lula you have done so much without your degree. You just need that piece of paper in case you want to go on to other things."* She was referring to my leadership of Civil Rights groups, my writing and self-publication of a book of poetry, exhibiting my paintings and, professionally, being in managerial positions from 1968 until 1980.

My third and final managerial position was as Director of the New Castle County Head Start Program headquartered in Wilmington, Delaware. In the latter case, I was responsible for the supervision of one hundred and thirty-three staff members, a million dollar budget funded by federal and state government entities to train and care for five hundred and twenty pre-school aged children.

In 1980, I took Ethel's advice and retired from public life to complete my college education. Like many women of my generation I had had college level training from 1951-54, but left to get married. In my case it was three years at Knoxville College in Knoxville, Tennessee where I had been a Dean's List student majoring in Elementary Education.

In 1968 I had discovered the Goddard College Adult Degree program information in an advertisement posted in the back of a *Saturday Review* magazine. Goddard College was located in Plainfield, Vermont. It pioneered an innovative program to help women continue their education through independent study.

The program was structured to have women come to their Vermont campus for two weeks to work with professors in the development of a Study Plan which would then be executed at home. The student was required to submit progress reports, complete annotated and general bibliographies, college classes taken, if any, and for periodic return trips to the college until completion of the required work.

Goddard's program had been in the back of my mind since 1968 and I never forgot its immediate appeal. By 1980, Goddard had a program headquartered in nearby Philadelphia, Pennsylvania, a half hour drive from my home in Wilmington, Delaware. This made the trip to Vermont for the initial contact, unnecessary.

I made my contact and submitted my resume. During my initial interview with William Meek, the Goddard Program Director, I was informed that I had more than enough life-experience to make up for the one year that I lost of college education. He recommended me for, and I was accepted into Goddard's Masters Degree program.

Because of my experience in program management, I decided to continue my education in that area. The more I thought about it, the more "dead" that felt to me and I decided to work on a degree in Creative Writing. I had not planned to write about myself. Instead, I decided to write about a woman, Grace Goens, whose life and upbringing I considered more important than my own.

After six months into my Study, I was called upon and I responded to my sister-in-law, Alice Thurman, an elementary school teacher of twenty-six years, who was dying of cancer. I assured her that I would come to Cincinnati to care for her. This I did for twenty-nine days around the clock with only naps in between. There were no eight hour nights of sleep. When she died I returned to Delaware.

While in my doctor's office, I picked up a magazine that I never would read. It was *Rod and Gun.* An article written by the friend of a local Wilmington family's son who had been murdered, caught my eye. The friend wrote, *"If there is anything that you plan to do, you'd better do it."* It was then that I decided to write my own story even though this meant giving up six months of research and ninety, ninety-minute taped interviews of my friend, Grace.

With this new direction, I engaged in the difficult task of removing a protective, inner shield behind which I had, unconsciously, hidden since childhood. Emotionally and physically I had for years tried to run away from any attachment to my grandmother who, among all of my relatives, was the one with whom I, as a very young child, spent the most hours of any given day. It was my escape from what I considered to be her shortcomings and my anger at her for the damage I felt she had done to me.

The anguished yet self-righteous attitude with which I confronted the troublesome events of childhood gave way as I worked through each of the memories. With their completion I was forced to feel and see through the dense, mental fog of suppressed anger and insecurity. Many times, with sobs and tears, I gained new insight. In the distance provided by adulthood I could recognize the care, warmth and protections I had received as a child. My family became a kaleidoscope of beautiful, flawed, human beings of whom I was a part.

Upon this deeper reflection, I gained a sense of my family's wholeness and gained a more mature understanding of them and myself. More important, I allowed myself to discover the true feelings buried within me as these related to each of the family members. I found laughter where I once thought was absurdity. I found sorrow where there truly was sorrow. I saw their triumphs where before I thought only failure existed. But the most important thing that I learned was that I loved them. This was the greatest gift from this writing.

Twenty-eight years after the completion of the original version, *Bittersweet,* the title no longer felt appropriate. For years I have observed many ravens as they flew around my current home and paused on the branches of the juniper trees. I have heard that these huge, iridescent black, birds are magical and bring good fortune.

I once heard the story of a Catholic monk who had become head of a monastery, and who had great power because he was so beloved. Threatened by and jealous of the monk's power, others tried to kill him. When one form of poisoning failed, the perpetrators gave him bread that they had poisoned. As the monk was about to put the bread into his mouth, a raven swooped down through an open window, snatched the bread in its beak and flew away - saving the monk's life.

The writing and revision of this work, like the raven rescuing the monk from the poisoned bread, has rescued me from years of anger, negative criticisms and the inability to be grateful for what family members were able to provide. These feelings and thoughts had been, like the bread, poisoning my soul. With this in mind, I changed the title from *Bittersweet* to *The Raven's Song.*

Now, I would like to introduce you to members of my maternal family.

MEMBERS OF MY MATERNAL FAMILY

STEWART FOLEY CORBIN

Stewart Foley Corbin, Maternal Grandfather
B. May 8, 1883; D. April 25, 1965

SALLY HATHAWAY GABBITT

Sally Hathaway Gabbitt, Great Grandmother and
Mother of Stewart Foley Corbin, born into slavery, then
freed. She bore my grandfather, the child of her post-
slavery, Irish employer.

MEMBERS OF MY MATERNAL FAMILY (cont'd)

LILLIAN GRAY CORBIN

Lillian Gray Corbin, Maternal Grandmother
B. March 25, 1889; D. December 25, 1965

MATTIE TYLER GRAY

JOHN "PAP" TYLER

Lillian Corbin's Mother, My Great
Grandmother
Mattie's Mother: Lucille Watson Tyler,
Full-blood Crow Indian (Absaroke)

Mattie Tyler Gray's Father
Born into slavery of enslaved mother and
Caucasian father.
My Great, Great Grandfather

PART I

THE FAMILY

1

Family History

My maternal family had its beginnings in the post-slavery era of the late 1800s in Danville and Lexington, Kentucky. My maternal grandparents, Stewart Foley Corbin and Lillian Gray Corbin, were children and grandchildren of the victims of slavery and the pre-emancipation years dating from the 1600s. Their family members experienced the oppression endured by freed persons during Reconstruction and the Post- Reconstruction eras.

My grandfather was the youngest of three children. His mother, Sally Hathaway Gabbitt, was born into slavery. Upon gaining her freedom she worked as a cook and laundress for a horse farmer of Irish descent living in Danville, Kentucky.

The story told within the family was that when this employer learned that Sally was pregnant with his child, he threatened to kill her and that she fled across the fields of his property in order to save herself and her unborn child.

With the birth of my grandfather, Stewart Foley Corbin, Sally became the single parent of three children, each by a different father. William Proctor, the eldest son, Mae Georgia Hathaway, the second child and only daughter and my grandfather, who was named after his Irish, horse farmer father.

Sally reared her children in a one-room, dirt-floored cabin with a fireplace to heat the room and to cook their meals. The two older children were responsible for my grandfather's care while their mother worked long hours.

My maternal grandmother, Lillian Beatrice Gray Corbin was the youngest and only daughter of financially stable parents who owned their own home in Lexington, Kentucky.

There is some family confusion surrounding the heritage of my grandmother's father, James Gray, Sr. One story has him being from a white family. Another story has him as the son of a white father and enslaved woman. There were three sons and a daughter of this union. The father made sure that his three sons were schooled in some Trade and established in their own businesses upon completion of their training. I believe this latter story to be closer to the truth.

My grandmother's father, James Gray, Sr. owned and operated a tinsmith business which provided a good living for his family. There was never any mention of James's mother, my great great grandmother. One of his brother's, Robert, called "Bob" was said to have considerable wealth and had a personal chauffeur. A family photograph of the two seems to confirm this.

His other brother, John, was not mentioned in the stories that were told; but of their only sister, Laura, my great, great aunt, it was said that she moved to Chicago in the early 1900s and passed for white. They never heard from her once she moved away.

My grandmother's mother, Mattie Tyler Gray, was the only child of John "Pap" and Lucille Watson Tyler. Her father, "Pap" Tyler was born into slavery and was the only son of an enslaved woman and someone of Caucasian descent whose station in life is unknown.

John "Pap" Tyler was known to be deeply religious and a Bible-carrying, Bible- quoting man of gentle demeanor who resembled Jesus. It was his fair complexion, long beard and hair that earned him this description.

Mattie Tyler Gray's mother, Lucille Watson, was said to be a full-blood Crow Indian. The Crow Nation's Native American name is Absaroke. Her Christian name was Lucille Watson. It was Lucille Watson Tyler who taught her daughter, Mattie, to be a skilled seamstress.

When my grandmother, Lillian, was growing up she was taught this same skill by her mother. The Gray household had two sources of income. One was from my great grandfather's tinsmith business and the other from my great grandmother's sewing business. James and Mattie Gray had three children, Frank, James and Lillian Beatrice. My grandmother's brothers, Frank and James, Jr., did not work with their father as tinsmiths. The city of Lexington was known for horse breeding. They preferred working with the horses.

The mixture of races and cultures in my maternal family was not unusual and owed its origins to the period of enslavement of Africans, brought to America, and Native Americans who were dispersed and established on reservations when they were removed from their lands, and their cultures compromised. During these times, enslaved persons were considered property or chattel. The women and men were often used as breeders to increase the wealth of their owners. Family structures among enslaved peoples were fractured by this system.

My grandparents met when my grandfather, recently divorced, left his home in Danville, Kentucky to look for work in Lexington. He was hired as an apprentice in the tinsmith business of my grandmother's father, James Gray, Sr.

Lillian, my grandmother, seventeen, beautiful and a high school graduate, fell in love with my grandfather who was very handsome, worldly and six years her senior. This attraction was a great disappointment to her mother, Mattie, who had high expectations for her daughter's future. She wanted her to marry a young man who lived nearby and who was training to become a doctor. This was not to be. My grandparents were married and continued to live in Lexington for a short while thereafter.

During this time Foley luxuriated in the beauty and youth of Lillian.

Before he married her, he was filled with a false pride and defiant manner. All the anger that he had felt towards his natural father was forced deep inside. He never forgave him for the rejection of him, his only son, that forced him to live for years abject poverty. He covered his temper with the physical pleasure and new life with Lillian, a child-like, lovely, innocent younger woman.

At some point my grandparents made the decision to leave their home in Kentucky and move to Ohio where they would settle and start their family.

2

Lockland, Ohio

In the early 1900s my grandparents settled in Lockland, Ohio, a manufacturing center fifteen miles north of Cincinnati. Cincinnati was a major urban center overlooking the Ohio River in southwestern Ohio. In the very early 1800s it also had been a major stop on the "Underground Railroad," the means by which escaped slaves were aided by abolitionists on their journey to Canada and freedom.

Lockland got its name because it was a lock on the Erie Canal System that made commerce between cities possible and spurred the economic development of many rural communities. It became the home to Stearns & Foster, a major producer of mattresses that originated in Cincinnati, Ohio in the 1880s before relocating to Lockland in the 1900s, when the Canal System was established. Many small businesses aided the economic strength of the area. Most businesses and the seat of government were located in the all-white section called East Lockland.

The "colored people," as African-Americans were called, lived in West Lockland. This section was bordered by the railroad tracks of the L&N Line on its western edge and by Wayne Avenue on its eastern edge.

The southern boundary for colored Lockland was Front Street, the main street that ran through this area. Front Street became Wyoming Avenue when it crossed the railroad tracks into the wealthy village of Wyoming. The northernmost street for colored Lockland was Stewart Avenue. It was a tree-lined street with large single family homes close to its intersection with Wayne Avenue. Smaller, more modest frame houses bordered the railroad tracks on its western end. These homes suffered the grime, cinders and jarring movement of long lines of freight cars rumbling over the nearby tracks as they passed. Beyond this section of Lockland was the rural area known as the "Sub-division." This unincorporated area was under Ohio State and Hamilton County jurisdictions.

From Front Street on the south and Stewart Avenue on the north of colored Lockland, ran the parallel streets of Walnut, Maple and Mulberry. The streets that ran in a perpendicular alignment to Wayne Avenue on the eastern edge to the L&N railroad tracks were Locust and Elm.

West Lockland's business district was established on Front Street. Cheap furniture and dry goods stores, a pawn shop, a small bank and convenience stores for food shopping were the main businesses. Fresh vegetables, fruits and meats were often peddled to the residents from the sides of horse-drawn farmers' wagons which followed a well-established seasonal and weekly routine. The fresh items were often subjected to canning as the way to preserve them for winter when there were shortages of such things.

The intersection of Lockland's business district at Front Street and Wayne Avenue was called "Schwartz's Corner." Not many of the West Lockland and sub-division residents understood the meaning of the word "Schwartz" or its implication when combined with "Corner." The name was used by the streetcar conductors bringing passengers from areas of downtown Cincinnati where larger stores, hospitals and jobs were located.

Accepting the name "Schwartz's Corner" when no such local edifice exhibited the name, nor any businessman was known by that name, was one of the peculiarities of west Lockland inhabitants. In those days if one person of color called another person of color, "Black," it caused many men and some women to lose their lives, especially on Saturday nights after a few drinks in a local wine bar or beer garden.

During the period of enslavement, two words with the greatest negative connotations were "black" and the "N" word used for Negro. Often these two words were used together reminding the enslaved person of his/her degrading station in life. There was a saying from those times: "If you're white you're all right. If you're yellow you're mellow. If you're brown stick around, but if you're black, get back."

Calling a person of color "black" was a fighting word. However, when the streetcar conductor made his stop at Front Streets and Wayne Avenue in colored Lockland and loudly called out, "Schwartz's Corner," the passengers of color quietly exited the streetcar.

Most of West Lockland's inhabitants, in the 1900s, worked at menial jobs in the factories and as house servants for the wealthy white families of nearby Wyoming and Glendale. The colored, professional class consisted of the ministers of the Baptist, Methodist, Congregational and Holiness or Sanctified Churches, colored teachers who taught in the neighborhood school for the colored children, Wayne Elementary School, a doctor and a dentist. West Lockland and colored Wyoming residents owned several of the businesses in their sections of the towns.

Some were grocery stores, a garage to make auto repairs and several places for people to have good times during the week, if they chose, but mainly on Friday and Saturday nights. Elite's Café was where the more serious drinkers spent their time while Little Rossie's and Tenny's Bar were as famous for their chili and barbecued ribs as they were for the beer, wine and whiskey. These sections of Lockland were known to be "rough" areas with a few small homes in between; and were primarily located on Walnut Street.

On Mulberry Street and a block away from the Congregational Church was the single house of prostitution. From its appearance anyone new to the area would never suspect what transpired inside. It was a lovely white, two-story frame house with a large wrap-around porch sitting several yards back from the street. Its lawn was well-kept and the window shades were always drawn to the outside world.

The number of people in the colored community living in Lockland was matched by the number of colored people living in the village of Wyoming, which was across the railroad tracks. The poorer children of both communities lived closest to the tracks where they fought each other with rocks and sticks.

Except for the few professionals living in Lockland most of the colored people attended the Baptist and Sanctified churches. The colored Wyoming residents and a few of Lockland's professionals considered themselves of a higher station than their neighbors. They attended the Methodist Church. The Baptist Church services were louder and longer. The Methodist Church services were quieter and shorter.

Another factor in the religious affiliation was the skin color of members. Except for a few, most of those of fair complexion appeared to attend the Methodist Church while those of the darkest complexions attended the Baptist Church. These two denominations had the largest congregations of the four in the area.

Religious affiliation did not matter when it came to Friday and Saturday night relaxation. People from both Lockland and Wyoming went to the beer gardens and wine bars, all located in colored Lockland.

One organization, the Young Men's Christian Association, provided avenues for socialization and athletics outside the churches. It sponsored programs for both girls and boys and was another place for the adults to take leadership roles as board and committee members to manage the Y's affairs. Other leadership opportunities were in the church and small businesses. In addition to the Y.M.C.A. there was a one-story movie theater or "show" as it was called.

Wayne Elementary School was West Lockland's only educational institution.

With the completion of eighth grade, the graduates were integrated into the East Lockland High School located in the white section of Lockland.

West Lockland became the new home of my grandparents.

The Corbins in Lockland

Lillian Gray Corbin, my grandmother, was accustomed to an environment of gentility and modest affluence in Lexington. She found the adjustment to Lockland's rough environment, difficult. Foley, my grandfather, experienced in his upbringing the life of poverty and struggle. He had a third grade education and tended bar before learning the work of a tinsmith from his father-in-law. He, unlike my grandmother, was more accepting of the Lockland's rough, working-class environment.

They settled into one of the small frame houses on Elm Street not far from the railroad tracks. My grandfather at twenty-four found work as a tinsmith with a small business across the tracks in Wyoming, while my grandmother at eighteen adjusted to the life of homemaker.

Between 1916 and 1921 the family grew to include five beautiful and energetic children. Robert, the eldest and only boy, was followed by Irene, my aunt, Ethel, my mother, and my two other aunts, Catherine and Crystal. All except Robert were known by nicknames within the family and to neighbors and their friends. Stories were told that "Corn" or "my little Corn" was Irene because she had attempted to smoke corn silk at one time. It made her sick and became a source of teasing and laughter. "Eckey" was my mother, Ethel. There was no story of how she got her nickname. "Hookey," my Aunt Catherine, got her nickname because she was said to be bow-legged or had hooked legs; and my Aunt Crystal, the baby, called "Lockey" or "Lockey Jane" because she had locked herself in the bathroom.

Foley and Lillian had had five children in quick succession. Lillian's mother, Mattie, died in the 1918 flu pandemic that occurred in the midst of Lillian's childbearing. This was a devastating blow and proved to be the beginning of a sickly, complaining and depressed Lillian. Her father's marriage so soon after her mother's death angered her and placed a deep strain on their relationship.

My grandmother held no fondness for her neighbors or their children. She especially resented the spinster Raymond sisters Maggie and Cora. Their house was the closest to the Corbins and they were the most inquisitive neighbors. They attempted to engage my grandmother in conversation whenever she was outside hanging up her wash or making purchases from the farmers when they were in the neighborhood with their fresh vegetables. When she did not respond they ignored her aloofness in their quest for information that would feed their gossip.

The Raymond sisters kept close tabs on the children as they played behind the little picket fence of the Corbin house.

Robert watched over his younger siblings and took this responsibility with great seriousness. He was devoted to his mother and espoused her quiet mannerly ways.

A Family Story

Monday was a usual washday. It was one of the few days that Lillian spent outdoors. Robert helped hang the clothes. Irene watched after her younger sisters.

The Raymond sisters spent hours in good weather sitting on the front porch of their quaint little house, watching the road, collecting information for gossip. They kept an immaculate house, rising early to complete their work so that the remainder of their day could be spent on the porch. In winter they peeked out from behind their curtains.

Maggie Raymond, a tall, strongly built, medium brown-skinned woman in her sixties adjusted her dust cap, the flower-banded cloth that protected her hair, and leaned over her fence and called out from across the street. "Miz Corbin that son of yours is the nicest child. The other day he helped me with my groceries and wouldn't take a cent. I don't know a soul that'd do that now-a-days."

Lillian Corbin made no reply. She took the wooden clothespin and jammed the end of it onto the clothesline securing the wet petticoat.

"He's such a handsome chile, too. You'll have to watch the girls. If I was younger, you'd have to watch out for me," Maggie laughed.

"He's the best child I have," Lillian said.

Lillian did not see Maggie Raymond nod her head in agreement.

"Robert doesn't have time for girls, Miss Raymond. He's the biggest help I have around the house," Lillian answered her, annoyance evident in her voice. She wasn't used to such brazen insinuations. It was an insult to her manners and sense of decorum.

Maggie Raymond ignored it. "I notice how he takes care of his little sisters. Playin' with 'em and keepin' 'em in that yard," she continued.

"Well, he tries to, but it's hard to do anything with Eckey. She gets away every time. I don't know what I am going to do with her."

Once she had given this much information, Lillian feared it was a signal for more verbal intrusion than she had intended.

"Hee! Hee!" Maggie Raymond laughed. "She sure is a little devil. She likes to play more than any child I know. I watch them a lot from my porch. Never seen children who could have so much fun with each other."

Whenever Lillian became pregnant, the Raymond sisters were the first to notice the change in her body. She remembered before Lockey Jane was born how they yelled across the street, "Miz Corbin, you puttin' on a little weight there?" That day she had responded, "Not that I know of." Under her breath she told her son, "They're the nosiest women. Why don't they tend to their own business?"

Robert, thinking he could rescue his mother from the neighbors said, "Mama, I'll hang up the clothes."

"No, I'll let Irene help with these."

"Do you want me to go to the store, Mama?"

"After while. I'll let you get me a nickel's worth of lard."

"I can go now, Mama, if you want me to." Robert tried to hide his eagerness. He considered it his duty to help his mother and to make her happy; but he loved to be alone, off by himself, walking the road to the store. In the spring and summer, his favorite time, he was free and could observe what the neighbors were doing. He was an intelligent and very curious child. As he made his way to the grocery store he stopped to chat with Maggie Raymond.

"Those are beautiful flowers you're growing, Miss Raymond. What kind are they?" He asked.

"Those are zinnias and over there are cornflowers." Maggie Raymond pointed to the bright red and sunny, yellow plants that were blooming in her flower garden on the streetside of the fence.

"Could you give me a few to take to Mama?"

"Why sho' chile. You sho' a thoughtful chile, thinkin' about your Mama."

Robert opened the gate and went inside. He sat on the porch talking with the Raymond sisters, displaying patience and a genuine interest in them for one so young.

Cora Raymond was always the quiet, observant one. She was fairer in her complexion than her sister and more subdued. Both had spent most of their years working for wealthy white families. A great deal of their sense of decorating their house, porch and yard showed in the lace curtains that hung from their windows and the variety of flowers they grew in their yard.

"How's your mama these days?" Maggie Raymond asked.

Cora sat forward in her rocking chair awaiting Robert's response.

"She's doing pretty well," Robert responded, squirming uncomfortably in the cane back rocker he had chosen. He knew his mother would be irritated if she knew that he was discussing her with Maggie Raymond. When she tried to ask another question he said, "I have to go now, Miss Raymond. Mama will be waiting for me to bring her the lard from the store. I don't want to be too long. Mama wasn't feeling well today."

Maggie raised her eyebrows. "Not feeling well. What's the matter with her?"

"I don't know, Miss Raymond."

"Well, the flowers will make her feel a lot better. How're yo' lil' sisters?" Maggie got in another question.

"They're all fine."

"Yo' mama sho' keeps them close in that yard."

"Yes, mam, she does," Robert answered politely; but he kept shifting back and forth, anxious to leave.

"How's yo' daddy?"

"He's just fine, too."

"Don't see much of him."

"No, mam. He leaves for work real early."

"Yo' mama's not makin' another little one is she?"

The question was finally out. Robert cringed. "I don't think so, Miss Raymond."

He was embarrassed. The blood rushed to his face. With his light complexion, he could not hide this reddening from Maggie Raymond. Robert stared down at his scuffed up shoes.

"I'd better go now, Miss Raymond," he repeated. "Thanks for the flowers. I'll tell Mama you asked about her."

"Yo're welcome, chile. You do just that," Maggie Raymond smiled.

Robert walked briskly along the road to the store, past the fenced yard of the James family whose children were their playmates. He spoke to everyone he saw as he went.

At thirteen, Robert loved Lockland. He loved the railroad tracks that ran behind their house and the adventure they provided.

On Sunday afternoons, when the weather was nice, his father took Robert and his sisters for a walk along the railroad tracks. They walked until they came to a thicket that led down to a small, quiet creek.

12

THE CORBIN CHILDREN

(l to r) My mother, Ethel Corbin, "Eckey," b. June 21, 1917 d. October 3, 1998. Uncle Robert Corbin, "Uncle Bobby," b. March 13, 1915 d. 1980. Aunt Catherine Corbin, "Hookey," b. October 9, 1918, d. February 21, 1991. Aunt Irene Corbin, "Corn" "Reenie," b. October 31, 1916, d. June, 2004. Aunt Crystal Corbin, "Lockey Jane," the baby being held by Robert, b. December 25, 1919. (As of July 2010 living in Cincinnati, Ohio).

4

A Story as Told of a Sunday Outing

It was a game the Corbin children played each weekend. Who would ask Daddy to take them to the creek?

"You ask him, Lockey Jane," Irene and Hookey begged the youngest sibling.

She was a plump, pretty child with skin the look of rich cream like her four older siblings. She had a face as full of freckles, like her father and long, silken braids. A streak of brownish red hair ran down the center of her head.

"Uh uh!" Lockey Jane shook her head. "I'm scared."

"Hookey, you ask him. He'll take us if you ask him," Irene said.

Hookey as they called Catherine, was slightly bow-legged with thick, short black-brown hair. She too had her father's freckles.

"No. I'm scared, too," Hookey replied.

"Scared? What are you scared of?" Irene asked.

She was the tallest with a thin, soulful face, quiet, alert and mature beyond her years. Laughter showed in her dark eyes.

"Never mind. I'll ask him," Robert said, tired of the bickering.

When their mother, Lillian, heard the children, she called out from the tiny kitchen where she was preparing Sunday dinner.

"I don't want you all to go nowhere in your good clothes. And don't go getting wet like you did last time."

Lillian, taught to be an accomplished seamstress by her mother, made the children's clothes. Each day the girls wore large, satin bows in their hair even when they wore play clothes. Their father listened to the chatter from a back room where he had been relaxing on his day off from work. He got up from his chair to join the others.

"They can't swim no how," Foley laughed. "Where's Eckey?" he asked, seeing that she was the only one missing from the group.

Ethel the second oldest daughter, was called Eckey.

"She went out to play with Anna," Lockey Jane volunteered.

Hookey hit her on the thigh for telling.

"I told her not to go out of this yard," Lillian whined.

"She's so hard-headed. Robert, go up there and bring her home right this minute; and tell her I'm going to tan her bottom good when she gets here!"

Robert did as he was told. He found his younger sister and herded her home in spite of her loud protestations.

"Mama's not going to let us go. Why can't I stay and play?" Eckey cried.

"Because you can't. Besides, Daddy is waiting for us," Robert scolded her.

At eleven Eckey was a beautiful child with three silken braids and a wide, satin bow in her hair. Everyone said that she looked just like a gypsy with thin, even features and strong, high cheek bones. Her eyes flashed with enthusiasm and determination. They revealed her free-spirited nature.

Eckey did not get "tanned" when she got home. Lillian fussed, but often did not carry out her threatened punishment. She was frail and complained most of the time. Robert and Irene took her sickly state to heart and did most of the work hoping to relieve her stress and encourage a smile from time to time.

After the children put on their play clothes, they headed for the trek along the tracks with their father. Lillian remained at home completing her preparations for their Sunday dinner and resting.

"I'm walkin' with my daddy," Hookey insisted.

Lockey Jane skipped alongside her older sister, Irene. Eckey ran ahead. Robert joined Hookey and walked beside his father happy to be out of the house. Foley scanned the tracks and smiled, "Now, if you hear a train comin' run for the side of the hill there. Don't want none of you gettin' run over by that fast one that comes through here."

He pointed to an easy incline away from the tracks.

"I'll keep watch," he said. "But you all have to be on the lookout. Remember you have to listen, too."

This was their father's standard direction no matter how many times they walked the tracks to the creek. A fast train could appear so quickly that escaping being run over was a major priority. The people living near the tracks were always alert to the danger.

"I been meanin' to get myself a watch," their father told them.

He never did and after years of living with the trains at his back door, their schedule was second nature to him-a part of his blood.

The long, arduously slow-moving freights pulled past usually near two in the afternoon when the sun sat catty-corner in the sky above the narrow, two and three room frame houses. At three-thirty the fast passenger train, a gleaming silver comet, moved past so fast that the elaborate dining cars became a blur of white made by the linen tablecloths. It was the only flash of elegance that people would see as the Silver Streak passed.

"Now it's the fast train we want to watch out for. Let's make it back home before that rascal comes through," Foley said.

The railroad tracks defied the monotony of the landscape, as they curved into the shimmering summer heat.

"Look, Daddy," Robert cried out.

He pointed a long, tanned arm skyward toward a dark, gliding creature.

"Is that a chicken hawk or a crow?" he asked. "I can't tell."

"Mighty big for a crow." Foley squinted. "But maybe not. Looks too small for a chicken hawk," he said, shading his eyes with his hands.

Eckey gathered the pebbles along the ties and pitched them into the weeds.

16

"Don't get too far ahead, Eckey," Foley warned.

"I'm not! I'm just right here." Eckey jerked herself towards him, annoyed.

Lockey Jane held tight to Irene's hand staring stonily ahead intently watching as her father had cautioned. "Is that a train coming?" she asked, pointing her small finger up the tracks.

"Where?" Irene asked, her heart starting to pound.

"Up there! Up the track."

Irene squinted, shading her eyes against the sun's glare. She had heard nothing, but knew you had to be very cautious. "No, Lockey Jane. That's no train. You almost scared me to death," she laughed.

"Well, what is it then? It looks like a train!" she insisted.

"It's just the heat from the tracks. You sure have a good imagination."

"Are you sure, Corn?"

"Sure, I'm sure! Listen."

They stood still not daring to breathe lest Lockey Jane mistake that for the sound of a train.

"Put your head on the track," their father called out to them. "That way you can feel the train's vibration, even if the train's a long way off."

"No, Daddy. I'm not going to do that!" Lockey Jane responded.

Robert laughed as he continued to watch the birds and tripped over one of the railroad ties.

"I've decided it's a chicken hawk, Daddy."

The bird swooped then glided for a time, was caught by a downdraft and then swept rapidly towards earth. Just as Robert thought it was about to collide with the ground, it quickly rose. To him, the bird's world epitomized freedom - soaring into the heavens, serene. He was mesmerized. Robert took off and in a burst of speed ran across the ties, faster and faster.

"Look at Robert go," Hookey shouted gleefully.

Eckey picked up his cue racing after him braids flapping behind her. Robert turned to race back to the group. Ethel waited for him and raced him to where their father stood laughing.

"Eckey, you think you'll ever beat him running?" her father asked.

"Unhuh. He's too fast now; but I'll beat him next time."

The air grew still. The sun grew hotter. As they neared the bend in the track, the children grew more tired. But, they were nearing the path that led down to the creek and the cool, still water.

Robert sprinted toward the weeds lining the path. The path was worn and dusty through high, tough, grass. Straw- like from the dry, hot days, it resembled the hay from a farmer's field. Then, Robert noticed the tall, golden flowers. "See those flowers over there?" he called out. "They're called cornflowers."

Robert puffed up with pride having learned the new word from the Raymond Sisters.

When they arrived at the creek, the water was low.

"Can we go in swimming, Daddy?" Robert asked.

"*You* can, but these gals just better wait 'til I rest up."

"Awwww, Daddy, can't we just wade along the edge?" Irene pleaded. She almost knew how to swim and was losing her fear of water.

Robert wandered towards a tree hanging over the deepest part of the creek. He took off his shirt and pants, stripped down to his shorts and hurled himself into the water. His, tan, muscular body cut through the murky water. He was cooled and refreshed.

"Robert swims like a fish," said an admiring Lockey Jane.

"You don't know how a fish swims," teased her father.

"I do, too, Daddy," she pouted. "And, I want to go swimming, too."

18

"All right! All right! Hold your horses you little piss ant." Foley removed his overalls covering his cut-off pants and waded in. Then, he beckoned to Lockey Jane.

"I don't wanna swim, Daddy," said a brooding Eckey. "I want to fish."

She had brought some twine from home and had gotten a fish hook from her father's tool kit. Both were stuffed in the pocket of her dress.

"All right then, but find a good, long stick and a quiet place not so far that I can't keep an eye on you."

"Corn got some chicken liver for bait so we can catch the crawdads."

"Where'd she get them?" Foley asked Hookey.

"She took a few from what Mama had in the ice box."

"I bet your Mammy fussed about that one. I can hear her mouth now."

Their father laughed.

Whenever he had something to tease about or to criticize Lillian, he called her, "your mammy." When he wanted to support Lillian, he told the children, "Do what your mother says, now."

"No she didn't, Daddy. I didn't tell her I got them," Irene divulged. A sly grin lit up her face.

"I want to catch crawdads to take home," Hookey announced.

"Okay. Okay. Just hold your horses," Foley told her.

Robert listened as they chattered away. He watched as his father took Lockey Jane on his stomach and began his backstroke with her holding tight.

He wished for a moment to be little again, not to know how to swim so that his father would carry him on his stomach like he was now carrying his baby sister. But then he remembered that when he didn't know how to swim, his father had just tossed him in and told him to "kick."

Now, he could do things for himself; and in this independence had lost the little physical contact that he once had with his father. They touched, but only with their comfortable silences and a few, short responses. At times his father spoke up for him when his mother requested that he do certain jobs, like the dishes. "Robert doesn't need to do dishes," he heard him say. "What're tryin' to do, make a sissy out of him?"

In his attempts to keep the peace, Foley often said one thing then proceeded to do exactly what he was criticizing. This time, he put on Lillian's apron, grabbed a towel and helped Robert as he laughed at how he himself looked in the woman's apron. "That woman's tryin' to make a sissy out of me, too," he had laughed.

'What's a sissy, Dad?' Robert remembered asking. "A sissy ain't nothin' but a boy who acts like a gal," came the answer.

It made no sense to Robert, but since his father was uncomfortable with him doing the dishes, Robert encouraged Irene to do the dishes as soon as she was big enough.

Robert floated on top of the cool, soothing water. He was physically away, but he mentally could not free himself from thinking about the family. If his father was a man of few words, his mother was a very talkative woman. Lillian talked from the time she got up until the time she went to bed. It was Robert and Irene who listened to every word.

When it was just the two of them, his mother talked at times of pleasant things. "When I was this high," she told him holding her hand a few feet from the bare, wooden floor, "my mother gave me my first piece to sew. It was a little six inch square of muslin. I made tiny stitches and long, basting stitches all by hand."

Robert envisioned his mother as a little girl quietly sitting by her mother, stitching.

She told him, "I worked with that piece every day, sitting by Mama as she sewed dresses for people and talked. When I was little, she made me the prettiest dresses. She made under things, too. She sewed all day while Daddy ran his tinsmith business."

"Mama's handwork was perfection," Lillian said. "My brothers, James and Frank, didn't stay around the house much. They were off with Daddy. But soon as they got big enough, they went to work around the race horses. You know Lexington was known for the horses. My brothers loved the horses. Daddy wanted them to work with him. But they didn't. They thought Daddy was mean."

Listening to his mother was the way that Robert learned about his relatives living in Lexington, Kentucky. They visited Grandfather Gray and he seemed nice enough to him. He did not seem "mean" like his mother said. His grandmother Gray died of the flu in the pandemic of 1918. This was shortly after Hookey was born. His mother said that she was alone in the world now that her best and only friend was gone.

On a few occasions his mother's Uncle Bob came to visit. How Robert's eyes bulged as they stood along their yard's picket fence, surveying his chauffeur-driven car. Their Great Uncle Bob was wealthy their mother had told them. She said that he had never married, and that he idolized her, his only niece. Her father may have been mean, but her Uncle Bob was extremely nice and generous.

Their Grandfather Gray never came to visit. Shortly after his wife's death, he married a woman twenty years his junior who was just a few years older than his daughter, Lillian. He and his new wife had five girls all just a few years younger than Robert, and his sisters. Lillian was so angry at her father that she never had a kind word for him as she seemed to continue mourning her mother. But still they, the children, liked their Grandfather Gray.

A shrill voice shocked Robert out of his reverie.

"Look, Daddy. I got one! I got one!"

It was Eckey rushing from the far side of the creek where she had been fishing. Her hand-me-down dress was now hanging off her thin shoulder. The hem hung lopsided. Robert emerged from the creek laughing to himself. Eckey dangled a tiny Sunfish from the end of her string.

"I'll be darn," Foley beamed. "Look at that. You little devil. You sure got one."

"Let me see it, Eckey," Robert asked. It was a pitiful little fish, he thought. "Are you going to keep it?"

"Ummmhuh. Going to take it home and show Mama." She turned it away from Robert's scrutiny.

"But, it's so little," he said. "Why don't you throw it back?"

"I'm going to keep it. I caught it," Eckey said with finality.

Corn and Hookey, who had been patiently and carefully turning over rocks, waded along the bank to where the little group was examining Eckey's fish.

"We got a whole lot of crawdads, Daddy. Over there's lots and lots of 'em. But, you have to be real quiet," Irene said.

Just then Foley looked up at the sky. From the sun's position he knew it was getting late. He turned back to the children. "Looks like we'd better start headin' for home."

"Aw, Daddy, not yet," the children whined. We just got here."

"If we don't get a move on, your Mammy's goin' to skin me alive."

They heard the train just as they were walking through a vast, patch of tall grass.

"Train's comin' now, Dad," Robert shouted from his watch at the head of the line.

"Too late doggone it!" Foley said.

The Silver Streak passed the tired but happy group. Robert counted the cars. "Fifteen, Dad! Fifteen! And not including the caboose."

When the caboose passed, Foley said, "Well, that's it. We can get goin', now."

They dragged themselves up the hill to the vacant, silent tracks and finally walked through the gate. They were home.

Lillian was waiting on the front porch, thin face, more sallow in its frown.

"Oh! Oh!" Foley said. "We're in a peck of trouble."

"Whyn't you just stay all day," Lillian pouted. "Just up and leavin' me by myself all that time."

"Well, I'd have thought you'd like some peace and quiet for awhile. You're always fussin' about not havin' a minute's peace," Foley said.

"Well, I do but it doesn't have to last forever."

"Look at the fish Eckey caught, Mama," Robert said. "…and the crawdads Hookey and Irene got."

"Well, who's going to clean 'em? I'm not." Lillian continued to be angry.

"Daddy took me swimmin' Mama," Lockey Jane volunteered. Hookey poked her again.

"I told you not to let them go in the water," Lillian scolded Foley.

"A little water never hurt anybody, woman. Might even do you some good," he retorted.

"What do you mean by that!? I take my bath every Saturday. I don't know why you'd want to lie like that," she complained.

"It was a lot of fun, Mama. You should've come with us," Irene responded. She wanted to soothe her mother and avoid trouble.

"We all can't go lollygaggin' all day. Somebody has to do the work around here. Standin' over a hot stove cooking all day on Sunday."

"I'll help, Mama," Robert offered. "I'll set the table for supper."

"You all get cleaned up first," Lillian said, retaining her irritability.

There was no soothing her. Robert knew it as they walked solemnly into the house.

In the early morning hours, Robert awakened to the sound of his mother's hysterical voice.

"You don't love me. You never did. I haven't known anything but misery ever since I left home."

"Aw, why don't you grow up?" his father was saying. His voice was low, but strained.

"All you do is whine and complain all the time. Your mammy just turned you into a spoiled brat." His father's voice grew quieter and his mother's louder.

"I should've stayed with my mother. She warned me about marryin' you."

"Your mammy didn't know nothin', Sister."

"She knew that a divorced man was no good."

Robert's heart pounded. Who was divorced? Was it Daddy? He thought to himself. What did his mother mean?

"Your mammy was nothin' but an old griper. She didn't know a damn thing about my business. I don't want to hear anymore talk," Foley said, his voice steeled.

His mother kept talking, "No wonder that woman left you for another man. You haven't changed..."

Robert wondered why they were arguing. What had happened to start it up again?

Was it their going to the creek and leaving her alone? As he continued his scared, cautious listening, his sisters slept soundly through the conflict.

"All these children to take care of...no money...no nothin'," his mother was saying.

Robert could hear as she started to cry.

"I'm not used to living this way. I don't know why I ever married you. I was too nice for you."

His father remained silent. His mother continued, "That's what it is. You want some old, slut. Some old, no account woman."

This was the first time, in spite of all the times she fussed, that Robert had heard his mother refer to his father's earlier marriage. Then he heard it, the crash, the loud sound of someone falling, hitting the floor. He heard his mother's scream.

In an instant, he was on his feet. He rushed up the narrow staircase to the only room on the upper floor of the tiny house. In his parent's bedroom he saw his mother. She lay on the floor near the bed, crying and holding her stomach.

"Daddy, don't!" Robert did not recognize his own voice. It was more like a croak...hoarse in its terror.

His father's face was contorted with rage. The sound of his son shouting at him brought him to himself. He lowered his foot.

Foley had pushed his wife out of bed; then he kicked her once and had raised his bare foot, a lethal weapon, to kick again.

Robert ran to his mother and helped her up from the floor. She leaned on him, sobbing. The other children, still sleeping, had not heard the commotion.

"It's all right, Mama. It's all right," Robert said, trying to reassure her. His thirteen years now seemed like forty. He felt ill. The vomit pulsed into his mouth and then receded. He must not be sick, he told himself.

He helped the whimpering figure back to bed. She seemed so fragile, so delicate with her dark hair, now damp with perspiration, streaming from her face to her shoulders. When she was not angry or hurt his mother was the most beautiful woman he knew. He adored her. Even Miss Raymond and the other ladies acknowledged that. Now, she seemed doll-like and vulnerable. Robert felt his own vulnerability. He could not protect his mother from his father's anger and rage. He could not protect her from hurt.

Foley, only a few hours earlier was smiling, laughing; the freckles dancing on his handsome, ruddy, face. Now, he slumped on the side of the bed. Memories of the past explosions, three to be exact, flooded his mind.

Yes, Foley Corbin remembered them well. As a little boy, he had once and only once disobeyed, his mother, Sally Hathaway Gabbitt. She was away at work all day. She told him to have the fire laid by the time she got home. He had been playing and forgot his chore. He had disobeyed. His mother said nothing when she got home. She busied herself and laid the fire as he, his sister, Mae Georgia, and brother, Will, watched.

Then, his mother asked him why he had not done his work. Embarrassed, he gave a flippant response. The next thing he remembered was the searing pain from the flames.

His mother had, with one swift fling of the back of her hand, knocked him into the fireplace. She walked away and just left him there.

All he remembered was the burning sensation and his brother, Will, screaming as he pulled him from the fire. Mae Georgia cringed in disbelief. His mother went about the business of preparing the evening meal for her three, fatherless children. The scar from that burn lasted him the rest of his life; and not only on his arm.

When he was a teenager his natural father gave him work on his farm. Foley desperately wanted to be recognized by his father, to be called son not just to get the meager clothes and the farmhand job he had been given. He wanted true recognition from the Irish farmer, who had not claimed him, who tried to kill his mother when he learned of her pregnancy. One day, when he had finished working in the barn putting in feed for the horses, he approached his father. He demanded money, his birthright, so he felt. Foley's father exploded with rage by what he perceived as Foley's arrogance. His father ordered him off the farm and never to return.

When he recounted his story to his mother, her response was that he was "just like his old, mean, white daddy." He never forgot this.

Foley's third bout of rage came as an adult. He had walked in on his wife with another man. The explosive anger, an inheritance from both his parents, welled up inside of him. He almost killed the man and seriously hurt his wife.

For all those who knew him or met him at the bar where he had worked, Foley was the perfect bartender. He laughed a lot. He was gentle and accommodating. He never said a mean or cross word. *This* Foley, the one with the volcanic blind rage, no one but those who lived with him, knew.

Foley felt justified in what he had just done to Lillian. He felt her behavior recollective of all the uncaring and unsympathetic people in his life.

The house was still now. His own son stood stark still in terror, tears streaming down his face in the wake of the violence. Robert could not, did not want to look at his father. His father, too ashamed, did not want to look at him. Robert gently pulled the covers over his mother, assuring himself that she was comfortable. When he saw that his father had calmed down, he left the room.

Robert did not sleep. He did not want to sleep. He only wanted to lie there waiting to hear if his mother cried out again if she needed him.

The next morning the doctor came. Lillian lay in pain throughout the day. Robert and Irene kept the children quiet and away from their mother. By evening it was over. Maggie Raymond came to help. Lillian had miscarried. It would have been her sixth child. She had been two months pregnant.

Robert could not erase that scene from his mind as much and as hard as he tried. Life suddenly became a cold crypt that sealed his feelings inside.

Foley returned to his calm, teasing and sometimes sarcastic self. He said nothing about the night and its violence. It was as if it had never happened. He never again raised his hand against his wife.

5

The Growing Family and a Great Depression

Catherine, called Hookey, the fourth child was pensive and unsmiling.

"How come she don't have hair like the rest of 'um?" Miss Raymond asked Lillian.

Maggie Raymond and her sister made constant comparisons of the Corbin children while they sat on their porch gossiping. Their talk was always about who had the "better" hair and who had the lightest skin coloring.

"She takes after her daddy. He had wavy hair, just like hers, when he was a boy," she answered.

Sometimes the neighbor women said, "She don't look like the rest of 'um, does she?"

They expected Lillian to agree with them. She didn't. But, this was no consolation to Hookey who, though unable to understand the words, sensed the meaning of the tone.

She was "different" that's what the words and tone of their voices said to her. To Hookey, her being "different" was different from the way that Lockey Jane, the pretty baby, or Eckey, the beautiful, stubborn child and Robert, the handsome one and "Corn," the pretty, nice, helpful one, were different. She felt that her being "different" meant that she was ugly "different."

No one had to say the word. Lillian tired of the questions and the hidden insinuations said to her husband, "It's as if she's not your child. Any fool can see that she looks just like you; and is just as mean and ornery as you!"

"Well, maybe she ain't mine," Foley teased Lillian as he awaited the calculated response.

"Well, who else's could she be if she ain't yours!? Lillian retorted. "I never had nobody but you."

"Can't prove it by me, Sister," he chuckled.

Lillian bristled, "I was a perfectly innocent child when I met you."

Hookey heard it all and so did others. Her siblings developed a protective attitude towards her and were tolerant of her quiet, unsmiling ways. Robert, Corn, Eckey and Lockey Jane became Lillian's children. Lillian said that Hookey was "her daddy's child."

Lockey Jane and Hookey were a year apart and close together in everything they did, as if they were twins. Being the baby in the family, Lockey Jane, was given the most attention. She was very quiet, but also very pleasant. This demeanor remained with her as she got older. Corn and Eckey, her oldest sisters, cared for and spoiled her as if she was a delicate, china doll.

Lillian insisted on keeping the children close to home and each other. She made her intentions clear by letting them know that the other children on Elm Street were unlike them. These children were, in her words, "black, dirty and snotty-nosed." This she said with obvious disdain in her voice.

All of the Corbin children listened as their mother extolled their virtues over those of the neighbor children, but the first chance they had to be outside of the fence, legitimately, they played and grew friendly with the other children.

Lillian imitated her mother by the manner in which she reared her brood. She wanted clean, pretty children kept close to home and raised properly. She ran an orderly house. Monday was for washing and Tuesday was for ironing; but with five growing children and her constant illnesses, it was a nearly impossible assignment for her to maintain. Still she clung to it issuing, from her sick bed, the call which Robert and Irene faithfully obeyed. Eckey did not.

Eckey was the third child, restless and in a hurry. Helping in the house was not her idea of fun. The picket fence that Lillian and Foley had around the yard was sufficient restraint for Hookey and Lockey Jane. It was not sufficient for the meanderings of Eckey. Eckey was afraid to argue back at Lillian, but forgot all of her mother's admonitions when sky, wind and warm weather beckoned her.

The boys in the neighborhood were Eckey's best friends. She often beat them up, outran them, and except for the closest neighbor, James, Jr. and the older Jones boys, out hit them in baseball. She was their equal in school as well. Like them, it took her forever to learn her arithmetic times tables and, like them, she had no love for books.

Irene, called *Corn*, *My Little Corn*, or *Reenie*, the eldest of the four daughters, quickly took on the role of caretaker because of her mother's illnesses. She joined Robert in accepting more and more household responsibility. The other siblings had a childhood. Robert and Irene did not. Except for Eckey, they obeyed their mother's rule about not going beyond the picket fence.

Wayne Elementary School was attended by all the neighborhood children. It was within easy walking distance of the Corbin home. Robert, Corn, Hookey and Lockey Jane were excellent students and were well-liked by their teachers. Eckey was the only one of the children who did not excel academically. She did not like school, but she was an excellent athlete and had a beautiful singing voice. As one of the prettiest girls in the school, Eckey was the teacher's pet when it came to stage performances and school sports.

The Corbin children received high praise from their father for excelling academically. Eckey received his admiration for her performances on stage.

Lillian's response to her children's successes was to recount how she had been the teacher's pet when she was a girl in school.

"You weren't no teacher's pet," her husband Foley chided, "You were just a spoiled, little brat."

"I was, too, teacher's pet. You don't know nothin' about school. You didn't go past the third grade," Lillian argued back.

"Didn't need to, Sister," he replied. "I just passed by the school and was smarter than you," he laughed.

"That's what you think!"

The children listened as their school successes were lost in their parents' bickering.

The picket fence was a boundary that Hookey and Lockey Jane did not cross. They were not going to incur the anger of their mother. Eckey left the yard whenever her mother wasn't looking. Robert was always sent to get her. She broke the rule so many times that her mother told her, "You galavant around just like a gypsy. I should have given you to them when they wanted to take you. You're hard-headed and never mind me!"

Lillian was referring to a story of the time when Eckey was a toddler playing in their front yard. A band of gypsies traveling through the area saw her and, according to Lillian, told her that Eckey looked like them and that she really belonged with them. They asked Lillian to give Eckey to them.

Lillian said that she was so frightened that she hurried all the children into the house and would not let them out to resume their play until there was no sign of the gypsies.

The "behind the picket fence rule" remained the rule for the two younger girls, but the rules changed when the three older children grew into their teen years. During these years Robert, Corn and Eckey were allowed to go to the Y.M.C.A. for sports and Saturday dances. Here, they could mingle with those in their high school classes.

Although Lillian continued to complain about her frail condition and unhappiness with their impoverished lifestyle the family appeared to be doing as well as any of their neighbors. Foley had his work and his drinking buddies at Little Rossie's. He rarely complained.

October 29, 1929 came. "Black Tuesday" and the Stock Market Crash sent the country into a disastrous, economic tailspin. Wealthy people jumped out of windows and off the nation's bridges. People of modest means, like the Corbins, slid further into the depths of poverty.

During this same period, Robert turned sixteen, Corn turned fifteen and Eckey turned thirteen. The two adolescent children, Hookey and Lockey Jane, were eleven and ten.

Within a matter of weeks after "Black Tuesday," Foley lost his job at Dougherty's Tin Shop in the nearby Village of Wyoming. He sat at home whittling to pass the vacant, idle days while Lillian pleaded with him to get the charity food and clothing being offered the poor, colored people of Lockland. A fierce pride and stubbornness kept him firmly seated in his chair at home, with his whittling knife and a block of wood in his hands.

"We'll starve if you don't do something," Lillian cried.

"Well, I ain't standin' in no charity line. We don't need no charity," he insisted.

"That's the dumbest, fool thing I ever heard when we don't have nothin' in the house to eat. You just have to do something," Lillian pleaded.

When it was spring, the weather warm and the dandelions in bloom, Foley took the children to gather dandelion greens. The tender shoots provided a meal. Sometimes the dandelion greens were mixed with Polk greens. Hard-boiled eggs and cornbread brought variety to this meal.

Foley said that he didn't have to do "nothin but die" and went his way with the children. The Corbin children listened to their parents' arguing and, except for their empty stomachs and fraying clothing, were torn between feeling terrible about the Depression and having fun picking dandelion greens with their father.

Lillian cried, blew her nose, put on her street clothes and called out for Robert to join her. These two stood in the charity lines for food and the hand-me-down clothes.

Hookey resented being poor. She did not like the "Mammy-made clothes" that Lillian created for them. She did not like wearing Irene and Eckey's hand-me-down dresses made out of the cheap, printed cotton, flour sacks that Lillian bought at the dry goods store.

Corn, Lockey Jane and Hookey, at times, refused to wear the old clothes and shoes, but Eckey paid them no attention. It was fine with her as long as the things kept her warm in winter and lightly covered in the summer.

The Lockland Y.M.C.A., located near the Corbin home next to the Lockland Wayne Elementary School, was a major social outlet for Robert, Irene and Eckey. They were able to get away, if only momentarily, from the unhappiness that pervaded their home and escape the Depression's heavy weight on the family.

Robert's interest was in the Y's body building program. He wasn't a tall young man, but he had a robust build. His body became sturdy and rock solid and he liked associating with boys his own age. Many were registered in the boxing program, but boxing did not appeal to Robert despite his build.

Participating in sports and the dances at the Y.M.C.A. were the best times for Irene and Eckey. They especially looked forward to Saturday night and the dances.

"Eckey, you goin' up to the Y in that old sailor dress?" Corn asked.

They were getting ready for the Saturday dance. The sailor dress was one of the items in the latest charity box. Eckey had selected it.

"Ummmhuh. Ain't nothin' wrong with this dress," Eckey answered.

"It doesn't have a belt and it's miles too big for you."

"No, it ain't."

"Yes it is, Eckey. Look here."

Corn held the billowing dress out from Eckey's thin waist.

"It's just fine with me," Eckey insisted and walked out, heading for the dance.

Corn said that Eckey got more dances than anyone there as she "sashayed" around in that old, charity dress and shoes that were too big.

Over Lillian's protest, the next week Foley gave in to Eckey and Corn's requests to have their hair "bobbed." Lillian did not want her girls looking "too grown." She did not want them attracting too much attention from the teenage boys. It was all to no avail.

Foley set a chair in the middle of the kitchen. Eckey was first. She sat very still as her braids fell to her lap. Foley cut through the thickness using his wife's best sewing scissors. He cut the braids three inches from the scalp.

"Now, you look like a little boy for sure," he teased. "Go look at yourself in the mirror."

Eckey rushed to see her new image only to find that her father was teasing. He had cut off only two of her braids. The third braid still hung, isolated, down her back.

"Aww, Daddy. You're not finished yet," she laughed.

The third braid fell off as Foley cackled, "Now, your head looks just like a duck's behind."

Scared, Eckey dashed to the mirror again, and again she saw that it, too, was to her liking. She said, "It looks just fine with me, Daddy. Thanks!"

Foley repeated his cutting steps with Irene who, having seen Eckey's hair being cut did not have any fears for her own braids coming off. She washed her freshly, bobbed hair, letting it dry into thick, silky, black curls. Eckey did the same.

While the two girls preened with their new, stylish hairdos, their father gathered up the long, thick braids from the faded linoleum that covered the kitchen floor.

He tied bright red ribbons on one end of each and secured the other ends with a string.

He placed the braids in the tin box in his top dresser drawer. Foley had kept this box since his youth. It was his place for old photographs of his mother, Sally Hathaway Gabbitt, his brother Will Proctor, now a preacher in Lexington, some agates and fading Confederate money. His daughters' braids marked the first phase of their "rites of passage."

With Corn's hair newly bobbed she did indeed look more grown up as her mother feared. She looked very stylish for her fifteen years and was able to get a job as ticket seller at the local movie theater. Each week she brought her pay home and immediately turned it over to her mother to help with expenses.

Eckey liked the freedom and the time she saved with her new, hair cut. Her friends and the neighbor women scolded her for cutting off all that beautiful, long hair.

The Raymond sisters said, "There's a many of us give a right arm to have hair like yours. Now look what you done. You jus' cut it all off. Mmmmmuh! mmmmuh! mmmmmuh! Ain't that a shame?"

The neighbors and their friends talked a lot about "good hair" and "bad hair."

The girls and Robert could not get over all the fuss about hair and color.

Corn continued helping with the ironing and housecleaning. She was never one to complain. She was a tireless worker who kept smiling, enjoyed joking and doing whatever necessary to keep peace in the family. She especially liked cooking and thought herself better at it than her mother. At least that's what her father said.

As if she did not worry and complain enough about the difficulties she endured, Lillian's concerns became more intense about her older girls and their increasing contact with the boys their age and older. She remembered her own attractiveness as a teen and how that very attractiveness could also become a problem. Lillian knew that her family's money and position, as well as her mother's protective manner had been her security until she met Foley. Lockland was not the same type of environment for her girls. It was wild and more unpredictable.

"Don't be foolin' around with no boys. Do you hear?" She warned.

Now that Lillian could only watch as her daughters' bodies blossomed into womanhood, she lived in great apprehension of boys with her girls. But Lillian did not take time to explain the "facts of life" to the girls. She was hesitant and embarrassed. The girls were left to get their information elsewhere. Lillian remained apprehensive.

Mike Martin, four years Eckey's senior, was a very popular athlete known especially for his performance in high school football and basketball. He was a frequent participant at the Y.M.C.A. where he could meet girls outside of high school.

Eckey loved sports. She was a major participant in the Girl's basketball group that played at the Y.M.C.A. She caught the eye of more than one of the young men frequenting the Y. But it was the older Mike Martin with whom she became infatuated. He was tall and very dark. He was called "Goodie."

Although her mother always spoke in disparaging terms about people who were black or dark skin, Eckey had never paid this much attention. She always found joy in competing and playing with the "dark, snotty-nosed boys" who lived on her street.

Mike Martin became her boyfriend and one her mother knew nothing about until her younger sisters, now eleven and twelve, told their mother that Mike Martin had walked Eckey to the corner of Elm Street after school one day.

Eckey's best friend was Anna Lawson, a thin schoolmate who was an athlete like her. It was Anna Lawson and not her older sister, Corn, to whom Eckey turned when she wanted answers to her questions about boys.

Since both girls' periods had begun Eckey did not let this interfere as she continued playing sports with the boys, on those days. On one occasion she almost lost her "rag," as the home-made monthly padding was called.

One day, his face flushed with embarrassment, Robert told his mother, "Somebody's left something in the bathroom. Eckey was the last one in there."

It was the "rag" left there by Eckey as she forgot all about it in her hurry to get to the Y and her girls basketball game.

When Eckey was pressured by Mike Martin to have sex, it was Anna Lawson that she asked for advice.

"If I do," she hesitated in her embarrassment. Then she began again. "If I do something with Goodie, will I get pregnant if it's the first time?" she asked.

"No," Anna answered authoritatively.

Eckey was fifteen and would turn sixteen in June the next year.

PART II

A SHORT PERIOD
BEFORE MY BIRTH AND MY EARLY YEARS

Birth – 4 years

1

The Lingering Depression

The Depression returned Foley to the only part-time work he could get. In his early "wild days" as he called them, he had tended bar in Lexington, Kentucky. This was before he met Lillian.

Foley went to work at Tenny's Bar and Restaurant. Although famous for its chili, Tenny's was a popular hang out for drinkers. Foley slipped easily into his old job. He liked being around the customers, serving them drinks and listening to their jokes. Occasionally he had to break up a fight, but for the most part he had fun.

"Beats not workin'," Foley told Lillian in response to her complaint.

"You call pouring liquor and beer, washin' and dryin' glasses workin'?" she asked. "No decent man worth his salt is going to be caught around a bar all day."

"Ain't nothin' but decent men there, Sister. A helluva sight more decent than that old, drunken daddy of yours," Foley retorted sarcastically.

"My daddy wasn't no drunkard," Lillian said.

"The hell he wasn't. You and your mammy was the only ones who didn't know it," he laughed.

"Well, if my daddy was a drunkard, you're the one who taught him," she said.

"Like hell, I did," Foley said. "He's the one who taught me to drink."

"You look like you drink more beer than you sell," Lillian observed.

"Aw, woman, why don't you be quiet for once in your life. Can't never satisfy you."

The economic pressure played itself out in the daily lives of the children as they continued wearing the charity clothes and receiving charity food boxes. Hookey was completing grade school while Lockey Jane had another year to go. Robert and Corn were completing the twelth and eleventh grades at East Lockland High School and Eckey was finishing tenth grade. During this time Eckey had daily contact with Mike Martin at school as they passed between classes and saw each other after sporting events.

Mike's family was dominated by an aggressive and determined mother, Molly Martin. Her boys were to be successful. This is where she placed her focus although the Martins also had two daughters, Louise and Agnes. Molly, a large, very dark-skinned woman had such a deep, husky voice that she sounded loud and harsh even when happy. She cooked, washed and cleaned to give her children the advantage of a good education.

There was a fierce loyalty among the Martins. Joe, the eldest of the Martins was a devoted big brother to his baby brother, Mike. Both had been known for their athletic ability while at East Lockland, but Joe was also a scholar. It was rumored that Joe was interested in Irene, but nothing ever came of this.

1931 came slowly to an end. The hopeless months 1932 began as Foley lost his hours at Tenny's causing him to get behind in rent payments. Lillian was pregnant for the seventh time.

Help came when another half-sister of Foley's from his mother's marriage to Mr. Gabbitt. Her name was Margaret. She and her husband Ben offered the family an apartment in their three-story home in Walnut Hills, Ohio. This was a section of Cincinnati not far from the downtown metropolitan area. Cincinnati was known as the "city of seven hills." Walnut Hills was one of the seven.

The Corbin family left the house on Elm Street in Lockland. They left the children's schools and the friends they had made over the many years they had lived in there. With this move to Walnut Hills, Eckey was separated from her boyfriend, Mike.

Walnut Hills and Lincoln Avenue, where the Corbin family moved, was far more sophisticated than rural Lockland. Buses stopped at several corners making it easy for residents to get around. But many people without transportation did not mind the long walks to larger stores, churches, a colored owned pharmacy and soda shop. This gave them opportunities to stop and visit with their neighbors as they strolled down Lincoln Avenue.

The colored community was spread out over a wide area of the Walnut Hills section. Lincoln Avenue was a busy street and a main thoroughfare from Cincinnati to Madisonville and O'briensville. Teachers, pharmacists, funeral directors, ministers, blue collar workers and the elderly who no longer worked, all lived in the Lincoln Avenue neighborhood that became the Corbins' new home.

The schools were very different. The Hoffman Elementary school and Withrow High School were integrated. Children of different ethnic groups lived in their separate communities, but they all attended the same schools.

Robert, Corn, Eckey and Hookey all entered Withrow High School. Lockey Jane could walk to her eighth grade class at Hoffman School which was a few blocks away.

The best news came when Foley was asked to work for Frank Reed who had bought Dougherty's Tin Shop once located in Wyoming, now moved to Lockland. The only problem was the distance he lived from work. But his problem was solved when Margaret's husband, Ben, provided transportation for just a few cents a week. Things were improving.

Margaret could not ignore the signs of Eckey's morning illness and her poor attendance at school. She approached Lillian with her suspicions that Eckey was pregnant. This greatly angered Lillian. She felt that she had enough to deal with, that it was a preposterous notion that Eckey could be pregnant. But when confronted by her mother, Eckey admitted that she had missed her period.

She had not told anyone, not even her best friend Anna Lawson. In her fear she was silent. But in her classes at her new high school, she began falling asleep. Her teachers complained about her lack of interest in her classes, but this was nothing new to her mother.

Lillian took Eckey to the General Hospital clinic and her pregnancy was confirmed.

Robert and Eckey's sisters were in shock. Their mother and their sister both pregnant! Now there was no end to their mother's illness and stress-driven complaints. Foley said little about both situations. He just listened to his wife's chatter.

Margaret insisted that Lillian go to see Molly Martin, Mike's mother, and tell her that her son had to take responsibility, as he was Eckey's only boyfriend. When Lillian confronted Molly she received an angry and degrading response from her.

Molly said, "Your daughter's nothin' but a street walker. Everybody knows that. My son's going to college!"

As far as Molly Martin was concerned, marriage was out of the question. Her son had a football scholarship and no matter what, he was going to follow through with it.

Lillian was furious. How dare she talk about her daughter that way! Lillian was also angry that anyone as black as Molly Martin would dare speak to her in such a manner. In Lillian's mind her light color and pretty hair automatically made her superior to the rough Molly Martin.

Lillian was very angry at Eckey for putting her in such a degrading position. She had expected some degree of understanding from Molly, but her rejection took her by surprise. When she told Foley of her experience he expressed no such indignation. Lillian was mortified by his lack of empathy.

Molly Martin sent her son, Mike, off to college on a football scholarship. Eckey was sent to stay with her Grandmother Gabbitt in Danville, Kentucky to hide the family's disgrace and embarrassment.

With these current happenings Lillian decided to move out of Margaret's apartment and into a place of their own. Here there was no privacy. She did not want Margaret interfering in her family's business no matter how helpful she wanted to be.

There was a vacant apartment on the same street but a block away. Lillian asked her Uncle Bob in Lexington for the money to move. He agreed to help his niece and the family settled into a ten-family complex called the Helena Apartments. Lillian felt herself far enough from Margaret that she would have the privacy she desired.

The move, however, brought more heartache for Lillian. She delivered her baby, a girl who was born with a heart defect. The baby died, shortly after birth, from the condition known as the "blue baby" syndrome. Lillian had named the child Beverly.

2

New Challenges

The new home at the Helena Apartments was a small four-room apartment. It was one of two apartments in the lowest level of the ten apartment complex. Although these two apartments were known as "basement apartments," the one in which the Corbin family lived was actually over the basement with its dirt floor. The second "basement apartment" was built on a cement slab.

Lined by holly hock bushes, a paved walk led to cement stairs that gave access to these lower-level apartments. For the benefit of all tenants, a room on this same level and next to one of the apartments, was to be used for extra storage.

The basement held the storage bins for the winter supply of coal. Each tenant had their own bin. Foley made a game out of rolling the lumps of black coal down the hill and into the open basement window.

These lower-level apartments and storage room were made possible when ground was excavated to make way for the huge apartment building. The mound of dirt, from the digging, was raised then leveled to create the hillside and upper plateau of the back yard. Here the tenants hung their wash and on occasion socialized.

With Eckey away living with her Grandmother Gabbitt in Kentucky and Corn having made the decision to marry, her neighbor, Francis Green, a minister's son, Hookey, Lockey Jane and Robert became good friends with the teenagers from the Bell and Robinson families in the new living quarters. Foley also socialized with the young people when they gathered in the backyard, but Lillian remained aloof and as self-isolating as she had been in Lockland and at Margaret's house.

The Corbins' new four room apartment had one bedroom where Foley and Lillian slept. This was in the rear next to the kitchen. A center open space off of which was the bathroom and a closet, connected the front living room and the second bedroom where Hookey, Lockey Jane and Irene slept. Robert slept in the living room.

You entered the apartment through one of two front doors. One door led into the living room and the other led into a teenage girls' bedroom.

The sunlight coming into the rooms of the basement residences was minimal. This lack of light relegated them to a dreariness that permeated the atmosphere inside the apartments.

Rickety wooden stairs led down the back of the building and were used by the tenants living in the upper apartments to get their wash to the back yard on wash days, and to pay visits to the Corbins and Doodlums who lived in the lower apartments.

The family did not have the airy lightness they had experienced living in Margaret and Ben's large, open house, but they did have a place of their own.

Shortly after their move to the Helena Apartments some changes occurred. Robert left school and the Helena Apartments to join the Civilian Conservation Corps. This program was established under the Federal Government and President Roosevelt to ease the effects of the lingering Depression, and to provide jobs for unemployed young men. CCC participants had jobs that were to improve and establish more national parks and the infrastructure to support them. Robert's enlistment would ease some of the family's financial problems.

Not much was mentioned about Robert's experiences with the CCC. However, it was not long after he joined than he returned home. No one ever spoke about the reason for this abrupt return.

Four family members, Foley, Lillian, Hookey, Lockey Jane and Robert settled into their new living quarters.

Hookey, soon to turn fifteen, left high school to work as a nursemaid for a Jewish couple and their two young children. Her other reason for leaving school was to help Lockey Jane, her baby sister, have the things that she needed, then at least she might be able to complete her education.

It was during this period upon his return from the CCC program, that Robert, now eighteen, experienced his first "spell." What happened was out of character for Robert, the gentle, kind and intelligent son and brother who always tried to please.

He was in the living room of the apartment at the time. On that afternoon Robert put his fist through the glass window with a thrust so powerful that he cut it badly. Blood gushed from the wound. Lillian rushed from the kitchen and stood in horrified dismay at what she saw. Robert stood quietly licking the blood from his fist. The shattered glass was on the floor. It frightened his mother Lillian.

They took Robert to the General Hospital, where an anxious Lillian waited while the cut on his hand was checked and bandaged. She kept saying it was just that he cut his hand.

Hookey and Lockey Jane were not so sure. Recently, when in Robert's presence they had seen strange signs. He was agitated, giggly and very much unlike himself. They had not paid it a great deal of attention. Now, they were fearful and quiet. Foley was stoic. He did not laugh, but he did not go to the hospital to see how badly Robert had cut himself either.

After a week of observation at the hospital, Robert was moved to the Psychiatric Ward for more in-depth testing. Absorbing this turn of events was extremely difficult for Lillian and was soon compounded when Robert was transferred to the Longview State Hospital for the insane.

Another tragedy occurred. No sooner had she cried herself sick over Robert's mental collapse than Lillian got word that her brother James, living in Atlantic City, New Jersey had been killed.

Years before, James had left a wife and two children in Cincinnati. He was never to return. He had lived in Atlantic City where he had taken up with another woman. Word was that he had been shot and killed in a barroom brawl.

The year before the "Crash," James paid for Lillian to come to Atlantic City for a vacation. Lillian had been sick and, in a deep depression after miscarrying her sixth child. It was her first trip to the East Coast and her first time to see the Atlantic Ocean. Upon her return she told the family that she had found "home" as she stared out across the vastness of the Atlantic Ocean. She said she basked in the sun during the day and was taken around by James to see his friends in

44

the evenings. He bragged about his pretty little sister. She felt special and youthful again.

At this latest news, Lillian could not fathom James' death. She remembered how much he had loved working with horses and had followed the racing seasons from Lexington to Atlantic City. He seemed so happy. Now, he was gone. First her son and now her last, living brother were out of her life. Frank, her older brother, had been killed when he was run over by a streetcar, in Lexington, years ago.

Lillian focused on her sewing to escape her grief. No one in her immediate family was left except her daddy and herself. She felt that her life had become too hard. She had not forgiven her father for his meanness to her mother when she was alive, and for remarrying so soon after her mother's death.

While this was the environment in Cincinnati, Ohio, a pregnant, teenage Eckey was living a very different life in Danville, Kentucky. She was living with her grandmother, Sally Gabbitt, away from the questioning, judgmental stares of the residents at home on Lincoln Avenue . In a way, she was being allowed to be a child even though she was physically preparing to be an adult and a new mother.

Eckey roamed freely over the country area of Danville, unrestrained by fences and mental barriers. She enjoyed sunny days and reveled in her experiences, joyously eating Sally's delicious cooking. She especially loved her grandmother's blackberry and apple cobblers. The fried chicken and light-as-a-feather biscuits were given her without limitations on the amount she could eat. Her grandmother Gabbitt loved having Eckey with her. She had not been able to spoil her own daughter, Mae Georgia, but she could spoil her granddaughter. There had not been the time nor enough money to entertain such a notion as spoiling her own children.

Sally had her own little home now, not a dirt floor cabin as before. She had fruit trees and a garden where she grew her own vegetables. The hard years were softened by the presence of the granddaughter she was now caring for.

Eckey would live in Danville away from her parents and siblings until a short time before she was due to deliver her first child.

SALLY HATHAWAY GABBITT

Sally Hathaway Gabbitt, author's great grandmother, in her vegetable garden in front of her home in Danville, Kentucky 1932-33. My mother, Eckey lived here during her pregnancy Mother of Stewart Foley Corbin, Grandmother of Eckey Corbin and my Great Grandmother

3

A New Life Arrives

Showing no signs of improvement, Robert remained in the Longview State Hospital. At times he attacked some of his fellow patients demonstrating very violent tendencies. When this occurred he was moved to the violent ward away from the others. Lillian visited him on Wednesdays and Foley visited him on Sundays, the two days set aside by the hospital for family visits.

Living in Walnut Hills made it possible for Lillian to take in sewing from some of her neighbors. Although she had strained relations with Margaret, this did not keep Margaret from getting clients for Lillian. These were the wealthy people for whom Margaret worked. This led to Lillian being recommended to others and in this way she developed a small home business. With this steady clientele of new customers she began making and selling slip covers. With her earnings she was able to buy a new Singer sewing machine.

In late September, Eckey left the protection and loving care she received from her grandmother Gabbitt to return home and await the delivery of her first child. Her return brought with it the same admonishments and anger that she had experienced before from her mother.

Eckey went into labor and was taken to General Hospital, the largest hospital in the area, and one that was known for its fine reputation for quality care.

Her labor was long and painful - more than sixteen hours. Eckey was unprepared for the severity of the pain. Her cocoon was cracking, splitting, tearing her further from her innocence. Something was wrong. The baby was turned in the womb, not coming into the world naturally or easily.

The doctors debated what to do. Would Eckey live and the baby die; or the baby live and Eckey die? Finally, through the searing white pain, the baby emerged feet first from Eckey's strained limbs.

On October 5, 1933 my first cries were presented to the world and my new family.

"Born ass backwards," my grandfather, Foley, said of my birth. "What do you think of that?"

At forty-six and forty years of age respectively, he and Lillian became grandparents.

My mother lay for days in awe of being alive. The numbing pain was ever present in her memory and a near-bald-headed, sleeping baby girl lay cradled in her arms.

She named me Lula Delores Martin. The "Lula" was for my mother's Aunt Margaret's sister, Lula Dee. Her Aunt Margaret promised that if my mother named me for her sister that I would never "want for anything."

Later the Bell sisters, neighbors in the top floor apartment, would give me the nickname "Sweetpea" because I had only fuzz and a tiny curl at the top of my head and reminded them of the comic strip character of the Popeye series.

My mother named Mike Martin as my father. Here, on the birth certificate, he had no control over his responsibility. I was, biologically, his child and my mother wanted that to be known. Whether he and his mother, Mollie, claimed me or not, my mother gave me the Martin family's name.

During the months that my mother lived in Danville, Kentucky with my great grandmother Sally Gabbitt and on the days that she lay in the throes of birth pains and recovery, Mike Martin was attending college in the South and liking his new found freshman experience. This was just as his mother Molly had planned when she renounced her son's part in my mother's pregnancy.

Fate had other plans for Mike, my father. He entered college to prepare for his first football season just a few months before I was born. He and my mother never spoke or saw each other after the meeting my grandmother had with his mother, Molly.

When Mike played his first most important game, he suffered injuries which reportedly ended his football and college careers. He returned home to Molly.

They said that he became a pathetic "hanger on," the weak Martin unable to be known as anyone but "Goodie Martin," Molly's baby boy. He lived in the shadow of his successful older brother, Joe who graduated from college and became a teacher and coach.

In the year after Mike returned home word was out that he had gotten another girl pregnant. But this time, Molly did not intervene. Mike was forced to marry. Ironically he had another baby girl. This one bore his name legally, a half-sister who was a year younger than me.

My mother took me home to 1339 Lincoln Avenue where the tiny, four-room, one bath apartment, awaited me. Here I was to live with my mother, grandparents, two Aunts, Hookey and Lockey Jane and my Uncle Bobby, when he was well enough to be released from the Longview State Hospital.

The poor economy of the Depression continued its heavy weight on my family as it had with other families in the Helena Apartments and elsewhere. My grandmother, Lillian, was more tense about their situation and insisted that my mother marry. My illegitimacy and the snub from Molly Martin had stung her pride to such an extent that she did not care what pressure she placed on the daughter who had caused all of this disgrace. An opportunity soon presented itself in the person of Cornelious, "Neil" for short, Price. My Aunt Irene (Corn), dated him when she attended East Lockland High School, a year before she married Francis Green.

Neil Price was tall and dark with a very agreeable personality. He lived in the sub-division with his family of several brothers and sisters.

The Price family was a good, steady and pleasant group. They were well liked by neighbors and friends. Neil was very serious about my Aunt Irene, but she was not serious about him. He was deeply hurt when the Corbins moved away. He visited them in their two new homes on Lincoln Avenue, hoping that he could persuade Irene to marry him. She refused and married Francis Green instead. It was then that Neil turned his attention to Eckey.

Neil had not contemplated any relationship with her because she was pregnant and away from Ohio; but after Eckey returned from

Kentucky and I was born, he took a renewed interest and asked her to marry him.

To appease my grandmother and to put a stop to the daily accusations and criticisms, my mother agreed to marry him. After their marriage my stepfather moved in with us. With five adults and a new baby, the apartment was very crowded.

AUNT HOOKEY AND MY MOTHER

L. Aunt Hookey, 15, R. My mother, Eckey 17, after my birth. Photo taken in the backyard of Helena Apartments.

4

One Left Behind

My mother became pregnant with her second child and in July of 1935 Albert Cornelious Price was born at General Hospital. He was nicknamed "Sonny."

With five adults and two infants living in the four room apartment, my mother and stepfather decided it was time to have a place of their own. As they arranged to move to a garden apartment several miles away, they were unprepared for the request made by my grandmother.

"Eckey, you and Neil have your hands full. Why don't you leave Sweetpea with me?" She said one day as my mother packed.

"No, Mama. She belongs with me. Neil wants to adopt her and give her his name. We can take care of her."

"But two little babies are an awful lot to take care of. You know how you always half did your work."

"I can do it," my mother insisted.

"Well I don't think you can. I never could get you to finish one thing I gave you to do."

"But, I'm different now."

"I don't see no difference. Since baby Sonny came you and Neil still sleep late. I'm the one getting up and taking care of the baby when he cries. Sweetpea belongs here with us. A little girl ought to be brought up right, and you know you never paid any attention to anything I ever said. Look where your hard-headedness got you. I don't think you can raise her right! Me and your daddy can."

My mother protested and cried. "But she's my baby, Mama. I can raise her right."

My grandmother cried, too. "But you have two babies. I've lost my little baby. You won't raise her like I would raise her. You'll be a terrible mother. You're too young and too wild. She's used to having

51

us feed her, and she's used to being around all of us. She'll be upset not seeing us and havin' to be around people she doesn't know."

My mother cried, and as she cried she knew she was losing the struggle. She had won so many little battles. When she was a child she succeeded in getting out of the gate of their old house in Lockland, and playing with friends that my grandmother had said she was too good for. She had even won when her Aunt Margaret said they could help her get rid of the baby. She had held out firmly on that one. "Nobody's going to make me get rid of my baby," she had said.

But this time she was losing. It slipped from her and out of her soul like water flowing through her fingers. She could see the words as they drained from her mind. Her baby would be taken by her own mother. She could not fathom the idea that she was giving her baby away. Her mother's will to have her baby had won out.

My mother became very quiet. The pain she was feeling was too intense for tears. This place where she now found herself was too hollow, too deep, and too distant for her internal cries to be heard. She felt as if she had sold her own child. The guilt, the anger and the devastation mingled forming a tornado of emotions. When she was finally able to speak the words, they came out in a whisper.

"Okay, Mama. You're right. She's better off with you."

My grandmother was happy in her triumph. She had been able to overcome her most stubborn, unyielding child, the one who never listened to her. She had handed over her baby. Lillian felt renewed life. Her depression lifted. She smiled.

5

Awareness

My home with my grandparents presented me with sounds and smells created by them and other family members that awakened my senses and attached me to my surroundings. Each morning my grandmother lingered over her coffee. She and my grandfather arose at six A.M. He washed, shaved and dressed for work. She remained in her nightgown and housecoat over which she placed a cotton, bibbed apron that she had made. Grandma prepared my grandfather's lunch and their breakfast simultaneously.

She packed a lunch of a fried egg sandwich and a piece of pie or cake. There was little or no variation, of his lunch, during the week. When Granddaddy complained about the monotony of the lunch or simply brought it back uneaten, Grandma packed him a lunch of a bologna sandwich with mustard and a dill pickle.

Breakfast consisted of bacon, eggs and toast for them, but for me, she put on a small pan of water for Cream of Wheat or Oatmeal. The warm, sweetened cereal was my favorite and the same fare each day. Unlike Granddaddy, I did not want there to be a change.

Those morning sounds of moving feet, running water, cooking food and snatches of conversation bathed my ears as I lay awake quietly listening and absorbing my environment.

Granddaddy's job as a tinsmith took him back to Lockland where he now worked for Frank Reed, the Mayor and insurance broker. Granddaddy rode with his sister Margaret's husband, "Uncle Ben."

My Aunt Lockey Jane arose in a rush to get ready for school. Then, there was a great splashing of water, the smell of Cashmere Bouquet powder and Jergen's Lotion. She had grown into a beautiful teenager, but in her eyes, she was an adult like the rest.

Whenever Grandma talked to my aunt, it was as if there was another child in the house. Her voice was soft and musical when she spoke.

"Lambsie Pie," she said. "How's my little, sweet, Lambsie Pie?"

My Aunt Crystal was called Lockey Jane because she had locked herself in the bathroom as a toddler. Now she had other nicknames as well. She became "Lambsie" and "Lambsie Pie." She never objected to the new nicknames and she was never asked about their origins. It was as if she had always been called "Lambsie Pie," no matter that Grandma was the only one using the term.

Some mornings "Lambsie Pie" complained to Grandma, "Sweetpea wet all over me last night. I didn't get all my sleep and I have a big test today."

She remained irritable until she slammed the door, books riding on her hip, as she left for Withrow High School.

During this time I do not remember my mother Ethel, called "Eckey," at all. There is no image of her in my consciousness - no sense of her sound or feel.

Other early memories are of the apartment's four rooms. The living room stood in austere, empty silence waiting for "company." It was a dark room except for the indirect light which came in from one large window and another small window that was part of the door leading from the outside. Both windows faced the cracked, gray, cement retaining wall that held back the dirt of the Tate property next door.

In the living room an over-stuffed, brown, mohair chair and matching, triple cushioned sofa provided seating against the inside walls. Each upholstered arm had hand-made, white, crocheted, heavily starched, decorative protectors. In the summer bright and bold flowered, chintz slipcovers, made by Grandma, added brightness to the room. Granddaddy sat in the living room at night reading his paper and listening to the radio.

A picture of Grandma hung on the wall over the sofa. This picture was taken when she believed herself near death. It was an image of a fragile, white-looking woman, hair parted in the middle and turned under just above her shoulders. The fullness of her face rested in her lower jaws. A strength generated by high, strong cheek bones

54

and a narrow, angular forehead was affirmed by piercing black eyes. She did not smile.

The eyes looked out from that picture diminishing the black dress and white, lace collar that Grandma had worn that day. It was a picture in harmony with the overriding gloom of the living room and was the powerful, silent, omnipresence of my grandmother's belief that she would soon join her mother, Mattie Gray, who died in the pandemic 1918 flu.

Grandma said that she wanted to leave something so that her children would never forget her. I saw a solemn, unhappy, but beautiful face, a younger replica of Grandma. As a child this picture frightened me.

By contrast, in the dark corner of the wall nearest the entrance from the living room to our bedroom, hung a picture of Lockey Jane. It was a magnificent, glowing, sepia-toned portrait. Her smile revealed her perfectly even, white teeth. Her high cheek bones were the same as Grandma's. She wore the same hairstyle as Grandma's, but this was a picture exuding beauty and happiness. It overwhelmed me by its dramatic contrast to Grandma's picture. They were polar opposites. I loved looking at the beautiful, happy, picture of Aunt Lockey Jane.

At the end of the living room was the closet where our outer clothes were hung. We only entered the living room to get to them, as only Granddaddy and Grandma spent time there after dinner. The closet had no light. In winter it was dark and cold. In summer it was dark and stuffy and our shoes, which sat on the closet floor, were filled with mold.

I spent most of my time in the front bedroom, which was across from the living room. This is where I slept with my aunt Hookey and Lockey Jane. Our bed was double-sized with rounded brown metal head and foot boards. It was placed against the wall near the one window which looked out and through the rickety steps, leading to and from the upstairs apartments, and into the back yard beyond.

A metal floor lamp with a silken cream-colored fabric shade provided light over the bed on dark rainy days and at night. A dresser against the inside wall, near the living room, was made of wood finished to resemble tortoise shell. A large rectangular mirror was attached to side anchors and could be adjusted forward, backward or simply straight up and down. Our underwear and night clothes were kept in the dresser. Flower- patterned wall paper decorated our walls. There was an inherent coziness to this room.

A black pot-bellied stove stood in the corner of our bedroom near the door, which led to the outside. The stove, quiet and cool in summer, was in winter the roaring main source of heat for the rooms and central hallway of the apartment. Additional heat came from the kitchen oven when Grandma left the door open. There was no heat for the bathroom.

One morning when I was three I was playing in our bedroom. The day was sunny. I was on the floor facing a straight-legged wooden chair. I used its seat as a play area for my dolls. As she usually did in the mid-morning, Grandma remained in the kitchen at the table drinking coffee. Except for my childish chatter the house was very still and warm.

Grandma called to me from the kitchen. "Sweetpea?"

She watched me from her chair at the kitchen table and awaited my response.

"Sweetpea?" Grandma called again. "Come here, darlin', Grandma wants to talk to you."

I reluctantly pulled myself up, moving away from my dolls, through the doorways and into the kitchen. Grandma still had on her housecoat with her apron over it. She sipped her cup of coffee. The breakfast dishes had been cleared away and sat stacked in the small white porcelain sink that stood atop wooden legs in the kitchen corner.

The morning sun streamed into the kitchen's two windows. The one near the ice box, opened to the back yard. The other next to the stove, looked out on the hillside and driveway of the apartment building next door.

Grandma motioned for me to sit on her lap and I did so with her help. There was no smile on her face. Her eyes seemed even larger as I peered into them through her rimless glasses. Grandma was never without her glasses unless she was washing her face. When she did that, she scrubbed with such vigor that I thought the skin would come off. She washed my face in the same manner, much to my displeasure. Her speech was slow and deliberate as she said, "Granny has something to tell you."

I waited intently watching her, studying her face. She seemed troubled. I sensed it and became apprehensive. Then Grandma continued, "You're not like other little girls. You don't have a father."

My response was immediate and invisible to her for by the time she had completed the sentence, "You don't have a father," I had already become two entities. I was the physical me sitting on my grandmother's lap, crying as tears welled up in my eyes and streamed down my face. My grandmother's words saddened and alarmed me because she sounded so very sad. Simultaneously there was a "me" that came into being that my grandmother could not see, but that I could see. This other "me" had sprung out of my body, a gray, ghostlike figure that was my mirror image.

This spirit "me" stood in the air above my right shoulder looking down at us. With both hands perched on either side of its waist and in a voice that was firm and defiant.

This second me said, *"Well, you may be sad and you may be crying, but I'm not going to be sad!"*

Then Grandma held the crying "Me" closer as she continued talking. "But that's all right. Grandma and Granddaddy love you and will take care of you."

The inconsistency of her words, the ones frightening enough to cause me to split off from my *Self* spawning a defiant, spirit me; followed by her cradling the crying, *physical* me in her bosom as she spoke words of comfort and assurance, created something new. It was the beginning of confusion, fear and suspicion about me and this grandmother, who said that she loved me. It was the birth of my duality and insecurity.

I continued to cry. I do not remember getting down from my grandmother's lap. I do not remember returning to play with my dolls. I know that from that moment forward I was intensely aware and alert. The world around me took on a peculiar aura. I was conscious. I was no longer an innocent child, but a child sensing that something was very wrong with it, but who had a spirit self who gave it a different way to be. That spirit never, ever left me.

I did not know whether there was an invisible wall around my grandmother, isolating her from me or an invisible shield around me, protecting me from her. Whatever it was after this incident, I would not approach her.

One morning Grandma was overcome with tenderness. She sat at the kitchen table in the quiet morning hours. She looked at me - her dark eyes dancing beneath her glasses. She smiled and held out her arms for me to come to her.

"Oh, my little sweetie, come here and give Granny a kiss."

"Uh huh. No, I don't want to," I said, with the previous incident fresh in my mind. I dared not risk hearing anymore frightening words. As I turned away from my grandmother she became angry.

"What!?" she looked at me surprised. Her eyes flashed. "You little, black bastard," she spat at me. "Just like those old black evil Martins."

The suddenness of her fury took me by surprise and frightened me even more. There was no mistaking the depth of her anger with me. Just as sudden as her anger was the suddenness with which tears came to my eyes. It was as if someone had poured water over my face.

"What're you crying for!?" she demanded. "I'm the one who should be cryin'. All the care I take of you and what do I get in return? Nothing! Not even a hug or a kiss."

It at once pained and embarrassed me. It made me ashamed of myself. "Black bastard" must be a terrible thing to be. But Grandma had said I was a "black bastard" and that I was "like the black, evil Martins." I did not know any Martins or about black or bastard. All of this was foreign to me. I was three years old.

I swiftly turned from the kitchen and ran to the bathroom crying. There, I made myself stop crying.

Grandma continued to verbally assault all the members of the family who she considered "ungrateful, never caring about her." Now she was no longer happy, no longer smiling. Her eyes no longer

58

danced. When I returned to the kitchen, she did not ask me for a hug or a kiss. She gave me my breakfast in a steely, enraged, self-pitying silence.

THE AUTHOR AGE 3

Lula Price Cooper, "Sweetpea" age 3

6

Aunt Irene's Illness

Francis Green, my Aunt Irene's husband, was the younger of two children and an only son. His family was very well known locally and nationally. His father was the Reverend Francis P. Green, Sr. who headed the largest colored, Baptist Church in Cincinnati and he was well respected in the national Baptist Church hierarchy. His wife, always referred to as "Mama" Green, was a graduate of the famous Madame Walker Beauty School in Harlem. The Green's older child was a daughter, Naomi, who was a college graduate and an accomplished musician.

Aunt Irene and Uncle Francis met when my family moved in with Margaret and Ben. The Greens lived across the street. Before his marriage to my Aunt Irene, Francis completed his freshman year at the all-colored Wilberforce University in Wilberforce, Ohio. Once married, he took a job in a factory that made cans. My aunt did not work.

The year after her marriage to Francis Green, my Aunt Irene had her first child, a girl she named Sylvia Naomi after her husband's sister. With Aunt Irene, sometimes called "Corn" and "Reenie," living a half block away she was able to maintain her close ties with her parents and siblings. The family was able to see each other several times a week, if not daily.

When Aunt Irene had not visited Grandma for several days, my Aunt Hookey went to check on her. She returned in tears. "Mama, Corn is sick in bed with almost no food in the ice box. When I went to fix her something to eat, there was only some bologna and a few slices of bread!"

Grandma was very upset. "Why didn't she let us know? She doesn't have to go hungry because Francis and his old cheap, parents won't help."

"Mama you know she'd never tell anybody if anything was wrong. She never did let us know if somethin' was botherin' her. She just kept it to herself."

Grandma had Aunt Hookey prepare some food for Aunt Irene. When she left with the hot meal, Grandma said, "That lazy Francis Green. He ought to be ashamed of himself letting "Reenie" live like that. I bet he's eatin' at his cheap mama and daddy's house while his wife is sick and hungry. And my Reenie laying there pregnant."

Some months later, Aunt Irene gave birth to her second child, Joan, just a year after Sylvia was born. Before she could be released from General Hospital, my aunt learned that she had tuberculosis of the stomach. No one in the family had heard of this before. They knew of tuberculosis as a lung disease, not a disease of the stomach.

Aunt Irene was hospitalized in a convalescent home built for those patients recuperating from tuberculosis. This facility was located miles from our area in a section of Cincinnati known as Mt. Airy. It was the highest place where the air was much colder and, as they thought, better for tuberculosis patients. My aunt was immediately isolated from the family, her newborn Joan, and one year old, Sylvia.

My cousins, Sylvia called "Mitzi" and new-born Joan, moved in with us. Once again there were young children in need of a lot of attention and care in our four room apartment. I had just turned three.

My grandmother asked the Greens, the girls' other grandparents, and their father, Francis to help with the children's care. She needed assistance with buying food and clothing. To her surprise the only assistance she received was a one time donation of a quart of milk or as my grandmother said, "Twenty-five Cents."

What was an even greater surprise was the fact that Uncle Francis did not come to visit his children, nor did he travel to visit with Aunt Irene the entire duration of her hospitalization. Grandma, Granddaddy and my aunts were her only visitors.

Aunt Irene remained in the convalescent home for a year before she was considered well enough to be released. When she came to our apartment to get her children, neither recognized her as their mother. It was particularly devastating to Aunt Irene when the baby, Joan, now a year old, would not go to her when my aunt held out her arms to take her.

My aunt returned to her husband and their small apartment and was determined that her children would never again fail to recognize her as their mother.

My other aunts, Hookey and Lockey Jane, were outraged by the lack of attention and support that their sister, Reenie had been given. They railed against Francis Green and his "so-called" minister father, the Reverend Francis Green. They considered all the Greens to be "heartless hypocrites." They came to refer to their sister as "Poor Reenie."

Aunt Irene did not want to speak of conflict and the past. She resumed her usual demeanor, telling jokes and having fun making others laugh. At times this would become caustic humor as she selected choice references to her husband. These favorite names were used when she was visiting with her sisters, Hookey and Lockey Jane. Then she called my Uncle Francis a "Fat Fart" or "Lazy Butt." The sisters doubled over, in hysterics, laughing.

FAMILY PHOTOGRAPHS OF GREEN FAMILY, EXCLUDING DAUGHTER NAOMI

MY AUNT IRENE

Aunt Irene Corbin Green
7 years after her release from the
sanitorium. Circa 1940.

UNCLE FRANCIS

Francis P. Green, Jr.
Married to Irene Green. Father of
Sylvia and Joan. Circa 1940.

"PAPA AND MAMA GREEN"

The Reverend Francis P. Green, Sr. and Wife
Parents of Francis P. Green, Jr. The Reverend Green was pastor
of First Baptist Church, the largest African-American Baptist
Congregation in Cincinnati, Ohio (Walnut Hills community)

7

Grandma's Burden

Although my mother had long since moved away, she continued to occupy the negative thoughts of my grandmother. My mother, Eckey, and my Uncle Bobby were the members of the family whose names were constantly on my grandmother's lips. From her seat at her sewing machine, she talked and cried about my mother and my uncle. From what she said and how she said it, my grandmother loved Uncle Bobby. She hated my mother.

But after my grandmother had told me that I wasn't "like other little girls"; and after this revelation had split me off from my real self as a three year old, I had from that moment remained leery, but alert, to anything Grandma said. I was a captive audience being alone with her every day. I listened, but I also applied myself to my imaginary play.

"Your mama was the worst child I ever had. She wouldn't do her work and was always leavin' the yard to go play ball with those nasty little boys up the street. I knew she was goin' to get into trouble. But, no, you couldn't tell her nothin' with her hard-headed self."

Most of the time when Grandma talked about my mother, she was at her sewing machine making beautiful slip covers and crying. This was the time when I learned more about her. Often I was just sitting at the kitchen table or in the bedroom.

My mother came alone whenever she visited me. I remember this beautiful lady who was very kind. She seemed very nice to Grandma, but Grandma talked to her with so much anger in her voice. She did not treat her like she did Aunt Irene, Aunt Hookey and Aunt Lockey Jane. With my mother, Grandma lashed out calling her a "liar" and talked about that "ol' black Molly Martin," and "ol' black Goodie Martin."

My mother arrived happy but she left crying. It seemed that she was always trying to correct what Grandma was saying. It never changed. My mother complained that they did not have much, but that she would try to buy me coats and shoes when I needed them. I was curious and confused about my mother's words.

When my mother did buy me clothes, my grandmother still found some way to talk to her that would make her cry. I felt so sad and even sorry for my mother. She did not seem like the person Grandma talked about all the time when she wasn't around.

My mother was the prodigal child, the bad child, the one who was the cause of my grandmother's grief and so much unhappiness. No matter what she did and no matter how regretful she was of her past transgressions. Grandma just said, "You're nothin' but a liar. Always were and always will be."

I don't remember any time that my mother spent with me, holding me, talking to me and or playing with me. I just remember my mother being criticized and bombarded verbally with Grandma's harsh words and her utter disdain for her own daughter.

This anger and disdain were not tempered by time. My mother was the negative spirit that occupied my grandmother's world. No one else in the family felt that way about my mother. Her sisters loved her and were kind and full of laughter when they spoke of her. My Uncle Bobby loved her and even Granddaddy never had unkind words about her. Grandma was the only one with such negative views of my mother. I never wondered why. It was just another one of those things that allowed Grandma to maintain her position as a victim of a regrettable circumstance.

As a result of these comments I felt that I was the cause of so much pain for my mother and for my grandmother. I did not feel a part of this world. It was all very alien and uncomfortable for me.

Uncle Bobby was a different matter altogether. He was my grandmother's "best child." He and Aunt Irene were her helpers, the ones who took care of her and the other siblings years ago. Before his illness Uncle Bobby was loving, kind and gentle with his mother. She said that he never disobeyed her. His mental illness seemed anathema to everyone since the time when it struck him at eighteen and without warning.

My earliest memories of my uncle are of his distinct presence and his equally distinct absences. When he was home he took me for walks to the store with him to get groceries for Grandma, out back to watch the squirrels and on long walks to Eden Park where we watched the boats on the Ohio River.

There were times when we sat on the park benches stationed along the edge of the Eden Park's duck pond as we observed the small, sailboats, tranquilly gliding on the still waters, delighting their owners and other children and adults.

These were the times when my uncle was serene and instructive as he showed me the birds and called them by their names. He whistled as he made the sound of the bird he called a Bob White.

"This is what the Bob White says, Sweetie," he told me pursing his lips. With a soft, warm breath he made the shrill sound, "Bob, Bob White. Bob, Bob White."

In our backyard with its tangled shrubbery and giant, cottonwood tree, he continued my instructions singing to me and reciting words that rhymed, but of which I had no knowledge or understanding at the time. I listened for my uncle's voice and sounds long after he had been returned to Longview State Hospital.

With my mother, Eckey, gone, my aunts and grandmother all became "mothers." I slept on Aunt Hookey's chest, wetting on her during the nights when she was home from her job with the Freulands, and Aunt Lockey Jane cared for me when she came home from her classes at Withrow High School.

MY UNCLE BOBBY

Robert Corbin, my Uncle Bobby when he was
home from Longview State Hospital - 1940's

8

The Day I Learned To Eat Fried Chicken

As we grew older, I remember the regular visits Aunt Irene made to our apartment bringing my cousins Mitzi and Joan. She usually came on Mondays when she also brought her wash. Since she planned to stay the entire day, she brought the food she would cook for supper.

Grandma was always happy when Aunt Irene came for the day. Grandma's place to do her sewing was in her bedroom next to the kitchen. From here she could carry on happy conversations with my aunt who was either busy in the kitchen, or doing her wash in the bathroom where Grandma kept the Norge washing machine. I could play uninterrupted with my cousins in the bedroom where I slept with Lockey Jane and Aunt Hookey.

On this particular Monday Aunt Irene brought chicken and fresh corn to cook for supper.

"Mama, you're almost out of flour," she told Grandma.

Aunt Irene had opened the metal canister that sat on the cupboard shelf and found it near empty. She had cut up the chicken and set the pieces in a large bowl.

Grandma replied from her bedroom, never looking up from her sewing, "No, I'm not "Reenie." Look in the closet in that big can on the floor. There's lots more flour if you need it."

My aunt wrestled the lid off the can where Grandma kept extra flour and then returned to her cooking preparations. She filled a brown, paper sack with the flour. She added salt and pepper and turned the bag upside down to mix the ingredients. Next, she put the cut up pieces of chicken into the bag and shook it vigorously.

Aunt Irene said that she wanted me and my cousins to be as close as sisters, but it wasn't long after they arrived that we began to squabble. I was older, taller and bossy. They resented that. So, I escaped to the kitchen and was absorbed in the movements and happy voice of my aunt.

68

"Peasy," as she always called me, "Are you going to eat a nice piece of my fried chicken today?"

"Uh-unh!" I shook my head "no" with the same vigor that Aunt Irene had shaken the bag of chicken.

"You can't get her to eat nothin' that's good for her," Grandma called out from her bedroom. "Mitzi and Joan love chicken, Peasy. Why don't you like it?"

Aunt Irene's voice was a gentle caress flowing over me. I wanted to tell her that I didn't like it when Grandma bought a live chicken from Thatcher's Fish and Poultry Market on Saturdays. She had that chicken strutting around on a long rope in the back yard. Then, with one hand, Granddaddy would grab the chicken around the neck, swing it like a bolo, round and round until the body of the chicken took off like a bullet separating its body from its head.

The chicken's body flopped around headless. The blood coated the weeds on the hillside and spattered into the air. Granddaddy stood in his work clothes with the head in his hand. The eyes of the dead chicken stared out with a vacant, lifeless look.

Later the body was dipped up and down in boiling water like Grandma's Monday wash. Granddaddy sat on the stone steps leading to the upper plateau of the yard, calmly plucking out the white feathers. One by one each was deposited into a pile next to him. The disembowelment was the most horrible to watch. I stood silent but dismayed as Grandma took a huge knife to cut open the naked carcass and pulled out the dead chicken's entrails.

When we sat down to supper they had the audacity to present me with a fried drumstick from that same chicken. It was a golden-brown remnant of the live chicken. It had a gray gelatinous piece near the muscle and grotesque, blue veins that had once carried so much blood. I would not eat it. No amount of coaxing would get me to eat it.

I responded to my aunt's question, "I don't like those blue things on the leg."

"Is that all?" My aunt looked at me calmly. "There's more to a chicken than the drumstick," she said.

Aunt Irene continued her cooking. The cast iron skillet on the gas stove had heated the white lard, for frying, and it was ready. She put the floured, seasoned chicken parts into the hot, melted fat. All the pieces were fried to a golden-brown. Aunt Irene then prepared biscuits that baked in the oven until they too were golden brown on top. Whenever my grandmother or aunts made biscuits, they were light and fluffy.

When Aunt Irene had removed the chicken pieces from the hot grease, she poured some of the grease into a can that Grandma kept near the stove. She left enough grease in the skillet to make the milk gravy that would go with the biscuits.

The yellow-gold ears of corn were shucked near the kitchen sink, their strands of silk removed thoroughly. Next my aunt took one of Grandma's sharpest and largest knives, positioned each ear of corn over a shallow pan, and proceeded to run the knife down the ear as the kernels fell in groups and singly into the bottom. Then she scraped each cob with the knife. When she had completed this, Aunt Irene took the corn over to the heated skillet and emptied the kernels into the small amount of hot grease to begin the cooking process. She then took some sugar, salt and a little flour in her hand tossed it onto the corn and added a small amount of water. A lid that fit the skillet was placed on top and the corn was left to simmer until Aunt Irene decided it was done.

I was mesmerized by the entire cooking process. I loved watching my Aunt Irene. I never spent much time in the kitchen when Grandma was cooking because she fussed too much.

When the food was ready, my cousins joined me and the three of us sat at the table to eat. The adults would eat when Granddaddy got home from work.

I was watchful as Aunt Irene prepared each plate. Joan, the youngest, was served first, then Mitzi. When it was my turn, I said, "I don't want any chicken, Aunt Irene."

"Okay Peasy, but I just want you to try one, little piece for me. You don't have to eat it if you don't want it. You hear?" She gently coaxed. She took a piece of the brown, crusted, white meat from the platter. "This is the breast," she said," and it doesn't have those blue

70

things that you don't like." She cut through the crisp skin and into the steaming white meat. She cut another, smaller piece and put this up to my mouth to test. "Taste this and see if you like it," she smiled.

I gingerly opened my mouth and accepted her offering. I slowly and stiffly began to chew it. The warmth of the piece of chicken became one with the warmth of my aunt and her gentle words. She was sitting close to me as she fed me. This was attention and patience I did not normally receive. "That's good," I said.

"See. I told you," Aunt Irene laughed.

From that day whenever we had chicken, which was mostly on Sunday, I only ate the breast.

"She won't eat nothin' but the breast," Grandma fussed. "I'd like to eat a breast some of the time," she said.

"You can never be satisfied woman," my grandfather said. "First you fussed because she wouldn't eat chicken at all. Now you fuss because she does eat it, but you want the part that she does eat. There are two breasts you know!" he retorted.

My grandfather ate all parts of the chicken, but Grandma insisted that she was only left the part that got over the fence last.

MY FIRST COUSINS

JOAN GREEN (l) and sister, SYLVIA NAOMI GREEN (r)

Joan Green, b. November 23, 1935
Sylvia Naomi Green, b. November 24, 1934

71

9

House Jobs

My grandfather had his jobs around the house. If any of Grandma's cooking pans had holes in them he brought out his toolbox which he kept in the kitchen closet, removed his soldering iron and bar of solder, and repaired them.

I was fascinated with the process as Granddaddy carefully spread, the day-old *Cincinnati Times Star* newspaper on the kitchen table, turned on the gas stove, and set the long-handled soldering iron directly into the blue-red flames.

When the iron was ready, Granddaddy applied the red-hot tip to the bar of solder. The silver-colored solder melted from the heat and formed small, metal beads that danced around on the bar. Granddaddy dipped the iron in an acid bath and then affixed the solder beads to the damaged pot.

"Watch out, now," he warned as he placed the iron in the acid. "That stuff will burn you."

I moved an inch or two away, eyes still glued to his movements as Granddaddy methodically worked from the stove to the acid to the solder and to the pan. He spread the solder bead over the hole sealing it, and then set the pan, upside down, back on the table to cool and the solder to harden.

When Granddaddy had finished, he carefully wrapped the cooled soldering iron in a cloth, gathered the bar of solder into another cloth, and placed them neatly away in his tool chest. This was returned to the closet and the door closed tightly.

I loved watching my grandfather at work on the pans with the glitter of the silver solder, the red hot colors of the soldering iron and the lighted, blue-gold flames from the gas stove. These were colors in motion and magic.

After supper, if my Aunt Lockey Jane was out, my grandfather did the dishes. Then he retired to the living room, took his seat in the mohair chair and read the newspaper.

There were other times when Grandma and my aunts came to Granddaddy to have their "corns" and toe nails trimmed. My grandfather had several pocket knives which he kept in very, sharp condition. The pearl-handled one, which he always carried in his pocket, was his sharpest, most efficient tool.

"Poppy," my Grandmother said in an unusually soft, sweet voice. It was late evening and after supper. "This toe hurt me all day," she said flexing her bare foot in front of him.

"Well, let me take a look at it, Sister," he said setting his newspaper aside. "Looks like you got a bad, ingrown toenail there."

He was carefully holding my grandmother's foot. He turned it towards the light, putting his face just inches from my Grandmother's toe. He never uttered a sound and seemed firmly concentrated on finding the real source of the problem. I thought he'd tell her that her feet stank, which would have set Grandma fussing, but he didn't.

After my aunts had left home, I remember awakening in the early morning hours, terrified by nightmares. I would run to my grandparents' bedroom, crowding myself between their legs at the bottom of the bed. I was aware of the odor of feet, but I could endure that better than the terror of sleeping by myself.

Granddaddy told Grandma to soak her foot, and then he'd take care of it. This she did for several minutes while he spread newspaper on the floor to soak up any spills. Then, he got a large towel from the bottom dresser drawer in our bedroom, adjusted the living room light and started to work.

Granddaddy carefully opened the pearl-handled knife, selecting the smallest blade. Setting the knife aside, momentarily, he proceeded to dry Grandma's foot. She sat back in the chair relaxed. Her eyes never left Granddaddy's hand as he worked. He trimmed the gnarled nail on the big toe. It looked like a piece of an old tree trunk. He scooped away the once dry, yellow part of the nail and began to trim the inflamed area. Grandma winced.

"Hold still, now," he cautioned, "I'll cut your toe off if you're not careful," he laughed.

"Well, it hurts," Grandma whined. This "whine" from Grandma was different. It was coquettish.

"I won't hurt the ole gal," Granddaddy responded. Without further concern expressed from Grandma, he cleared from the toe's edge the hard part of the nail that had been digging into the soft, fleshy part of her toe.

I watched this intimate picture of them. They were at ease with each other. They were calm. My grandmother was like a child in the arms of a parent. The soft light from the lamp cast a glow over my grandfather's stooped shoulders. The two appeared transported into some state of intimacy, tenderness that was different from their normal behavior. There was, it seemed to me, a sacred hush surrounding them.

10

Molly, Mike and Mama

Each morning Grandma washed and dressed me. She changed into her house dress and began her work making slipcovers. Her Singer sewing machine, kept under the window in her bedroom, hummed away as Grandma pumped the treadle.

Over her bed, Grandma spread the large, heavy, pieces of slip-cover material. Sometimes she used the floor in the living room to pin the patterns, which she made from newspapers, onto the material. At times she thought her eyesight too limited for the darkness of the living room and she would return to the bedroom.

The material with which Grandma worked had brightly colored, floral patterns. She made the cording for the finished covers from pieces she cut on the bias. Cutting on the bias meant that Grandma cut the material cross-wise instead of cutting in her normal, straight-ahead manner. Her final products were always a wonder to me. They were works of art.

Grandma charged twenty-five dollars for matching sofa and chair covers, and she often completed her work within a week. In this way she supplemented the meager income my grandfather made working for Mayor Reed's Tin Shop in Lockland.

Grandma's expertise was spread by word of mouth. Although the telephone had been in existence for quite sometime, we could not afford this luxury. Grandma worked for different kinds of people the wealthy and not so wealthy, black and white alike. She did her sewing after breakfast, took a break for lunch, then she returned to her work until it was time to prepare supper.

If Grandma was in a hurry to complete the work, she continued to sew into the night and on Saturdays. This provided me with a great deal of time to be to myself in the apartment or to wander up the back stairs to visit one of my favorite families, the Bells.

The Bells lived in one of the top floor, front apartments in our building. Mr. and Mrs. Bell, Frank, the younger son and two teenage daughters Elva Marie, called "Sister," and the youngest Christine.

They liked treating me like a doll, bathing and dressing me and, in the summer, taking me for walks to get ice cream. "Sister" Bell said that she was the one responsible for my nickname, "Sweetpea."

Sometimes, while Grandma prepared lunch, I ventured into her bedroom and toyed with the scraps of material that had ended up on the floor. These I placed under the sewing machine needle.

"Don't play with my machine, Sweetpea," Grandma said. "You'll break the needle." Sometimes she said, "Don't bother my machine. You'll get the thread tangled up."

I was fascinated by the sewing machine. Disobeying my grandmother and imitating her movements, I slipped the scraps under the needle, pressed my foot on the treadle and watched as the needle swiftly, but erratically grabbed the material turning it into a bundled mess.

"Now, look what you've done," Grandma said. "I told you to leave my machine alone. What makes you so hard-headed?

But there were many days when I sat playing alone in my bedroom and heard only the words that came from Grandma and the sounds from her sewing machine.

"I will never forget," I heard Grandma say, "that ol' black Molly Martin sitting there calling me a liar to my face; and calling your mama 'nothing but a common, street walker.' I didn't bring my children up to walk the streets. Your mama was just hard-headed. You couldn't tell her nothin'. 'Stay in the yard and don't go out of that gate', I'd tell her over and over when she was little."

I could watch my grandmother from my bedroom doorway as I played. She sat hunched over her sewing, crying and blowing her nose. Once again she began talking about my mother and the Martins. It was one of the days when she felt depressed and unloved. Then, she began retelling the story she had told many times before, and always with the same degree of anger and intensity as the first time.

The humiliation Grandma felt never left her. I was a captive audience as well as the end product of this story and my grandmother's misery. My mother was always the focus. Her name was woven into the fabric of my environment, although she was not there. Her presence was rare, as she only visited me occasionally.

My grandmother gave no thought as to how I felt sitting there listening to her. She cried as if her life was utterly lost. She sat sewing, making beautiful slipcovers when suddenly some remorse or sad thought entered her mind and the story began.

"Your mama just never would mind. If she had listened to me instead of those terrible friends of hers, she wouldn't have gotten into trouble. I raised her right. I did all I could for her and all she did was bring me trouble and misery. Always the tomboy, not content to play like other girls. No-o-o-o-o, not her! She had to play ball with the boys! Couldn't get her to do nothing around the house. I'd try to be nice and let her do some things and look how she repaid me.

"I couldn't hold my head up in Lockland no more. She made me the laughing stock. And that Molly Martin, pretending to be so much in the church with her big, black self! 'My son didn't have nothin' to do with your daughter', she had the nerve to say to me."

Grandma picked up the scissors, clipped the thread, put the completed cushion cover on her bed and started another one. Her feet pumped away at the latticed pattern, metal treadle. She continued to stitch and cry.

"You can't trust black niggers," she said, angrily. "That Molly Martin and all her black younguns'. 'Can we go to the dance at the Y?'" Grandma mimicked my mother and the others.

"I didn't like them galavantin' up to that Y with all the riff raff. But, then I'd try to be nice and let them go. 'Now be back no later than nine o' clock.' I told them. Irene, Hookey and Lockey Jane would come home with Robert just like they were told, but not your mama. They were good as gold and be home right at nine."

Grandma's voice turned vitriolic and my mother went from being "your mama" to being "that Mammy of yours." During these tirades, I felt sorry for Grandma and responsible for my mother. I wished Grandma wasn't so upset.

"No sir. She wouldn't come home. 'Robert, you go right back up to that Y and get Eckey. Bring her home even if you have to drag her home by her hair.' And he would, too. He'd have to drag that little hussy home by her hair. I should have let those gypsies have her when she was a baby. They said she looked like she belonged to them. It would have saved me a world of trouble and a lot of misery.

"But that ol' black Molly Martin got hers with her important self. She thought she was being so smart sending Goodie off to college so he wouldn't have to marry that mammy of yours. He got hurt playing football, too. No better for him. Almost died, too, and they sent him home. No more college for him. It don't pay. All he did was turn right around and get another girl in trouble. But this time he had to marry!

"Molly Martin couldn't do a thing about that! I shouldn't have let her bawl me out like that, like we were some common, alley people. I wasn't never poor in my life until I married your grandfather. What a fool I was. Mama told me not to marry him. He was too much older. But, I didn't listen to my mama and look what it got me."

I formed mental pictures of Grandma's story. I gave faces to the people she talked about, ol' black Molly Martin, Goodie Martin. These were people I did not know, but who were somehow connected to me from my mother going to a dance. These people and my mother made my grandmother angry as she sat at her sewing machine.

I didn't know the Martins. I rarely saw the person who was my mother. She came and went like Aunt Irene, Aunt Lockey Jane and Aunt Hookey, who were her sisters, and like Uncle Bobby, when he was home from the Longview State Hospital.

11

Grandma's Wash Day

Monday was washday. Grandma sorted the dirty clothes into piles of white things and colored things. A path was left between the piles so we could walk through the hall, where the clothes lay, to the kitchen. White things were washed first, colored things last.

Our Norge wringer washing machine was kept behind the tub in the bathroom. During the week, it held the dirty clothes until wash day.

"Can I wring the clothes, Grandma," I asked.

"Yes, but I'll have to help. I don't want you to get anything caught in the wringer."

Grandma was breathing heavily as she stooped over, picked up the dirty clothes and put them into the washer's tub. The water was heated on the gas stove in the kitchen and carried into the bathroom. The bathtub, which sat in front of the washer, was filled with cold water and bluing. Bluing was used in the rinse water to make the white clothes whiter.

Clean clothes sped through the wringer falling directly into the blue, rinse water. I enjoyed watching this operation of steaming, sudsy clothes as they made the plopping sound when they fell into the cold water.

Grandma used Oxydol soap powder made by Proctor & Gamble, a large Cincinnati company. She and I listened to "Ma Perkins," the soap opera, which came on the radio every afternoon. It was sponsored by Oxydol.

"Can I put the soap in, Grandma?" I asked.

"No. You might get too much, then I'll have soap suds everywhere. Look out!" she screeched, "I'm comin' through with hot water. Don't get in the way. I don't want to burn you. Get out of the way, now. Why don't you go in the other room until I get finished? Move! Move! Move!" she cried out.

I was happy when Grandma let me put the clothes through the wringer.

"Now be careful. Here, let me get the clothes out and you put them in the wringer. Watch out for your fingers," she shouted, frightening me. "Your mama got her hair caught in the wringer once. We had a devil of a time getting her loose. Her head was sore for weeks."

I envisioned my mother screaming as her braids were pulled into the soft, cream-colored rubber, wringer rollers. I imagined her head right next to the division between the upper and lower ones. I wondered what had happened next. Did her head go through and get mashed like the clothes?

"Good thing the washer cut off or it would have been real bad," Grandma said.

I saw this happen when I put too large a clump of wet clothing up to the rollers. The wringer halted making a loud noise. I thought the noise said, "come quickly! She did something wrong." My heart pounded whenever this happened. Grandma always rushed in and quickly slapped the side of the wringer with the heel of her hand. Immediately the metal restraint flew open, releasing the wad of clothing from the rollers. I could then remove the wet clothes and put in just one small piece at a time.

"Don't try to put so much through at once," Grandma said. "Just take a small piece."

Once the novelty had worn off, I left the washing, wringing and rinsing to Grandma.

"You're not much help," Grandma said.

On sunny days the clothes were taken in huge baskets out through my bedroom and up the stone steps to the flat ground of the backyard.

"Come here, Sweetpea. Hold the door for me," Grandma called.

I stopped my play to hold the door as Grandma came through with the basket of wet clothes. The smell of Clorox and bluing floated beneath my nostrils.

For hanging clothes on rainy days, our apartment building had a dark, dank, storage room next to our Aunt Mae Georgia and Uncle Doodlum's apartment. This unlit storage room was always open and you could see inside of it whenever anyone went up or down the cement steps leading to the street above. It had not been cleaned in years. It smelled of mold. Layers of gritty dirt covered the floor from years of accumulation. A former tenant of the Helena Apartments, as our building was called, had left an old piano in the storage room. Sister and Christine Bell played the tune *Heart and Soul* when they had to hang their wash in there.

When Grandma hung our wash in the storage room, I was scared as I stood outside the doorway watching. I thought of ghosts and horrible monsters and was anxious to get back to the apartment.

12

Granddaddy Gets a Nickname

When my family first moved to the Helena Apartments, my Aunts, Hookey and Lockey Jane, met the teenagers from the Bell family in the backyard, where they gathered to socialize and get acquainted. Frank Bell, the youngest boy and his older brother, Walter, were typical teenage boys with their eyes on the Corbin girls. Walter was determined to win Lockey Jane's affection. She said that Walter was too "serious," and Frank was too "fresh."

In the backyard was a huge cottonwood tree. Its gigantic trunk grew upwards from the base of the stone steps, while its branches covered the hillside and spread over the dilapidated, wooden shed below them. On the lower sturdier branch was a swing made of an inner-tube that hung from two very strong hemp ropes.

One afternoon Granddaddy joined my aunts and the Bells, on the hillside under the tree. Frank liked to hoist himself up the broad side of the Cottonwood and hang by his knees over the lower limb. They said he liked to "show off." Lockey Jane was perched in the center of the inner-tube gently swinging back and forth.

My grandfather stood at the crest of the hill, watching. He had decided to try the swing and to show the "young whipper snappers" a thing or two. He was going to let them see that he could beat them at their game.

When Lockey Jane alighted from the swing, granddaddy made his move. He walked over and took hold of the two ropes that held the inner tube. Then, he steadied himself on the hilltop, pushed himself back onto the inner-tube and prepared to take off.

He yelled just as he let his feet leave the ground, "Watch out now! Here I come!"

Before the swing was halfway down the hill, the ropes gave way and Granddaddy went sailing through the air. He landed with a thud that was louder than old man Tate's when he rolled off the roof of his dilapidated garage and onto our shed.

Everyone was shocked into silence as Granddaddy landed. Stunned, my grandfather got up and brushed himself off. He said he was all right. He said nothing was broken. He tried sheepishly to laugh it off. Fortunately for him he was all right, but he was covered with black and blue bruises on his back sides.

For three weeks after the incident, Ralph, his partner at work, had to do all the climbing when they went to repair roofs for clients. Grandma called Granddaddy an "old fool." But it was Frank Bell who nicknamed him "Tarzan" after *Tarzan the Ape Man* who swung from tree to tree in the jungle, giving out a loud whoop as he went. The name stuck with Granddaddy, who laughed along with everyone else when he was called by his new nickname.

"How about a swing, Tarzan?" Frank Bell asked one day after the fall.

"I'll never do nothin' dumb like that again," Granddaddy said. "That damn thing like to've killed me."

After that, Granddaddy limited his backyard activity to feeding the gray squirrel, which scampered up and down the cottonwood tree; and rolling the winter's coal down the hillside into the cellar beneath our apartment building.

13

The Helena Apartments

When I was almost five, I discovered a new sense of freedom and independence. I was considered old enough to explore the outside of our apartment by myself. The red brick Helena Apartments at 1339 Lincoln Avenue in Walnut Hills must have been a plain, but quietly elegant structure at one time. It continued to carry the name and house ten families, but it was an aging, grand, old "lady" with decaying roof overhangs, gutters and downspouts through which rain water cascaded as if from a mountain waterfall.

Eight upstairs apartments, four each on the two upper floors, were separated and at once joined by a central hallway. These hallways, the common passageways for the tenants, looked as if they had not been swept in years. The chalk-like plaster walls had never been painted. Light filtered down onto the hallways through a thick, frosted glass skylight in the roof. The first and second floor apartments, located at the front of the Helena apartments, each had a porch from which tenants could sit outside as they watched the street traffic and neighbors walking by, when weather permitted.

A cement sidewalk led to three, wide wooden stairs allowing a common area and entry to the porch and a large doorway into the hall. Everybody's mailbox was tacked to the wall inside the doorway. They were all the same sized, black metal with a flap that the mailman closed once he had deposited the mail. I don't remember seeing locks on any of the boxes.

I liked visiting the Robinsons, who lived on the first floor, because they had a front porch and I could sit there with Mrs. Robinson. Grandma told me not to go in or near the street. I loved watching the cars and buses as they went past, and by sitting on the porch, I got to know some of the other neighbors. Miss Jones was a school teacher. She walked everywhere. Whenever she passed the Helena Apartments, she was always dressed up with a hat, gloves and purse. She was a beautiful, stylish lady.

These apartments also faced lovely, two-storied homes with stained glass windows. They were on the opposite side of our street,

Lincoln Avenue. The lawns of these homes, as well as the areas of a smaller apartment building, were kept watered and manicured in summer. Also, at that time of year, bright, striped awnings shaded wide front porches with their rocking chairs and glider swings.

The Bells, who lived on the second floor of our building, also had a front apartment with a porch. I loved visiting with them. Eventually they would move to one of the back apartments. These back apartments had no porch, but the tenants living in them had a view of the backyard. It was very quiet and was where everyone hung their wash. They had to use the rickety, back stairs that really needed to be repaired to get to the backyard.

Each apartment on the upper floors was accessed by a door off of the hall.

From Mrs. Robinson's porch, I could see the Home for Aged Colored Women. Its sign was unrecognizable, as it had faded over the years and not been restored. The old ladies sat in their rocking chairs and observed the activities along Lincoln Avenue. This was their primary entertainment.

The Robinsons had twins, Paul and Pauline, who were the same age as my Aunt Lockey Jane. Pauline and Paul were both light-skinned with sandy colored hair. They were pigeon-toed and very intelligent. Both were musicians. Paul played the saxophone and Pauline played the piano. Their dog, Rex, a mutt, always disturbed the neighbors with its howling when Paul practiced his saxophone.

Mrs. Robinson was a plump, dark brown, quiet woman. She maintained an immaculate apartment and when talking with neighbors, she liked asking lots of questions. She had a habit of saying, "Ummmmhuh. Ummmmhuh. Ummmmmhuh!" the entire time an answer was being given.

Paul and Pauline were excellent students at school. Rarely did I see them idle. They were very serious. I sat with Mrs. Robinson on her section of the front porch, listening as Paul practiced hour after hour on his saxophone, while Pauline practiced the piano. I don't remember Mr. Robinson. He left for work early each morning and returned late each night.

Sitting with Mrs. Robinson was always a pleasure. We watched the buses as they passed on schedule. One of the stops was at the corner of Lincoln and the Victory Parkway. This was a very short distance from our apartment building and made travel, to General Hospital Clinic or shopping at the Sears Department Store three or four miles away, very easy as you did not have to transfer.

The many oak trees lining Lincoln Avenue, shaded the homes and apartments and made lacy patterns on the sidewalk. The front apartments of our building were kept cool all summer by the large trees from the neighboring houses. Sitting on Mrs. Robinson's porch was a good way to cool off from my running and playing in their small front yard.

Great Aunt Mae Georgia, who was Granddaddy's half-sister, lived in the apartment next to ours with her husband, Uncle Doodlum. She had a daughter from her first marriage. Her name was Cleo. She and her son, George, came to live with her.

With their teenage son Delaney living at home, the apartment was as full a place as ours. I rarely visited with them, but when I passed their apartment on my way up front, I would talk with Great Aunt Mae Georgia, Cleo, George, Jr. or Delaney through their screen door.

Cleo, Aunt Mae Georgia's daughter, was considered "high yellow," as was her son, George, Jr. She had huge eyes and an engaging, lyrical voice. She sang in her church's choir. George was slight in his build. He had a nervous twitch and restless eyes. Grandma said he had "shifty" eyes. He chain smoked and spent a lot of time in the County Jail for stealing.

Cleo, with her happy voice, hovered intensely over George. She was very protective of him. It was difficult for me to get a picture of George as a thief. Opposite in mannerisms from George, was great Cousin Delaney. He was dark-skinned and calm like his father, Uncle Doodlum. Grandma said he was honest and very funny.

Our apartments shared a common wall between the living rooms. When our radio was broken or when Grandma refused to allow me to listen to it, I sneaked into the living room to listen to the "Lone Ranger" coming from the Doodlum's radio through the wall.

Holding my breath and putting my ear hard against the wall, I could hear the episode of the "Lone Ranger." Delaney and I both liked "Gang Busters" and the "Lone Ranger." We never used the living room except when company came and this was rare, so listening to the Doodlum's radio was an excuse for being in there.

When the sun was shining, it streamed into our kitchen window. It was the kitchen and Grandma and Granddaddy's bedroom that got the morning sun. The kitchen was the main gathering place for us and this was where we spent most of the time.

Grandma's crisp, lace curtains hung at all the windows in the front part of the apartment. There was one small, lace curtain at the window of the door leading in and out of the living room, and two panels of lace curtain at the large window next to the door. Then, another small panel at the door in and out of our bedroom and two panels at the window next to our bed. These curtains gave a degree of elegance to an otherwise mundane living space.

The mold from the basement below was always a source of irritation for my grandmother and aunts. It molded shoes and left its "musty odor" on the clothes and mattresses. In warm weather, Grandma and my aunts dragged the mattresses out to the backyard where they were placed on two chairs, turned upside down, and left to air in the bright sun.

Grandma hated dirt and unclean odors. In the spring the lace curtains were taken down, washed and stretched on wooden curtain stretchers. The stretchers' wooden frame had small, sharp pins located an inch apart on which the wet curtains had to be hooked. These pricked Grandma's hands making them bleed, but this she endured in order to have white, starched, clean curtains at the windows.

Before winter, delivery men brought our coal. It was delivered a ton at a time.

The trucks, bearing the loads, had to use the neighboring apartment building's driveway in order for us to get the coal. They dumped it on the hillside. From here Granddaddy rolled the large and small lumps down the hill and through the basement window. At times Aunt Hookey helped him. I was allowed to help as I got older. Grandma and Aunt Lockey Jane did not like getting coal dust on themselves. They stayed inside or watched and directed the work from the top of the hill. I really liked it when I was allowed to roll those shiny, black lumps of coal down the hill. At other times, my grandfather had me stand by the basement window and push through the lumps that did not go in when he sent them down.

The coal was stored in individual bins separated by wooden plank walls.

The apartment dwellers shared coal with each other when one's bin got low and it wasn't yet time for another delivery.

The Helena Apartment Building encased me in the world that was outside. It, Lincoln Avenue, with its beautiful as well as decaying houses, and all the interesting people walking by became my universe as a child. When the rain fell in torrents, dodging the "waterfall" that came down from the rotting downspouts above, made getting into our apartment without being drenched an adventure. It was the reason I learned to run so fast and to get over the cracked cement walkway with such agility.

THE HELENA APARTMENT BUILDING
As it appeared, refurbished, in 1976
1339 Lincoln Avenue – Walnut Hills (Cincinnati), Ohio.
I lived here with my grandparents, aunts and uncle.
1933-1942, 1943-1947

14

Punishment

Mr. Tate's poll parrot broke the summer silence at odd times during the day.

"Awk, awwk…Polly wants a cracker. Awwk, awwk. Ann. Ann. Shut up, Ann."

Polly sounded like Mr. Tate who spent most of his day shouting at Ann, his only granddaughter.

Ann was six years my senior, fat, light-brown skinned and very bossy. She spent most of each day sucking her two middle fingers and pulling at her hair. She had perfected her finger sucking to such a high degree, that she could talk to you without removing her fingers from her mouth. Her mouth was fast becoming the primary challenger to her hips in spreading beyond control.

All summer long, the parrot squawked, "Shut up, Ann…An-nnnn…awwwk, awwk. Go to your room, Ann. Awwk!"

Ann's mother, Miss Helene, was the Tate's only child. She had been married, but was divorced and back to living with her parents. Miss Helene taught school in downtown Cincinnati. She was quiet and very dignified. She, too, was stern with Ann.

During the school year, she forced Ann to excel in her studies. But during the summer, Miss Helene went to Michigan where she worked for a white family taking care of their children as they "summered on the Lake." Ann meanwhile, disintegrated in boredom with her ailing, aging, irritable grandparents.

Both of the elderly Tates looked white. They were recluses who rarely ventured beyond the confines of their property.

There were times when Mr. Tate spent most of the day sitting in his rocking chair on their stone, slab porch. At other times he could be seen, from upstairs Helena apartment windows, lying on a day bed. The bed was so high off the floor that it reached the sill of their dining room window where it had been positioned. The poll parrot's cage stood next to it.

After Mr. Tate fell off his dilapidated garage roof and landed on the shed in our backyard. It took time for his broken hip to heal. Living with a permanent limp, his personality grew intensely meaner.

The Tates lived in a very large, three-story house. It was constructed of gray stone and although narrow from the front view, it was very long. The rooms inside were large and overcrowded with the furniture from the two households. Miss Helene had brought all of her furniture when she returned. The parlor stayed dark and cool all summer as Mrs. Tate, a hefty woman with silver hair, sat with her needlework behind the venetian blinds that she kept closed. French doors, which led to the hallway and front living room, were also kept closed. Like Grandma, Mrs. Tate always had an apron over her dresses.

Mrs. Tate wore lovely, print dresses that almost came down to her ankles. Her ankles were always swollen and stuck out over her heavy, leather shoes that she wore. She was never without some kind of stockings. She wore her silver hair pulled back, twisted and formed into a huge bun that sat regally on her neck. She secured it with a very large, tortoise shell hair pin.

The dining room had a large, round wooden table with heavy legs and "feet" that looked like a lion's. This was the first of its kind that I had seen. There was a monumental, gleaming sideboard that took up most of the wall near the kitchen. Mrs. Tate kept a very old mirror over the sideboard. It had unusual looking speckles around its beveled rim. The mirror appeared to distort images.

On the opposite wall stood a bowed, front, glass and wooden china cabinet stocked with flowered, china plates and a delicately patterned assortment of cups and saucers.

A Tiffany lamp swung low over the large, dining room table. It provided light through its lively colors. The yellow, red, green and blue stained glass flowers gave the room a look of a burst of spring in contrast to the dreary pattern of flowered wall paper. The Tate's flowered wall paper was dingy, it's once bright flowers muted with age and winter's coal dust.

A cold, steel-blue and green patterned linoleum, cracked and damaged around the edges near the doorways, covered the dining room floor. A large sepia-toned picture of Jesus and the Last Supper, hung on the wall opposite Mr. Tate's day bed, sealing the room in gloom.

The day bed, like the Tiffany lamp, was a gay contrast. It was covered with a quilt of elegant, multi-colored, shiny velvet and silk patches. These patches were soft and puffed high in cloud-like ridges. They were stitched together with cream-colored embroidery floss, in the Crow's Foot pattern.

It was not often that I got invited to the Tate's house; but when I did, I was amazed at all the things they had inside and the mixture of beauty and gloom that I felt it portrayed. When I saw the quilt and its Crow's Foot stitching, I wondered if it was Mrs. Tate who could have made such a beautiful thing. Was this what she did with her time and her needlework? She stayed out of sight, most of the time, controlling the dining room and backyard from the kitchen where she kept an eye on Ann from the windows.

Ann often played in the backyard where it was shady and cool. Mrs. Tate kept watch very well from her vantage points. It was from the backyard that Ann could see what I was doing, when I was outside, and could talk to me while I played.

There were other older children in our building, but the Tates would not let Ann associate with them. They thought them too old for Ann. They felt that these were children of working-class families, not the professional like their daughter, Miss Helene. The girls in the Helena had more responsibility helping with the laundry, cleaning and cooking. Ann had no such responsibility and at my age, neither did I.

Ann looked down at me from the buckling, wire fence that ran along that side of the Tate's property. I looked up past Ann's fat legs, past the fingers in her mouth and sometimes spoke with her. She could not hold my attention for long. My neck got tired looking up and above the retaining wall from our lower level to the Tate property.

I was flattered that Ann would talk to me. My aunts were like mothers and the Bells were like mothers. They all tended to me and gave me orders. Aunt Irene was the only one who conversed with me for fun. Uncle Bobby talked with me, but he was not there very much. Ann seemed lonely and just needed someone, anyone, with whom she could communicate.

On one rare occasion, Mrs. Tate allowed Ann to come over and play with me. I was surprised and very happy to have an older girl who wanted to spend time with me.

"Pappy's gone away," Ann said excitedly running down our cement stairs.

It was seeing Ann face-to-face that let me know how big she actually was. She was so much taller and much fatter. Granddaddy said I was so skinny because I didn't "eat nothin'." I thought that Ann must have eaten a lot and often. I felt grown up playing with Ann. She was delighted to play "tea party" with me.

My Aunt Lockey Jane had a beautiful luster-ware tea set that she received as a Christmas present years before. She kept the set wrapped in its original box and put away in the living room closet. I asked Grandma if I could play with it. She always said "No," but this time, with Ann as my guest, she said it would be alright, but I must be especially careful with it.

Ann and I made tea cakes out of mud and sliced them with the remains of a Wilson Condensed Milk can that we had retrieved from the garbage. We picked plantain stems and leaves and made make-believe "corn." We used the leaves of a giant weed that resembled cabbage and made our "play" dinner.

Grandma stopped sewing and came to the screen door. "How are you children getting along?" she asked.

"Fine," we said, pretending to eat our food.

"Ann, how's your grandmother?" Grandma asked holding the screen door ajar.

"She's just fine, Mrs. Corbin," Ann answered.

When Ann wasn't sucking her fingers, she had a beautiful voice. She had perfect diction, like her mother. Granddaddy said that Ann was going to be pretty, if she'd stop sucking her fingers. Otherwise, she would have a mouth that spread all over her face.

I tried to envision Ann as "all" mouth as I was "all" legs and feet. But, Ann's cheeks were so large; I could not imagine her mouth outstripping them.

"How's your mother?" Grandma asked.

I grew impatient. I wanted her to go back to her sewing so we could play. I never had "company" and I only got to play with my cousins, Mitzi and Joan, when Aunt Irene came.

Whenever Grandma and Granddaddy had company, Grandma ran me out saying, "Don't be sitting there staring down my throat at every word I say." I was so embarrassed that I could have melted into the floor. Granddaddy said that "children should be seen and not heard." I didn't feel bad about that. So, as Grandma stood there talking to my company, I wanted to tell her to go back in the house and mind her own business. I knew that I'd better not say that or Grandma would blame Ann for my acting up in front of her. Then, she would not allow Ann to visit again. I just sat tolerating Grandma's intrusion. Ann, on the other hand, seemed to enjoy the pleasant way in which my grandmother was speaking to her.

"Mother's having a nice time in Michigan," Ann told Grandma. "She sent a postcard of the lake and a picture of herself. It was beautiful up there. The picture was of her with Mary and Paula."

Mary and Paula were the white children Miss Helene was caring for. When Ann got the picture, she held it close to the fence so I could see it. But, all I could see was the white uniform that Miss Helene was wearing. This was quite a contrast to the soft, colorful, winter wools she wore when she taught school. Ann cherished that picture of her mother. Mrs. Tate made her bring it in the house and put it away so she wouldn't damage it.

"When is she coming home?" Grandma asked, dragging out the conversation.

"In August. It won't be long now, and she said that she's bringing me some nice things for school," Ann reported.

"Well, that's nice. She's a good mother."

Ann shook her head and smiled. I took a sip of make-believe tea from Aunt Lockey Jane's delicate, tan, lusterware teacup.

"Would you like some lunch?" Grandma asked.

Ann immediately replied and I followed suit, not because I was hungry, but because I felt I was losing my company to Grandma.

Grandma let us eat lunch outside at the tea table. It was nice and cool where we sat shaded by the Cottonwood tree. Lunch consisted of a bologna sandwich made on Taystee Bread with cherry Kool Aid. After serving us, Grandma returned to her sewing. Ann and I cleaned up the tea party and carefully restored Lockey Jane's dishes to its box.

Ann and I played "toss" in the upper part of the backyard and took turns swinging in the inner tube swing. When we tired, we rested on the safest of the rickety, wooden steps leading to the upstairs apartments. Ann decided that it would be a good idea to tell stories. She knew lots of fairy tales suitable for my age. She liked "Little Red Riding Hood." The wolf was frightening me, so she told the story of Hansel and Gretel. I was fascinated by her command of the tales.

As the afternoon wore on, we both became tired and bored. Ann had been very patient spending so much time with me, five years old at the time. After all, she was eleven and should have had more friends her own age with whom she could play. This wasn't the case.

Ann suggested that we play nurse and doctor. This seemed like a good idea. I had had many doctors at the clinic. They were all friendly and very kind. So were the nurses, in their white caps and uniforms. They wore white from head to toe. Their white shoes never showed one scuff mark. Everything was pure white. "I'll be the patient and you be the doctor," Ann said.

We looked around for something to use for the doctor's tools and found an old umbrella next to an empty garbage can in the storage room. We hurried out of there because it was so dark and scary. "We can use this!" Ann said, ripping one of the metal ribs out of the torn, broken umbrella.

"What do I do with it?" I asked, puzzled.

"Well, I'll lay down here," Ann motioned to the wooden riser, "and you pull down my bloomers, like the doctor does. Then, you stick this in here."

I worked at pulling down Ann's bloomers. Her legs were fatter and smoother than I had imagined. She took up so much space on the stair that she almost fell over.

Ann had fuzz in the same area as my aunts. But, they would never have wanted me to see their private parts. Ann did not have a problem with this.

I always turned my head when Grandma or any of the others, Hookey, Lockey Jane or Sister Bell, washed my "private part." I was always embarrassed, even though I did not know why. Grandma called it my "pocketbook."

"Ann," I asked, "where do I put this?"

"Right here," Ann pointed her finger at her "pocketbook."

She was irritated by my ineptness. Wanting her not to be upset with me, I took the long, thin, metal rib and was about to stick it any-where, even if it didn't hit the right place. Just then, my grandmother appeared at the corner of the steps. She was enraged by what she saw.

"I thought you two were too quiet out here," she yelled. "Sweetpea, you get in this house right now! Playing nasty games like that. Where'd you learn to play bad!? You know I don't let you do things like that. You're going to get a lickin' for this."

Ann shot up from the stair, retrieved her bloomers and started to talk. Grandma stopped her.

"You go home right this minute, Ann. You're older than Sweet-pea and you ought to know better. Your grandmother's not going to let you come over if you act like this, and I am sure going to tell her."

Grandma was angry and adamant. I was scared. I felt like a thief, but not sure what I had stolen. I hurried into the apartment, frightened and out of breath.

Ann began to talk really fast. "Mrs. Corbin, we didn't mean any harm. We won't do it again."

"I know you won't because I'm not going to let you come over and play anymore. Miz Tate!????? Miz Tate!????"

I could hear Grandma calling Ann's grandmother. Soon Mrs. Tate appeared at the fence and looked down at Grandma.

"Ann's been playing bad with Sweetpea. I caught them and I'm sending her home. I don't know where children get their ideas of pulling down their bloomers and that nasty stuff. I don't want her over here for a long while," she huffed.

I listened from behind the door, too embarrassed to be seen.

"Mrs. Corbin, I'm glad you're sending her home. She's gotten just so sassy. She tries to be too grown up. She'll be punished," Mrs. Tate said.

"And I'm going to give Sweetpea a tannin', too," Grandma said.

I froze in horror. Ann went home and Grandma told me to get in the bathroom. I began to plead, "Don't spank me Grandma. I won't do it anymore."

Grandma said, "I know you won't if I have anything to do with it, 'cause I'm goin' to give you a whipping you won't forget."

She was firm about this. I could not talk her out of it. She reached for Granddaddy's razor strap that hung on a nail in the back of the bathroom door. Granddaddy used this to sharpen his razor. It was a long, brown, thick leather strap. My eyes got big. I had been fussed at and yelled at. I had been whined at and Grandma had pleaded with me to go away and stop pestering her. I had been slapped on the bottom sometimes and switched on the legs, but never had I been whipped with Granddaddy's razor strap.

I started hopping up and down, wishing I had on a something to protect my legs, but the sun suits Grandma made for me to wear in the summer offered me no protection. I couldn't run, because Grandma had closed the bathroom door. There was only a small space between the toilet and the bathtub. I was trapped.

Grandma sat on the toilet seat, held me between her legs, doubled the thick strap in one hand and hit me several times. With each landing of the strap, she said, "Are you going to be bad anymore? Huh? You know better than to be bad, you nasty, little thing. Now don't you do that anymore as long as you live! Do you hear me?"

She hit with the words. She breathed hard and hit with the strap. It stung. It burned. It burned the welts onto my legs and onto my bottom. It was pain like I had never before experienced. I could not get out the cries because I could not breathe.

Grandma let me up and ordered me to my bedroom saying, "And don't get up the rest of the afternoon." She was breathing so hard, she had difficulty getting out all the words.

I ran to my room sobbing from the pain. I lay down on the big bed trying to get my breath, wanting desperately for the pain to go away. It did not. I could hear the same scene being repeated at the Tate house. Ann's loud wails floated through the open window. I continued to cry.

Long after the horrible sounds of the beatings had subsided, the atmosphere remained thick with their echoes. The summer air now seemed like a blanket of pain that had settled over me. I heard the hum of Grandma's sewing machine as she peddled away.

I went off to sleep, my body still stinging. I went off to sleep hearing the muffled, angry voices of Mr. and Mrs. Tate. I went off to sleep hearing their poll parrot, laughing, croaking, "Awwk, awwk! Shut up, Ann. Shut up, Ann. Go to your room, Ann."

15

I Visit my Mother for the First Time

I knew that Eckey was my mother and that I did not live with her because Grandma did not think she could "raise me right." But, one weekend Grandma allowed me to visit her for the first time.

I'm not sure how we got to her apartment, but when we did arrive, my half-brothers, Albert Cornelious, called "Sonny," and James, called "Jimmy," were waiting for us.

My mother and her family lived in a ground-level, garden apartment a short distance away near Gilbert Avenue. It was one of a series of apartments that opened onto a wide grass-covered courtyard separated by sidewalks leading around their complex to each apartment's door. When we arrived, children were playing safely on the grass just outside the apartments as there were no streets with automobile and bus traffic. I was so happy to see that I, too, could so easily get to the outside.

I remember the overnight stay and my mother fixing our breakfast of hot cereal in the morning. She was talkative, just like Grandma, but she didn't say angry things. I don't remember her hugging me, although she probably did, like Aunt Irene did when she came to see me. Another way that I could see that my mother was different from Grandma was that she spent time outside chatting with her neighbors. She had a wonderful laugh. Grandma rarely talked with anybody. She stayed in the house most of the time talking to me and herself. My mother seemed to be outside more than in.

My brother, Jimmy was just learning to walk, so my mother held him on her hip as she talked with her friends. My brother, Sonny, was four so he and I played together in the courtyard. We had to play quietly for awhile because my stepfather, Neil, slept until mid-morning because he worked nights driving a truck for the Darling Company.

Then, my mother left us to play while she got his breakfast before he left for work.

I also remember that at night, while my stepfather worked, my mother left us with a teenage girl while she went to the Beer Garden nearby with some of her lady friends. Grandma never went out at night and she only drank gin on Saturdays with Granddaddy. I didn't sleep well at my mother's although she left a light on in the bedroom where I slept with my brothers.

Even with this limited memory of my first visit, I recalled that I liked being able to walk out the front door of my mother's apartment to play. There were no broken, cement stairs to climb, no cement wall to stare out at from my bedroom or living room windows, and no cars and buses rushing down a busy street that I had to avoid. But I did wonder why my mother left us at night when it was dark.

One day, not long after my first visit, Aunt Irene came with my cousins to do her wash. While we children played, I heard Grandma and Aunt Irene talking about something that had happened to my little brother, Jimmy.

They said that my mother was doing her wash and had just filled a galvanized tub with boiling hot water. My mother didn't have a washing machine like ours. She had to heat the water in a kettle on the stove. She had placed the tub onto a step stool nearby. My toddler brother, Jimmy was crawling around on the floor playing while my mother worked. When my mother turned her back, he pulled himself up by holding the legs of the step stool. The tub of scalding water came down on top of him.

Jimmy was burned over eighty percent of his body and remained hospitalized for months. There was a photograph of him that appeared in the local newspaper, the *Cincinnati Enquirer*, covered with white, gauze bandages and only his eyes and a part of his mouth showing. He looked like a mummy I had seen in scary movies.

My grandmother blamed my mother. She said she was "careless" and "never did like doing housework." She added, "She doesn't pay those children no attention any way! I knew Sweetpea would be better off with me!" she emphasized.

My aunt thought it a terrible accident and just kept saying, "Poor, little Jimmy. Poor Eckey."

I could not imagine the awful pain little Jimmy experienced being burned so badly. It took months before my brother could return home. He bore the scars on his hands, face and body. His eyesight was affected as well.

Before Jimmy's accident, they said that my mother spent every night at the Beer Garden a few blocks from her apartment. She only went there when my step-father was at work. Aunt Irene and Hookey told how my mother drank lots of beer and got into arguments with the men. They said that if they were with her and any man tried to get "fresh," she was prepared to fight them.

I always sat very still, either on the bed or in a chair at the kitchen table, so I could absorb my aunt's and Grandma's conversations.

My Aunt Irene remarked to Aunt Hookey, "Eckey always was the one who'd fight for anyone of us! Remember when some guy got smart with me and Eckey just got right up in his face and dared him to say another word?"

Aunt Hookey nodded her head affirming Aunt Irene's statement.

"You're right, Corn (as Aunt Irene was sometimes called)," she said. "Even the big men were afraid of Eckey."

For awhile after Jimmy's accident, my mother continued this pattern of going to the Beer Garden, but then she got pregnant and bore her third son and fourth child, Ronald. With three little boys at home, and one of them badly burned, my mother spoke of a life changing experience.

My mother's sisters heard it first. She told them, that one night while on her way home from a drinking bout at the Beer Garden, she stumbled and fell to the sidewalk. She said that a voice from above said to her, "Saul, Saul! Why persecutest thou me?"

My mother told them it was the voice of God speaking to her, just as it had spoken to Saul, who later became Peter, one of Jesus' greatest disciples.

From that moment, my mother was in regular attendance at a Pentecostal Church nearby. She never again went to the Beer Garden to drink beer. She covered her body with long dresses and cleaned her face of make-up. She never again cut her hair, but let it grow long like it had been in her childhood. As a "Saved woman" my mother wore her hair parted into two sections, French braided on each side then pinned up along the back of her neck with huge, tortoise shell hairpins.

She came to visit me and Grandma one day several months after my visit. My mother sat on Grandma's bed while she was sewing at her machine. She told Grandma of her being a changed person. She said, "I've been saved by the blood of Jesus Christ."

Grandma never turned away from her sewing to acknowledge my mother's presence. That day, and in the same angry voice she said, "Saved! Huh! You always were a liar and always will be nothin' but a liar."

In spite of my mother's protests to the contrary, my grandmother remained adamant and accusatory. This visit from my mother ended like all the others. She left, our apartment in tears.

It was not long after when I learned that my mother, stepfather and brothers had moved away to the sub-division, an area fifteen miles north of Walnut Hills where we lived. It was a country area without electricity and indoor plumbing, but it was closer to my stepfather's family, the Prices, and the Darling Company where he worked.

My mother found another Pentecostal Church. This and their members became her new family. Neil, my step-father, did not join nor attend my mother's new church. She went alone to Wednesday night prayer meetings, and took the boys with her to Sunday Services.

ECKEY, MY MOTHER, AGE 19

1936, A YEAR BEFORE SHE JOINED
THE PENTECOSTAL CHURCH

Ethel Corbin Price

TEENAGE AUNTS WITH WHOM I LIVED AND THEIR
CLOSEST FRIENDS – 1936

L to R: Minnie Payden, best friend
My Aunt Catherine Corbin, "Hookey"

MY AUNT LOCKEY JANE, AUNT HOOKEY AND FRIENDS

L to R: Crystal Lucretia Corbin, my Aunt Lockey Jane, unknown, unknown, Catherine Corbin, myAunt Hookey

16

First Time Alone

Grandma put on her brown felt hat, her brown cloth coat and fastened its three huge buttons. With each of these movements I grew more anxious, more tense. She said she was going to cut patterns for slip covers for a customer.

Then Grandma said, "You'll be all right. I won't be gone long. Now, don't open the door for no one, you hear?"

Frightened by her leaving, I nodded my head affirmatively. A lump in my throat kept me from speaking. I was four years old. Grandma retrieved her purse from the white, flower-patterned, chenille bedspread that covered her bed. She checked inside her purse, removed the metal door key then firmly closed the clasp. I had never been left alone before. Grandma or one of my aunts was always there with me. Someone was either in the kitchen or the bedroom.

Grandma kept talking and giving me instructions as if she wanted to keep me occupied while she was away.

"Don't go into my dresser drawers. Don't play in the water or you'll catch a cold. Don't play in the bathroom. You can drink some milk and have some vanilla wafers, but don't eat them all. If anyone comes, don't open the door; just tell them, through the door, that I'll be back soon!"

I wished I could go with Grandma or stay with Mrs. Bell, but Mrs. Bell was working with the Mayo's getting ready for a big party, and Sister and Christine were at school.

"Now, when I go out, I'll lock the door behind me."

Grandma went out through my bedroom door. She used her long, metal key to lock the front door, and then deposited it in her purse. I saw her pass the living room window. I heard the sound of her feet scuffing along the walk growing fainter as she went up the cracked, cement steps. I knew that she would walk to the corner to catch the bus.

The apartment was ominously still, but as I looked around at the pot bellied stove, the bed and dresser, they seemed to be alive. I rushed to the safety of the kitchen where the morning sun filled the room. I had just finished breakfast, but was hungry again.

I went to the refrigerator and stood with the door open for a long time, searching for something I could eat. Nothing appealed to me. In my aloneness, I thought I heard Grandma telling me to shut the refrigerator door, but there was no voice.

I shut the refrigerator door and went to the kitchen closet. First I settled on the vanilla wafers but changed my mind as I spied the bottle of Karo Syrup. Grandma used Karo Syrup to make me syrup and butter sandwiches.

I set myself to my task at the kitchen table. First I got the large, green bowl Grandma used to serve hot vegetables for supper. I poured a great quantity of the thick, brown syrup into the empty bowl. Then, I put in a stick of butter.

I retrieved a fork from the cabinet drawer and, imitating Grandma, I began mixing the butter into the syrup. I kept stirring until the once deep brown Karo Syrup had turned a golden, caramel color. My hand ached from the mixing. I paid it no attention.

Never before had I been able to have all the syrup and butter that I wanted. I licked my fingers and the fork, savoring the taste. Wasting no time, I pulled the fresh loaf of Taystee Bread from the bread box on the cabinet, ripped open the end, removed the slice behind the "heel" of the loaf and began sopping, first one slice then another, into the mixture.

I stuffed the sandwich into my mouth, chewing huge chunks at a time. The syrup ran down the bread's crusty edges and dripped onto my dress. I scooped if off with a fresh slice of bread. Then I decided to fold the syrup-laden bread in half in order to avoid another accident. I leaned over the bowl and devoured another syrup sandwich.

In a very short time, I felt sick to my stomach, yet I had only removed half of the mixture from the bowl. I couldn't eat another bite, but, I dared not leave the syrup for Grandma to see when she got home. She would really fuss.

I decided to hide the bowl, with the remaining syrup mixture, under the kitchen sink. I thought the cotton curtain that Grandma made to go around the sink's wooden legs would be a sufficient cover. This was a safe place!

I remained in the kitchen, but as the time passed I became more apprehensive. Surely, at any minute, something was going to come through the kitchen door. Surely, some great ghost or monster from the scary movies I had seen with my cousins was ready to emerge out of thin air and destroy me. I kept my eyes glued to the doorway, waiting, breathing harder and faster. I began to perspire.

I pulled a chair away from the table and dragged it over to the window between the stove and the cabinet. The sun was warm and comforting on my face. I turned my attention from the doorway to the window and the outside.

I stared at the golden-brown autumn leaves that had fallen from the cottonwood tree and now made a heavy cover for the side of the hill near the apartment. They would turn into a compost pile against our apartment building's wall.

As I stared at the leaves, they came to life. They began to curl in on themselves. Some of them turned into yellow, polka-dotted snakes which began to crawl up the outside of the window where I sat. I could see their, flat, bright yellow underbellies, against the large, bottom window glass. I sat frozen, petrified. *"Grandma, please come home soon!"* I said to myself. *"I am so scared."*

I was too terrified to move from the window. I had a choice between the monsters waiting to come through the kitchen door or the snakes crawling up the window soon to come into the house when they reached the top. I decided to take my chances with the snakes.

The moment that I was certain of my demise, I heard Grandma's key in the lock.

I scrambled down off the chair, burst through the doorway past the imagined monsters and met Grandma as she came through the door. Never had I ever been so happy to see Grandma, to have her home.

After supper, Granddaddy left the kitchen for the living room where he relaxed, in his favorite chair, to read his paper. Grandma put hot water from the tea kettle into her dishpan to wash the dishes. She opened the curtain that surrounded the sink in order to scrape the dinner food scraps into the garbage pail. My heart stopped. Grandma spied the apple-green vegetable bowl with the syrup and butter mixture that I had made earlier.

It was taking her awhile to determine the contents as she sniffed it and held it up to the light. I could see the question on her face, but then she figured it out.

"What in the world!?" she said, "Sweetpea, why would you waste my syrup and good butter like this? A whole bowl full!"

"What'd she do, Mama?" Granddaddy called from behind his evening paper.

"Mixed a whole, bowl full of syrup and butter and then hid it under the sink. Good thing I found it. We'd have ants crawling everywhere!"

Grandma poured hot, soapy water into the bowl and let it sit on the edge of the sink to soak.

I felt ashamed that I had been found out. But there was no threat of punishment.

I was relieved.

"That's what she is," Granddaddy said, "She's a little, piss ant."

Grandma continued muttering about the waste. Granddaddy continued reading his paper. I sat in silence at the kitchen table glad that my grandparents were home with me.

That night, nothing else mattered now that the snakes were gone from the window and Granddaddy was sitting in the living room, with the lights on, where the monsters had been.

17

The Metropolitan Insurance Man

The Metropolitan Insurance man came every Monday morning. Grandma kept her insurance policies secured in an envelope marked *Metropolitan*. It hung on a nail that had been hammered into the door frame between her bedroom and the kitchen. The envelope was so high up I could only see the bottom edge when I was close to the door. It was a tan color with dark printing on the front. Since the envelope had no flap and was open at the top, the policies were quite visible when I stood on the other side of the room.

The nail was tiny, but sturdy enough to hold the policies in clear view and easy for Grandma to retrieve. The gas and pot bellied stoves deposited a film which discolored the top of the envelope. The film, from the coal-burning and gas stoves, formed on the wallpaper making once beautiful flower prints, dull and lifeless. Wallpaper cleaner came in a can. It was a rubber-like substance that when formed into a ball was rubbed over the grimy paper collecting the dirt. The wallpaper then looked like new again.

The insurance man, whose name was Jim, came every Monday. When he came, it was like having company. I ran to open the door. Jim was a large, ruddy colored, white man who always wore a dark, business suit, white shirt and tie. He was never without his hat, which he removed when he entered our apartment.

"Hello," he said. "Is your grandmother home?" "Ummmhuh," I answered.

Grandma heard the knock on the door and had already retrieved the envelope, with the policies, from the nail.

"Good morning, Mrs. Corbin. How're you today?" Jim asked Grandma.

He was very mannerly and respectful to Grandma. I liked Jim. When he came, I usually sat on the side of my bed with a coloring book to keep me busy; but which also allowed me to legitimately stay in the room where I could pay attention to the conversations. This way Grandma could not easily dismiss me as she and Granddaddy usually did if they had company. They always said that children should be seen and not heard.

Grandma smiled, then frowned as she replied, "Oh not too good today Jim. My arthritis keeps actin' up."

Grandma never answered the question "how are you today" by just saying "fine." She never failed to use every opportunity to go through a litany of complaints. Sometimes she told Jim that she had a "lot of gas" or that her diabetes was "acting up." Jim listened patiently, a look of honest, heartfelt concern gracing his plump, but strong featured face. He was more kind to Grandma because Granddaddy would have told her to stop complaining.

Jim was not old like Grandma, Granddaddy and Mr. Tate. He had sandy colored hair that seemed just a shade darker than the color of his face. His black insurance book always preceded him through the door. He then set it comfortably on his knees as he took his usual seat in the high backed-chair that stood in the bedroom, where I slept with my aunts. Grandma used Jim's visit to rest herself in the rocking chair, close to the pot-bellied stove, just inside the living room doorway.

Jim took the insurance policy from the envelope, removed the payment card and noted the amount being paid by Grandma. When he finished, he handed Grandma the payment card, which she returned to the envelope. He then turned to watch me as I colored in the coloring book Aunt Hookey had bought for me.

"Mrs. Corbin, how old is your little grandchild now?" He said turning back towards Grandma.

"She's four going on five. She'll be five in October," Grandma answered.

"Well, I was wondering if you had given any thought to her education?" Jim said.

"What do you mean?" Grandma asked.

"About her getting a good education after high school. Going on to college?" Jim waited for Grandma to take in what he was saying.

I could tell that Grandma was thinking about what Jim was saying because she didn't say anything right away. Then, she answered. "Nobody in our family has ever gone to college, except some of my relatives in Kentucky. None of my children has finished high school yet, with this Depression. I used to love school myself," Grandma said, "but my husband didn't go past the third grade. I was smart, too. All my teachers just loved me."

"I know a lot of families in your same situation," Jim replied. "They don't have the money when the time comes to go to college, if they get that far. But, they all want their children to have a better education than they did." Jim sat forward in the chair, a serious look on his face which Grandma studied intently.

Then he continued, "I know you don't think you need to consider college now, but that's why I wanted to talk with you. You take such good care of your granddaughter and you seem like a very intelligent lady. I decided that if I did talk to you, you would give some thought to what I said." Jim took a deep breath, tucked his shirt into the back of his pants and sat back in his chair. "Our company has a policy, an Education Policy, which will help you plan for your child's future. And only if you start now can you assure her of a good educational, foundation."

"But, I don't have money for another policy," Grandma said solemnly.

"Hear me out," Jim advised. "With this type of policy, our Company makes it possible for people, like you to pay a little each week then by the time their child reaches college age, there will be enough money to go to college."

As hard as I tried, I could not understand what Jim was saying. I was pleased that he and Grandma were talking seriously about me.

Jim continued, "You pay only twenty-five cents a week. That's about the same amount you pay for a quart of milk. Then, when your grandbaby's finished high school, you can cash in the policy. There'll be enough money for her to attend college."

Grandma thought for awhile. "It really would be nice to have at least one of the children go on to college. I thought my other children would make somethin' of themselves, but it didn't turn out that way. I know I won't be able to count on her mother to do nothin' for her." Grandma's voice turned harsh as it always did when she spoke of my

110

mother. "Her mother didn't think nothin' of her own education. She liked baseball and being a tomboy all the time."

"Well, your little grandchild appears to like doing other things. I've seen her looking at books when I've been here. Does she read?" Jim asked.

"No, not yet. But she likes coloring and looking at her aunt's school books."

Grandma was right, I did like looking at Aunt Lockey Jane's notebooks. This was the first time I knew that Grandma had been paying attention. Aunt Lockey Jane got mad when I bothered her books.

"She needs to be encouraged," Jim told Grandma. "Only an intelligent lady like you can make her life better." He paused, and then continued, "Tell you what! You think about what I just said and next week we'll talk some more. But, don't put it off too long. It's an inexpensive policy and you'll need to start soon if there's to be enough money for her college." Jim rose to leave.

"I'll think about it, Jim. I'm glad you told me. I'll probably be the only one she can depend on. Nobody else will think about her education," Grandma said.

Jim smiled and patted Grandma's hand. He told her she was a very considerate grandmother. Then, he collected his black, hard-back payment book and departed.

When Jim came the following Monday, Grandma was again happy to see him.

"Jim," she said, "I've decided to get that educational policy you were talking about."

Jim smiled broadly and sat down in the high backed chair.

"I knew you were a smart grandmother. Now, all we need to do is get some information on your grandbaby and you'll be all set with her educational policy. You won't have to begin your payments until the first of the month. That will give you some time to set aside the twenty-five cents."

One Monday morning in the spring, Jim came to collect the insurance payments, but this time he had another man with him. The man was younger-looking than Jim and was a full head taller. He was thin, gangly and impatient. His face was the same color as Granddaddy's face when he was out in the summer sun, working all day on rooftops. But unlike Jim, this man had a head full of bushy, red hair and red eyebrows.

"Mrs. Corbin, this is Bill Conley. He's going to be your new insurance man. Bill, this is Mrs. Lillian Corbin. You will be collecting from her each week," Jim said. Bill didn't smile, just nodded his head.

Grandma was very surprised. "But Jim, what about you? Where are you going? We can't lose you. Are you leaving the Company?" She asked.

"No, I'm not leaving the company, Mrs. Corbin. I have a new job. I will be leaving the area, though."

"You're still goin' to sell insurance aren't you?"

"No, Mrs. Corbin, I won't be selling anymore insurance policies. I'll be working behind a desk in the main office."

"They're tryin' to make a big shot out of you," Grandma teased.

Bill Conley did not smile. He fidgeted with his striped tie and kept shifting the black insurance book from one hip to the other. He cleared his throat impatiently, to get Jim's attention.

Jim turned away from Grandma just as she was saying, "I am going to miss you, Jim." She was sincerely disappointed by his leaving.

"Oh, well, yes, Mrs. Corbin," Jim said with his back to Grandma. "I hope it will be a good promotion for me. But, now, Bill here will write up your payments for today and from now on."

Grandma was looking at Bill Conley, waiting for him to smile or give some indication that he was acknowledging her presence, but Bill Conley's eyes were glued to his tie and the black insurance book. He never looked at Grandma, or me. I could tell he wasn't friendly like Jim.

112

Bill sat down in the chair where Jim always sat. Grandma sat in the rocking chair. He took the envelope from Grandma and said nothing.

Jim said, "There are two policies. The most recent one is the Educational Policy." He looked over Bill's shoulder as he removed the policies.

"Mmmmhuh," Bill muttered. He did not look up.

Grandma asked him, "You been an insurance man very long?" Grandma didn't smile. She sounded as if she wasn't sure she wanted to ask Bill Conley anything.

"Yes, I have," Bill said an artificial, lilting, singing quality to his voice.

Still there was no smile on his face. The room was more still than I had ever known it to be with so many people inside.

"There! That takes care of it." Bill looked up and handed Grandma the payment card. He got up from the chair. "I'll be coming the same time each week," he said.

"Ummmhuh," Grandma said, "just like Jim." Grandma's tone was cool. She sounded like she wanted this Bill Conley to know that she didn't need to be reminded of something that had been routine.

Bill looked at her. "Yes. Yes. Just like Jim."

"I'm going to miss seeing you, Mrs. Corbin," Jim said. "I want to thank you for being such a fine customer, always paying on time and for being so pleasant. It was a real pleasure serving you."

"Jim, I'll miss you, too. But you're going to be a fine man to have in that main office. You take care of yourself." Grandma took Jim's hand and shook it vigorously. The warm smile had returned to her face.

I turned away from my coloring book to witness Grandma's goodbye to Jim. Bill Conley said a short goodbye and hurried out the door as if he didn't want to be there any longer than necessary. Jim stood shaking Grandma's hand. But Grandma's eyes followed Bill Conley's fast movement out the door. She had a strange look on her face.

Bill Conley's Monday visit to collect the insurance payment was not like having company come to visit. He was matter-of-fact, unsmiling and cold.

"May I have your card, Lillian?" he asked Grandma.

I had never heard Grandma's first name used with such familiarity by someone whom she had only recently met and who was so much younger. Most people in our neighborhood Bill Conley's age always referred to the older people as "Miss, Mrs. or Mister." I thought Grandma was going to correct him, but she didn't.

The first time Bill called her Lillian, she just overlooked it. She tried to be amiable. She asked Bill questions in the same manner as she had asked Jim. I thought Grandma wanted to see if he could be cordial.

"Do you have a family, Bill?"

"Unhuh," he said, his eyes glued to the payment card.

"Any children?" Grandma probed.

"Unhuh," Bill crossed off the square for the day, but volunteered no additional information about his private life. He did not unbutton his suit jacket, no matter if it was a scorching, hot day.

By the third visit from Bill, Grandma no longer tried to be cordial. She did not ask Bill about his family. When she used his first name, it was the same, cold familiarity that Bill used her name. She no longer sat in the rocking chair. She stood holding the door. I watched a very different Grandma. When Bill Conley finished marking the payment book and was about to make his, unsmiling, officious "goodbye," Grandma exploded.

"Mr. Conley," she raised her voice. "I have never had no insurance man who was as nasty as you. You act like this house is dirt and that I'm beneath you. Well, I'll have you know that I know everyday,

114

ordinary people with better manners than you. My mother taught me to be courteous to people. But, your mother sure didn't teach you no manners; and if you think you can act that way in my house simply because I'm a colored lady and you're white, you just better have another think comin'."

I had heard Grandma and Granddaddy arguing during their Saturday lunches, after they had been drinking, about each other's old, white daddies. I heard Grandma criticize Granddaddy's boss, Mayor Reed for not paying him enough. These were always white people who were not physically in our apartment. But on this day, Grandma exploded at this white insurance man. I was frightened. I stopped coloring. My eyes were glued to the two, my angry grandmother and a startled Bill Conley.

She snatched the payment card out of the Bill Conley's hand. His face turned redder than his hair. Before he could say a word, Grandma said, "And if you can't act no better than you've been actin', you needn't bother to come back here."

Bill Conley stammered. He was scared. "I-I-I-I'm sorry, Lil… uh, Mrs. Corbin. I certainly didn't mean you any offense. I just have so many stops to make that…"

Grandma didn't let him finish what he was going to say. She interrupted, "I don't care how many stops you have, this one won't be one of them long." Grandma was relentless.

"Well, I don't want you to do that…I'll just not worry so much," Bill laughed nervously.

"I hope for your sake that you won't," Grandma retorted.

Bill smiled, quickly saying, "I'll see you next week, then, Mrs. Corbin?" and he exited hurriedly. He was like a freed, once-caged animal.

Grandma shut the door with such force that the noise resounded through the four rooms and hallway. The windows in the kitchen shook. Grandma had even forgotten that it was too hot to shut the door. It cut off the cool breeze we got from this shaded sided of our building.

Grandma fussed and fumed for another hour after Bill had left. She wouldn't let go of her pent-up indignation. "Old, red-headed, peckerwood," she fumed. "Makes me sick actin' like he's better'n me. Ain't nothin' but an old, ill-mannered peckerwood."

The next Monday when Bill came to collect, he was a different insurance man. He smiled and talked to Grandma. He told her he had a wife named Margaret and three children, all boys; and that he liked to bowl. Grandma smiled and said, "That's nice."

I wondered what he meant when he said that he "liked to bowl!"

18

Home from Longview

One winter, my Uncle Bobby came home from the Longview State Hospital for the insane. A few Wednesday's before was Grandma's day to visit Uncle Bobby. She always took banana pudding, his favorite dessert, which she had carefully prepared.

That Wednesday when Grandma got home, she told us the news.

"The doctor said that Robert's well enough to come home," Grandma said as she served me and Granddaddy our supper.

"You talked to the doctor?" He asked.

"Yes. He said Robert has done so well since he was admitted that he can come home for good."

"When's he coming, Grandma?" I asked excited by the news.

"Soon, maybe in a week or two. I'll know when I go to the hospital again next Wednesday."

Grandma dished up the steaming mashed potatoes from her green vegetable bowl.

Granddaddy and I waited. It was Wednesday evening and Wednesday was liver, onions and spinach night. Grandma cooked the liver and onions in her black, cast iron skillet. Then, she smothered the combination with water to make gravy. She left the liver and onions to simmer while she checked the spinach, to see if it was ready.

We bowed our heads and Granddaddy said Grace.

"Thank you for this food we are about to receive for the strength and nourishment of our bodies, Amen."

The verse never varied. The steam rising from my awaiting dinner bathed my face as I grew ever more impatient to eat. Wednesday supper was one of my favorites.

"Stop fidgeting so much," Grandma scolded.

"What'd the doctor say," Granddaddy asked.

"He was a nice doctor. Not like some of the others. I've never talked with him before. He was young with blonde hair," Grandma said.

I envisioned Grandma sitting in a hospital room talking to a faceless man with blonde hair and a white coat, the kind that I had seen the orderlies wear when Granddaddy and I visited Uncle Bobby on the violent ward.

"What did he say!?" Granddaddy repeated. He grew impatient and irritable.

"Just that he's doin' well. They let him start workin' in the Commissary and they've moved him to building Number 7."

"I asked the doctor if he knew what had made Robert sick. He said that it was as if there was a record player in Robert's head with a record going round and round and that ever so often, the needle just got stuck," Grandma continued.

I envisioned the record in my Uncle's head with a stuck needle like Uncle Francis' record on his Victrola record player. I kept eating.

"Does he think he will be home for good this time? He's come home before," my grandfather said skeptically.

"Oh, yes. He says that he reviewed all of Robert's records and he's better than he's ever been."

Granddaddy said nothing, his large jaws moving up and down as he chewed his food.

"Take your elbows off the table, Sweetpea!" Grandma snapped at me. "You'd think you hadn't been taught no manners."

I jumped, startled by the new admonition, then let out a long, slow sigh.

"Don't be sighin' like some smart aleck, either," Grandma said. "Just eat your supper and don't be sassy."

She continued speaking to Granddaddy, "He looked so well today. His eyes were clear and the color in his face was good."

118

Grandma put her finger in her mouth and extracted a gray looking piece of vein from the liver she had been chewing. She dropped this, unceremoniously, on her plate.

I was so happy. My Uncle Bobby was coming home. This time he would be home for good. Grandma said so.

He arrived one very cold day with his belongings in a brown paper, grocery bag.

"Uncle Bobby! Uncle Bobby!" I cried running to meet him.

Grandma lingered behind to pay the taxi cab driver who had brought them home.

"Hi Sweetie!" My uncle said. He threw down the sack with his clothing and stooped down to grab me as I ran to him. He hugged me, laughing and rubbing the top of my head.

"Well, I'm going to be home for good this time," he told me. "We'll have lots of fun."

I squeezed his hand and skipped along beside him as we headed down the cement stairs and to the door to the apartment.

"Grandma made you banana pudding," I informed my uncle.

"We can have a good time eating it after supper," he laughed.

I held the door open for him. The pot bellied stove in my room sent heat throughout the house making it very cozy.

"It feels good in here," my uncle said blowing on his hands.

'I can put the coal in by myself," I said proudly.

"You can?" he asked.

"Yeah. And I can do the dishes, too. But I don't like doing dishes," I said.

"Well, I can help you now." My uncle had a big smile on his face.

"Granddaddy helps me sometimes if I take too long and Grandma starts to fuss."

My uncle took off his coat and sat in the mohair chair in the living room. He calmly looked around the room. Grandma came in out of breath.

"How's it feel to be home? You hungry? I made banana puddin'," she said.

"I know. Sweetie told me."

"You didn't get into Robert's puddin' did you?" Grandma stared at me.

"Unhuh! I just had vanilla wafers."

"Well, for once you did what you were told," Grandma said.

"Mama, why don't you sit down and rest now. I'm not hungry. I'll wait 'til Dad gets home," my uncle said.

"All right, honey, whatever you say. It's so good to have my son home."

My grandmother's voice changed. She leaned over and patted Uncle Bobby on the cheek and started talking in "baby talk" to him.

"Goin' to be home a good, long time, too," she cooed. "You want to go in my room and lay down for awhile?" Grandma continued.

"No. I'm not tired. I think I'll put my clothes away, though," Uncle Bobby said.

"Grandma cleaned a drawer for you in my dresser," I volunteered.

My uncle quickly and happily became acclimated to the home environment. I followed him around while Grandma prepared supper. Now the apartment was once again filled with three big people and me.

After a week of adjusting and running errands for Grandma, Uncle Bobby announced, "I think I'll go see Mrs. Rainey about my old job."

120

"Are you sure you're ready to do that, now?" Grandma questioned.

"Yes. I liked working for her and she told me that anytime I wanted my job back, I could have it."

Uncle Bobby's old job was going door to door selling Mrs. Rainey's homemade pies, yeast rolls, and bread. He carried them around in a large basket with the items covered with a clean dish cloth. He started out with warm baked goods. Not many people could resist Mrs. Rainey's bread and pies.

The Rainey's lived in a very nice, single family home around the corner from Rosen's grocery store on Ashland Avenue. They operated their bakery from their kitchen. Uncle Bobby did return to work and I looked forward to the little apple pies and rolls he would sometime bring home at the end of his delivery day.

It was two weeks after he had begun work that Mrs. Rainey told Uncle Bobby she couldn't use him anymore because they did not have enough customers. Uncle Bobby broke the news to us over supper.

"Well, if she doesn't have the business, she doesn't have the business," Granddaddy said matter-of-factly. "You'll get another job." He consoled my uncle.

Later, we learned that some of Mrs. Rainey's customers were afraid to have Uncle Bobby delivering their bread and pies. Several had heard that he had been in Longview. They were scared and began canceling their orders.

Grandma got mad and fussed, "People make me sick," she said slamming her scissors on the machine as she sewed. "Robert wouldn't hurt nobody. He never has!"

Uncle Bobby did find another job. This time it was with the Tastee Bread Company. It was on the street behind the Sears Roebuck Department Store where we caught the bus when we went to visit him at Longview Hospital. Tastee's was several blocks away from our apartment, but Uncle Bobby could choose to walk or take the bus. He loved walking, so most of the time he walked to work.

This time he worked inside loading delivery trucks. Every evening when he got off work, he brought home a surprise for me.

"Brought you some jelly rolls, today, Sweetie," he said handing me a package.

He had brought these home in a large sack which he set on the kitchen table and carefully removed one package at a time. Taystee allowed its employees to take home any of their products that had the least bit of damage done to them in the loading or packaging process.

"Now don't eat any of that 'til after supper," Grandma said. "Robert, don't let her have any of that now," she repeated.

"All right, Mama. Sweetie, we'll put these away until later," he smiled.

"Awwww," I pouted.

"No use pokin' that lip out," Grandma said.

After supper I rushed to get the jelly rolls. The fresh, soft cakes with red, strawberry colored jelly spread over them then rolled into the little cakes. They came two to a package. The outsides were generally a little brown and crusty. This part I left, while eating all the rest.

"Look at how wasteful you are," my grandfather said perturbed. "If I was Robert, I wouldn't bring you anymore.

My uncle did not pay attention to the corrections I was getting from my grandparents; he was dressing to go out. This was a rare change.

"Where're you goin'?" Grandma asked. She was surprised since Uncle Bobby stayed home most of the time when he was not working. Granddaddy eyed him over the edge of his paper.

"Where you think he's going? He's got a big date."Granddaddy laughed as he teased Grandma.

"I thought I might go up to the drugstore, then over to visit this girl I met at work," my uncle told Grandma.

"Girl? What girl is that?" Grandma asked.

"It's none of your business, Sister. Leave the man alone," Granddaddy said.

"Her name is Dora. I just met her the other day and we talked," my uncle said.

"How do you have time to talk when you're supposed to be workin'." Grandma sounded annoyed.

"We talk at lunchtime, Mama," my uncle answered.

Grandma raised her eyebrows and stared at him. I got up and threw the crumbs from my jelly roll into the garbage can Grandma kept under the kitchen sink.

"Can I go with you, Uncle Bobby?" I asked.

"Not this time, Sweetie. Maybe next time," he said. I was disappointed by his answer since my uncle rarely refused me.

"Robert who is this Dora?" Grandma persisted.

Granddaddy groaned, "A man can't have no privacy and peace around you two," he said.

"Dora works with me, Mama."

"Oh?! Where does she live? Who are her people?" Grandma pressed my uncle for answers.

"She lives on Kerper Avenue," Uncle Bobby said showing infinite patience.

"*Kerper!*?" Grandma acted as if she had been stung.

I thought my uncle said purple.

"Don't nothin' but real, rough people live over there, son," she cautioned.

"Naw, it's not so bad, Mama. I don't know Dora's people. I just started talking to her the other day."

"Well, don't be gone too long now," Grandma advised.

Granddaddy gave a sarcastic laugh and kept reading his paper.

Uncle Bobby returned a little after nine. He brought me a package of Charms, his favorite candy.

"Sweetie, I put some candy on the dresser for you to have tomorrow." He spoke quietly and I heard him although I was half asleep.

By spring, Uncle Bobby had spent a lot of time with Dora. One evening he told grandma, "Mama, Dora and I are thinking about getting married."

For several seconds Grandma was speechless. Then, she managed to say, "Son we don't even know this Dora. What's she like. Who her people are. Don't you think this is a little soon?"

"Oh, I was planning to bring her around to see you, Mama. We aren't going to get married right away. We're just thinking about it."

I was sitting at the kitchen table having a glass of milk when Grandma broke the news to my aunts. She was very upset.

"Robert's talkin' about marryin' some woman he met at work. I don't know nothin' about her, who she is or nothin'. He's goin' to make himself sick again," she cried.

My aunt Hookey thought it would do my uncle good. "He needs to be on his own, Mama."

Aunt Irene said, "Awww, ain't that sweet."

Grandma felt betrayed. She continued her campaign to gain sympathy.

"Robert's not ready for marriage. He ain't been home from the hospital long enough."

"Mama, this is the first girlfriend Robert has had. All those years his friends were that sissy Freddie Cisco and "Big Meat" down in Kentucky.

Grandma stared at Aunt Hookey in utter amazement. "Hookey, that's a terrible thing to say. Freddie is a sweet child."

I wondered what my aunt meant.

124

"Aw, Mama, you don't know the half of it. We all love Freddie. His being sissified made not one bit of difference to us. We danced and had a lot of fun when he came, but we still knew that he was kinda funny."

"You're just talkin'. Anybody who is good looking and decent, you always have something bad to say about them," Grandma said.

"Mama, why don't you use your eyes sometime?" Aunt Hookey continued. "Didn't you ever pay any attention when Freddie'd come switchin' in here out of the blue from Cuba or some place like that? He showed us how to do the Rhumba and all the latest dances."

I remembered Freddie Cisco. He was always traveling to one place or another; but when he came back, he stopped at our house to see everybody and to ask about Uncle Bobby when he was at Longview.

I didn't understand what Aunt Hookey was saying because they all squealed and laughed, talked and danced right in the kitchen whenever Freddie came. He was as handsome as a movie star, with beautiful, even teeth and straight, black hair. His voice sparkled. Whenever Freddie was around, our apartment had an air of festivity. He was my uncle's best friend.

"Well, I don't care what you say. Robert did not go around with no 'sissies'," Grandma said.

That closed that conversation. Grandma went back to talking about Dora. "But, I don't know nothin' about this gal Robert's talkin' about marryin'."

"You don't have to know everything," Aunt Hookey bullied.

"Just never mind. There ain't no use in my tryin' to talk to you and your evil self," Grandma retorted.

One day after work, my uncle brought Dora home to meet Grandma and Granddaddy. I knew there was going to be trouble the minute I saw Dora. Dora had very dark skin and Grandma did not like black people. I had certainly heard enough of her talk about the black Martins, my real father and his family, to know that.

My uncle was very gentle as he introduced Dora to Grandma and Granddaddy. Dora had a nice smile and was a very, soft spoken and kind person like my uncle. She was not unattractive and dressed very well. Grandma was stiff and formal. Granddaddy was almost gallant he was so nice.

"Hello, Miz Corbin," Dora said in her slight, southern accent. "Robert talks about you and Mr. Corbin all the time."

"That's nice," Grandma said not smiling. "We've heard a lot about you, too, and I told Robert that it was past time for us to meet you."

Uncle Bobby escorted Dora to the sofa where they sat down. He called to me to come sit by him. "And," he said turning to Dora, "this is my little niece Sweetpea."

"Oh, my goodness," Dora said smiling broadly. "He just loves you. Talks about you all the time and every time there are some goodies, you're the first person he talks about takin' 'em home to." She laughed. I liked Dora.

"It's nice of you to come see us," Granddaddy said, smiling. "Are you the one making all those good cakes up there at Tastee's? Robert says it's your own recipe," Granddaddy winked.

Dora thought he was serious. "Naw, Mr. Corbin. I jus' package them." She laughed again.

"You lived around here long, Dora?" Grandma asked.

"Yes, Ma'm. I've been her ten years."

"Where from?"

"Well, my peoples is from Georgia but we lived in downtown Cincinnati for awhile. We moved to O'Briensville. You know where that is?"

"Yes. That's not too far from here," Granddaddy answered.

"Where downtown did you all live?" Grandma asked.

She interrogated Dora like she was on the witness stand. Uncle Bobby became uneasy. He moved from side to side in his seat.

126

"We lived down there near Sixth Street. You know where the Cotton Club is?"

"That's a pretty rough part of town to grow up in," Grandma sniffed haughtily.

"Yes, Ma'm. Sho' was, but we didn't mind it," Dora answered.

"Do you know that Robert's been sick most of his life?" Grandma's asked.

Her question punctured the air like a javelin being thrown at a distant target. Uncle Bobby turned gray.

"I told Dora all about that, Mama. There's no need to worry any more."

"Well, I just want to be sure that she knows what you all are getting' into."

"Yes, Ma'm. We've talked about it. Robert knows my situation and children, too. We gets along fine." Dora patted my uncle's hand. I sat closer to him.

"I didn't know you had children," Grandma said.

"Mama, I told you Dora has two children," my uncle said defensively.

Granddaddy laughed in hopes of reducing the rising tension in the room.

"You know your mama hears just what she wants to hear."

"Oh, shut up! You don't know what you're talkin' about," Grandma said.

Grandma told Dora that Robert had no money. Dora said she knew that, and after several more tries at dissuading Dora and making her more uncomfortable, Grandma finally gave up. Dora seemed very resilient, but then it could have been that she just didn't sense Grandma's hostility and thought these legitimate questions for a mother to be asking.

Granddaddy got Dora some lemonade. A silence fell over the room. Finally, my uncle who had become decidedly uneasy rose and told Dora it was time for them to leave. "You can come with me to walk Dora home," my uncle said to me.

"O.K. Can we stop at the Drugstore?" I asked.

"There she goes spending every penny she gets. 'Fraid it might burn a hole in her pocket," Granddaddy laughed.

"Just like my kids," Dora laughed. "Spends every penny they gets on bubblegum."

"We can stop, and we'll get something for the others, too," Uncle Bobby said.

He seemed a little more relaxed. Grandma got up. She told Dora it was nice to meet her, but that she'd better get back to her slip-covers. She abruptly left the room. We were happy about going and paid little attention to Grandma's behavior.

Granddaddy saw us to the door. "Don't be gone too long," he said, then went back to his chair and his paper.

I skipped ahead of Uncle Bobby and Dora. They walked behind me holding hands and giggling. We stopped at the Soda Shop on Chapel Street instead of Mangrum's Drugstore. I had an ice cream cone while Uncle Bobby played the Juke Box. It was the year when the song *Drinkin' Rum and Coca Cola* by the Andrews Sisters was very popular. Uncle Bobby sang along with the record and danced. He was so happy. We left the Soda Shop with the music ringing in our ears and enjoying the walk in the warm, night air.

Grandma was relentless in her attacks on Dora. Uncle Bobby was just as relentless in his defense of her.

When anger didn't work Grandma cried. "Don't nobody care about how I feel or what I think. Why is everybody so ungrateful? Give all my life's blood and what do I get in return? Nothin', not even respect."

My uncle grew more and more unhappy. Gone was the cheerful manner when he came in from work. He changed clothes without eating supper and left.

128

One evening after work Uncle Bobby brought home a bag of cakes as usual.

"Brought you some cakes, Sweetie," he said.

Uncle Bobby was happy, almost giddy in a strange way.

"Come see," he called out. "Look at this and this, and this!" He said dumping the cakes out in the center of the kitchen table, giggling. "Here, eat this!"

Uncle Bobby stuffed a cellophane wrapped cake into my mouth.

"Unhun," I said, taking it out and moving away from his outstretched hand. "I don't want any now."

"Well, then how about some Charms? Here, I got a whole pocketful of them. Bought out the store." My uncle giggled, shoving his hand into the pocket of his work clothes extracting the candy.

"Robert?" Grandma said from her place at the stove. "Don't give her any of that stuff now. It'll spoil her dinner."

"Okay. Okay. Mama says you can't have any now, Sweetie. Wait til' after supper."

My uncle piled all the candy back into the paper sack and threw it into the corner by the sink. He left to go into the bathroom, laughing strangely all the way.

Grandma did not sense the change in his behavior. I did. I recognized that this was a different Uncle Bobby. I recognized something that was familiar from other times.

The next morning as my uncle prepared for work he remained in the bathroom running water in the sink.

"Robert," my grandmother cried out, "Come on out of the bathroom, son. If you don't hurry, you'll be late for work." Robert did not answer. "Don't run the water too long, now," Grandma said.

When Uncle Bobby left the bathroom his hair was wet, but he was dressed for work. He left and did not return home. He had, instead, run away to Lexington to Grandma's Aunt El who was a Teacher and a Funeral Parlor owner and director.

The call, from her Aunt El, came to Grandma through a neighbor. Uncle Bobby was brought home and returned to Longview State Hospital.

We never saw or heard from Dora after that. On Sundays I went with Granddaddy to visit Uncle Bobby and on Wednesdays Grandma went by herself to visit him. After one Wednesday's visit, Grandma came home crying. She said that Uncle Bobby was very disturbed. She said he wasn't himself and that he yelled at her and said, "You're not *my mother! I don't have a mother!*"

On Sunday when Granddaddy and I went to see Uncle Bobby we were told that he had been transferred to Ward 18, the violent Ward, and wasn't ready to have visitors.

The time finally arrived when Uncle Bobby could have visitors again. The Sunday after Easter was to be the time that Granddaddy and I could pay him a visit as we had done before his violent outburst.

I had gotten a new coat and black, patent leather shoes for the holiday and Grandma made my Easter dress. I wanted to look especially nice for this first time seeing Uncle Bobby after so much time had passed.

Whenever there was a holiday like Christmas and Easter, Grandma gave me Shirley Temple curls. She washed my hair over a basin that she had filled with hot water and set on the kitchen table. She dried my hair with a large towel, then had me sit on the floor between her legs. She sat in a kitchen chair and put the large jar of Vaseline with the comb and brush next to each other on the table.

My hair was not completely dry as she parted sections of it then placed her finger in the Vaseline jar and came out with a lump o the pale, thick Vaseline. This she put part on my scalp and put the rest on the section of hair that she had separated. Then, she took the brush and brushed this section around the largest and longest of her fingers. When she released the hair from her finger, she had a long, shiny, "Shirley Temple" curl. She repeated this process until my entire head was full of Shirley Temple curls. Before going to bed, Grandma covered my head with a scarf to hold the curls in place.

I loved my Shirley Temple curls. They were thick and just as bouncy as Shirley Temple's. She was a favorite child, movie star and we loved it when Aunt Irene took me and my cousins, Mitzi and Joan, to see her movies. We wanted to be stars like her. We wanted to learn how to tap dance and sing like Shirley Temple did when she acted with Bill "Bo Jangles Robinson", a rare, colored movie star. Although I could not dance like her, I could sing very well and at least have the "Shirley Temple"curls.

I knew that Uncle Bobby would really like my Easter clothes and curls. He would be so happy to see me. I was glad that me and Granddaddy were finally getting to see him.

19

Frank Reed's Tin Shop

Granddaddy's boss, Mayor Frank Reed, was a short, pudgy, cigar smoking, white man. He had been re-elected Mayor of Lockland for two consecutive terms. In addition to his mayoralty duties, he was a successful small businessman. He operated an insurance company as well as the tin shop where my grandfather worked.

The family story was that Frank Reed had first met Granddaddy when he had been working for Dougherty's Tin Shop in Wyoming, Ohio when my aunts and uncle were young. My grandfather learned to be a tinsmith from Grandma's father, James Gray, Sr. He had his own business putting on roofs and installing tin downspouts on houses. They said that during the Depression, Dougherty's sold his business to Mayor Reed. He called on Granddaddy to work for him off and on, as business allowed.

In 1933, after I was born, Granddaddy got a permanent job working for Mayor Reed. He ran the two man shop, teaching Ralph, his helper, all that he had learned about working with sheets of tin, slate and other roofing materials.

Ralph drove the truck to the job sites since Granddaddy had never learned to drive. Years earlier, he had been in a car accident. A friend was driving when the car in which the two were riding, crashed into a tree. Granddaddy's collar bone was broken. He said he never "fooled with the damn things" (cars) after that.

One Sunday, on a rare outing, Granddaddy's relative, Margaret drove us out to see Granddaddy's shop. It was exciting for me because I rarely had rides in cars, and rarely went anywhere on Sundays except to see Uncle Bobby with Granddaddy.

Mayor Reed's Tin Shop where Granddaddy worked was in a separate building in the rear of the red brick building where Mayor Reed operated his insurance business. When Granddaddy took out the key to open the door to the shop, I felt that he must be very important to have his own key.

132

The shop was a gray, clapboard building with two large rooms cluttered with sheets of tin, large squares of slate, gutter and downspout parts, and tar paper, all for the roofing jobs. Soldering irons, bars of solder and all the tools for laying down the materials on roofs, were stored in the shop's rear work area.

I was amazed at all the tools and long metal pieces, called downspouts. These downspouts didn't have holes in them like the downspouts on our apartment building that allowed the rain to pour down on me when I ran into our apartment.

Next door to Mayor Reed's building was a small municipal park with a gazebo. Granddaddy said that on days when he hadn't eaten his lunch on a job, he'd have it inside the gazebo.

Mayor Reed's office and tin shop staff formed a congenial work team as Granddaddy told of them. From his stories, it seemed that their lives revolved around the Mayor. Granddaddy talked as if they felt that Mayor Reed's importance made them important.

During the week, when Granddaddy came in from work, he, at times, spoke lovingly and kindly of Betty, Mayor Reed's secretary, Ralph, and "The Boss," as he always referred to Mayor Reed. He took an interest in all they did at work and what they said about their home lives. In an inexplicable way he seemed happier with these people, whom he did not really know, than with Grandma. He wasn't critical of them as he often could be with Grandma.

I could tell by Granddaddy's tone of voice that he loved his "Boss." He always had a happy look on his face. Mayor Reed called Granddaddy "Ground Hog."

One night after work, Granddaddy had been sitting in the mohair chair reading his evening paper, the *Times Star,* while Grandma was in their bedroom at her sewing machine working on a slipcover. I had pulled the ladder-back chair, that normally stood in a corner of the bedroom, to the side of my bed to sit in. With the bed supporting my papers, I was able to busy myself drawing pictures. The bed supported my papers as if it were a desk. There was a single floor lamp standing at the head of the bed in front of the window that looked out into the backyard. This lamp was the one source of light at night. It had a silk-looking, beige-colored shade and the lamp cast a soft light over my paper. The lamp cast its soft light over my paper and disseminated into the rest of the room making shadows on the wall.

I took my eyes off my drawing as I heard Granddaddy get up from his easy chair. I saw him go through the open area that led, from all of our four rooms, into to the kitchen. I heard him retrieve a glass from the kitchen cupboard and proceed to get a drink of water. He didn't return to the living room immediately, but I heard him stop and talk to Grandma from the kitchen doorway that led into their bedroom.

"The Boss's goin' to Florida on his vacation next week. Goin' for two whole weeks," Granddaddy told Grandma.

"Who cares what he does, but you? He don't pay you nothin'. When do you ever get a vacation? Huh! When do I ever get a vacation for that matter?"

"You get a vacation every day, Sister," Granddaddy laughed. Sarcasm filled his voice. "What'd you ever do but run your mouth? That's the most work you do."

"You're just a big liar. Who keeps your house clean? Who takes care of your clothes? Who fixes your meals, but me?" Grandma said. "You do all his work and don't have nothin' to show for it," she nagged.

"How can I have anything, livin' with a spendthrift like you?" Granddaddy retorted.

"Spendthrift! Spendthrift? Who's a spendthrift?" Grandma shouted.

I could hear Grandma pumping away on the treadle of her Singer sewing machine even as she was shouting at Granddaddy.

"Well, I don't need no vacation nohow. I'm thinkin' of retirin' in a couple of summers," Granddaddy said, a little subdued.

"You been sayin' that since you started work."

Granddaddy changed the subject. "Betty said Ralph and I both looked like Kentucky briar hoppers."

I wondered what a "briar hopper" was. I hadn't heard Grand-daddy use this word before. I knew our family was from Kentucky but what was a briar and a hopper in Kentucky. Was it like a grasshopper jumping around? Granddaddy only walked. He never ran or hopped anywhere. I had never seen Ralph, his partner. I only heard Grand-daddy talk about him. Grandma's voice stopped my mental question-ing.

"Betty! There you go. Now I got to sit here and listen to you talk about Betty. You sure do love those white folks. They don't care a dime about you."

"They do, too! Me and Betty and Ralph get along just fine to-gether, Sister."

"Betty this! Betty that!" Grandma mimicked. "You must be in love with Betty."

"She's not a fuss-budget like you, Sister. She doesn't sit around running her mouth all day. She works!" Granddaddy chuckled.

"Who runs their mouth all day?" Grandma asked. "I don't have nobody around here to be runnin' my mouth with."

"You don't need nobody around. You just run your mouth any-way."

I heard the hum of the sewing machine stop. I heard the screech of the metal legs on Grandma's chair on the bedroom floor li-noleum as she slid it away from her machine.

I could see the picture in my mind, one that I had observed many times when I was sitting at the kitchen table while Grandma sewed. I was sure that she put her hand on her hip, stared at Grand-daddy as he stood in the doorway and rolled her eyes at him.

But, this time, she didn't say anything. I heard Granddaddy walk back to the living room and plop down in the mohair chair. I heard him pickup his evening paper and snap the pages as he did when he was just starting to read.

Then, once again I heard the sound of Grandma pumping away on the treadle of her sewing machine. The four rooms were quiet ex-cept for the sound of my pencil on my paper and the hum of the sewing machine. Grandma didn't call out for me to go to bed so I just stayed up and waited for my aunts to come home.

My grandfather, STEWART FOLEY CORBIN
as he usually appeared when he returned home from
work at Frank Reed's Tin Shop in Lockland, Ohio

1940s

GRANDMA AND GRANDDADDY

1940s

20

The Little Lamb

It was the last of March. The winds were threatening as they howled through the limbs of the cottonwood tree. The barren tree was the same stingy gray as old Mr. Tate's three dilapidated garages next door. Granddaddy came home from work smiling.

"Me and Ralph went out to a big farm, today," he said, removing the old overcoat Mayor Reed had given him. It was miles too short, but Granddaddy wore it because the "Boss" had given it to him. He worshipped the "Boss."

Granddaddy went into the bedroom, next to the kitchen, where Grandma was busy sewing away on a sofa cushion cover she was making. He hung up his coat in his bedroom closet and returned to the kitchen and sat down at the table with me.

Granddaddy seemed extra tired as he slumped down into the chair. He bent over slowly to remove his work shoes. He stretched his feet and tossed the shoes under the table.

"We're putting a slate roof on old man Hosey's place up there in Loveland. Big, old house, too," Granddaddy continued.

I was busy with my coloring at my seat at the kitchen table. I didn't look up. He kept talking.

"What're you tellin' me for? I don't know nobody named 'Hosey'," Grandma said.

Grandma had cooked our supper earlier in the day, but she was postponing serving it until she was at a place where she could stop with the cushion.

"Didn't say you did, Sister. Just said we were out there today. Me and Ralph."

"Well, so what? I don't care nothin' about those old, white people. You're the only one who licks their asses all the time," Grandma said, not looking up from her work.

"Today, we saw all the farm animals. Cutest little baby lambs runnin' 'round." Granddaddy said, ignoring Grandma. I looked up from my coloring.

"They were the cutest things you ever saw," Granddaddy said.

"Baby lambs?" I asked.

"Yep!" Granddaddy said. "You should've been with me and Ralph. Hoseys have all these animals - pigs, cows and chickens. Think I'd like to have me a farm someday." Granddaddy looked off into space.

Grandma put away her scissors, got up from her chair and placed the cushion, on which she was working, onto her empty the seat. She came into the kitchen, washed her hands and dried them on her apron. She removed the supper dishes, spoons and forks from the cabinet. She put the spoons and forks on the table and set the the dishes on the stove next to the pot of food she had made.

"You wouldn't know what to do with it if you did," Grandma said, rolling her eyes around at him. She was standing over the gas stove giving one last stir to the beef stew we were having for supper.

"That's all you know, Sister."

"You don't take care of this place," she said.

"I'd have me a garden and a pond so I could go fishin'," Granddaddy said, continuing to look up at the kitchen ceiling.

Grandma snickered. "You wouldn't go fishin'. You've been talkin' about goin' fishin' for thirty years. You wouldn't know what a fish looks like."

"Oh, Granddaddy, could we move to a farm one day?" I asked. I was caught up in the excitement of Granddaddy's daydreaming. I en-visioned myself living on a farm like the children in my coloring books.

"Sure will. I'll have me a place with enough room to hide from your Grandmammy's mouth."

138

"Hide from me! You wouldn't have to worry about hidin' from me," Grandma said.

"Granddaddy, tell me about the baby lambs," I encouraged.

"Well, me and Ralph was up on the top of the roof gettin' ready to put on the slate. I was takin' a little time lookin' out over the farm. It's a big farm. Never been on a place that big. Then, I saw this group of sheep. I didn't know old Hosey had sheep. Then, here come these frisky little lambs. Cutest things. Me and Ralph just got tickled watchin' them jumpin' around."

"Me and Ralph! Me and Ralph! You act like you can't breathe without Ralph." Grandma tossed her head back and forth mimicking Granddaddy. He kept smiling.

"Could you bring me one of those baby lambs, Granddaddy?" I pleaded.

"Yep! I'll bring you one tomorrow," he said smiling at me.

"You ain't gonna do no such thing," Grandma said "So why are you sittin' there tellin' her that lie?"

"I will too, Sister. You just wait and see."

I was so excited over the prospect of having a baby lamb that I could not eat my dinner. Grandma attributed my loss of appetite to having "Spring Fever."

"Give her some sassafras tea," Granddaddy laughed.

"You're mighty happy tonight," Grandma observed. "You and Ralph must have stopped off somewhere after work."

"Wouldn't tell you if we did, Sister." Granddaddy said putting a spoonful of beef stew in his mouth.

"Do you think we can keep the baby lamb in the backyard?" I asked, creating my plans for the lamb.

"Sure. Plenty room back there," Granddaddy said.

"How big will the lamb be, Granddaddy?"

"Oh, it's just a tiny thing, with a little stump of a tail." Granddaddy finished his supper and got up from the table.

"I'll put a red ribbon around his neck and take it everywhere," I said following him into the living room. He sat down to read his evening paper.

"Where'd Mr. Hosey get the lambs? I bet he's got lots and lots, all running over the farm playing," I said. Granddaddy did not answer.

"I have to get something to feed it," I told Granddaddy, talking to him through the newspaper he had been holding in front of his face. Granddaddy still did not answer.

I peeked over the edge of the paper. Granddaddy had fallen asleep while reading and had not heard much of what I was asking.

I went back into the kitchen and tried to talk to Grandma about the baby lamb.

"I'll put it in a pen in the backyard," I said. I was happy and excited.

"Don't pay your granddaddy no mind. You'll be blue in the face waitin' for him to bring some lamb home. That's his beer talkin'," Grandma advised.

"Yes, he will, Grandma. He said so."

I rejected any notion that Granddaddy would not bring the baby lamb.

The next evening, the suspense was great. I kept flipping the pages of my book waiting to hear Granddaddy's footsteps as he descended the cement stairs. When I didn't hear him, I imagined I heard him coming. Finally I asked, "Grandma, can I go up front and wait for Granddaddy?"

"All right, but don't go past Mrs. Robinson's porch, do you hear?" She said.

Granddaddy arrived with Aunt Margaret's husband, Uncle Ben, who stopped his car at the curb. Granddaddy got out but he didn't have the baby lamb.

"Where's the baby lamb?" I asked, trying to hide my disappointment. I grabbed Granddaddy's hand, holding it as we walked down the stairs to the apartment.

"We didn't go out to the farm today. We'll go tomorrow," Granddaddy answered.

"And you'll bring the lamb tomorrow?"

"Ummmmhuh. You'll see," Granddaddy assured me.

"Tomorrow" came and the day after and the day after that. I refused to believe that Granddaddy wasn't going to bring the baby lamb. I dreamed about the lamb at night. In my dreams I played with the baby lamb, running with it and feeding it from a baby's bottle.

One day I stopped asking Granddaddy about the baby lamb; but I always secretly hoped that the time would come when he would surprise me and have the baby lamb with him when he got home from work.

MY GRANDPARENTS 1940s

LILLIAN and FOLEY CORBIN

21

Roll-Your-Own

Granddaddy smoked home-made, roll-your-own cigarettes. These cigarettes were not as reliable as his Lucky Strikes or Camels, which he smoked on occasion. Each roll-your-own was different as if it had a mind of its own. This was determined by how the tobacco was packed into the thin cigarette paper, and how they came out of the cigarette rolling machine.

It was after supper and just before my bedtime. I was killing time in the kitchen when Granddaddy got up from his chair in the living room and returned to the kitchen. He removed his cigarette making machine from the kitchen closet. The machine was made of blonde-colored wood and had a metal crank on one side.

The machine was small, perhaps ten or twelve inches long and four or five inches wide. Granddaddy sat at the table so that he could be directly under the bare light bulb that hung from a rubber-encased wire from the ceiling. I moved closer so I could watch. He retrieved a packet of tissue-like paper, called cigarette paper, from his pant pocket then set to work.

He put one sheet of the paper in the wooden groove on top of the machine. Next he got a small pouch of tobacco from his blue, work shirt pocket, pulled on the yellow drawstring that opened it, and sprinkled the brown bits of tobacco neatly along the paper's length.

One end of the paper was plain, but at the other end there was a thin line of tan glue. Slowly, Granddaddy gave the crank a half turn. He checked his progress, and assured that it was going just fine, he gave a final swift, firm turn of the handle.

Two jaw-like pinchers rose from the machine, grabbed the thin paper and sucked it inside out of view. Then, it suddenly extruded its contents as one, white, elongated cigarette. I was mesmerized. It was magic. Then, Granddaddy carefully lifted the incomplete cigarette from its resting place at the lower end of the machine. He gingerly picked it up, placed the end with the glue toward him, put the cigarette to his lips and licked it.

Next, Grandaddy pressed the glue-end on top of the paper holding the tobacco and pressed the two sides together sealing the cigarette. If bits of tobacco got on his tongue, he unceremoniously spit them out. If bits were sticking out of either end of the cigarette, he tapped each open end on the kitchen table and packed the loose pieces in place inside the cigarette.

Sometimes, the cigarettes came out in compact, neat rolls. At other times they came out lumpy in the middle with barely any tobacco at the ends. When this kind of cigarette was sealed, Granddaddy ended up with a flat ended cigarette which burned in a flash when he lit it. These cigarettes did not settle down to steady burning until the long ash on the end fell off. Whenever Granddaddy lit one of these irregulars, he said, "Look out now. This damn thing just might burn a hole in my shirt." Then, he lit it anyway.

"Let me make some, Granddaddy," I begged.

"Okay, but take your time. Don't waste my tobacco."

I carefully removed a thin, cigarette paper from the packet as I had seen Granddaddy do. Then, I sprinkled the tobacco in the center. I didn't get the tobacco evenly distributed.

Granddaddy said, "Wait a minute, you little piss ant. You tryin' to make me burn myself up with that one? Put some more tobacco in there," he teased. "All right. That's enough," he added.

I liked making the roll-your-own cigarettes but, I did not like the taste of the glue on the edge of the papers so Granddaddy licked them for me.

PART III

SCHOOL YEARS AND OTHER LEARNING

AGE 5-7

1

Kindergarten and Miss Denman

I was four going on five when I started Kindergarten at Hoffman School. I looked forward to going, although it was with some trepidation.

Hoffman School was an immense, brown, brick structure with a huge tower that rose above the center of the building. A cream-colored material was used between each brick and the school took up half of an entire square block. The other half was taken up by an athletic field and a cement play yard that formed a semi-circle around the back of the building.

Commanding a large portion of the front of the school were four levels of wide, stairs which had to be climbed. This section faced the Victory Parkway, a wide boulevard and major thoroughfare below. Staring down from the roof-line of the building were grotesque, finely sculptured images that resembled masks of my imaginary monsters.

I knew nothing about these figures. I just knew that they were the scariest things that I had seen outside of scary movies. I did not like looking up at them. I wondered why these figures, with their bulging eyes and gaping mouths, were used to decorate a school building for children.

Hoffman School's students came from a variety of communities nearby. The colored families lived northeast of the school and close to the Gracelawn Cemetery. Their area also took in a section at the end of the Parkway along Gilbert Avenue. Jewish and Irish families lived to the south along Woodburn Avenue. Their sections took in Hackberry Avenue and a large area behind the school. We were all called either colored or white children based on skin color. The Jewish and colored populations in our area were very large. The Irish population was not as large, but still substantial.

I wanted to be grown up in the way I remembered my Aunt Lockey Jane. She had school books and notebooks when she was at Withrow High School. I would have my own notebooks and pencils. Whenever she left her school things in the living room, I poured through her thick notebooks. I was impressed by the thickness of page after page of notes and the even gliding words in cursive. Transported into a wonderful and strange new world inside my aunt's notebooks, I felt myself in a land of mystery and magic that overwhelmed me. It marked the beginning of my love for the kind of writing I saw that day. I was careful not to let my aunt catch me because I knew she would tell me to leave her things alone. I turned each page, entranced with the hieroglyphics of notes she had accumulated from her English, history or health classes. In the kitchen, I sometimes heard her complain to Grandma, "I can't do that old algebra. It's too hard. I don't know how Mr. Schifford thinks I can do that in one night."

I heard the Norge refrigerator door close hard and milk being poured into a glass.

I could not understand Aunt Lockey Jane's lack of love for school. She seemed very smart and her writing was neat and very even. All of this was accomplished with blue ink and the fountain pen which I would have loved to get into my hands. But she was adamant. I was not to bother her things. I was careful so she would not catch me as I quietly, and without detection, looked through her notebook.

Once home, Aunt Lockey Jane did not look at her books again until night when Aunt Hookey could help her with the algebra.

Aunt Hookey said, "I always liked algebra, Lockey Jane. How come you don't?"

"Hookey, you were smart at math. You should've stayed in school. I like all the other subjects, but math is just hard. I don't know why x+m equals z or whatever that stuff is," Aunt Crystal whined. I felt sorry for my youngest aunt and so did Aunt Hookey.

Even though she worked all day, Aunt Hookey sat down with Aunt Lockey Jane and with great patience tried to help her understand

Algebra, but Lockey Jane did not get it. Finally, from sheer weariness, Aunt Hookey worked the problems for her.

As her two daughters worked on homework Grandma would chime in from her work at the sewing machine, "When I was going to school my mother put me in the prettiest dresses with big, satin bows in my hair. The teacher let me clean the blackboard and pass out paper because I was so smart."

It was Grandma's story about her time, but she never mentioned algebra.

Now, it was my turn to start school. I was excited. I wondered what a blackboard looked like.

The night before, in preparation for my first day of school, Grandma washed and polished my white, high top shoes and got out the dress and under things that I was to wear. Everything was neatly placed on a kitchen chair.

That morning and every morning thereafter, I stood like a manikin as Grandma sponged me off in front of the open oven door. On nippy mornings, the gas oven was turned on to take the morning chill off while I was being washed. The door to the oven was the support for the shallow wash pan Grandma filled with warm water. The heat from the oven kept me warm as she scrubbed my body.

Grandma sat in one of the chairs close to the oven. I said nothing, just stood very still feeling the warm, soap-filled wash cloth scrubbing my body. I closed my eyes as my face, ears and neck were washed and rinsed.

Next, Grandma retrieved a towel from the table to dry me. Then she washed my arms, hands, under my arms, chest and back, and then my legs and feet.

Last, I stood up and spread my legs as my "pocketbook' was washed. I felt embarrassed and looked away. Because I frequently wet the bed at night, Grandma made sure that I was thoroughly clean and free of any urine odor.

The wash pan was round and shallow. The wash water and the rinse water were one and the same and therefore the warm water

146

cooled quickly. When I was carefully dressed, Grandma combed my hair. In order to accomplish this, she had me stand between her legs with my back to her as she held me in a viselike grip with her knees.

"Ouch!"

I pulled away as Grandma combed through one of my three long thick braids. Grandma grabbed me and began again.

"Ouch, Grandma, that hurts."

I hated having my hair combed. The tangles made it difficult to comb through my hair without it pulling. Soon my scalp became very sore. They said that I was "tender headed."

"Well, if you'd just hold still, it wouldn't hurt."

She tugged with the comb until she had successfully combed through all three braids. One dangled limply off to the front right side of my head and two dangled down my back. Each section had to be neatly parted, exposing the bare scalp. The comb was black with thick teeth. I cringed whenever Grandma had to rework the part in my hair.

"This gets on my nerves," Grandma complained. "How'd you expect me to have you ready in time if you keep pulling away?"

"But it hurts," I whined.

"Well, be still then and it won't hurt!"

There was never any other answer to my pain. The more "still" I was, the more it hurt and the more I jumped.

"Your mama acted the same way when I combed her hair. She was always tender headed and she had more hair than you."

"It hurts right here." I pointed to the top of my head.

"It always hurts you there. Your head didn't come together all the way when you were a baby," Grandma advised me with great seriousness.

I placed my finger on the spot and felt it with new questions. *Didn't come together*? Why and how was that possible? The spot in the center of my head now seemed more soft than sore. I thought I could feel the sink hole in the top of my head.

"It'll close and get hard when you grow up," Grandma assured me.

I thought, "Now there's something terrible about my head." It was soft on top and hadn't closed right. I must have been the only child living who had a head that "hadn't come together."

To get to school, it was a half block from our Helena Apartments to the corner of Lincoln and the Victory Parkway. Then you had to walk down the Parkway. Both Lincoln Avenue and the Victory Parkway were busy streets, but the Victory Parkway was far busier than Lincoln Avenue. Only cars were allowed on the Parkway. Lincoln's traffic consisted of buses, cars, trucks and even the Rag Man with his horse and cart.

It was Christine Bell's last year at Hoffman Elementary School. Grandma said that she would pay her fifty cents a week to take me to school each morning; and walk me back home at noon when she left school to have her lunch at home.

That first morning of school I heard Christine rushing, but carefully, picking her way down the rickety unsafe back steps. I grew more apprehensive by the minute. My scalp, still hurting from having my hair combed, did not ease that condition.

Grandma stood at the living room door as Christine took my hand and we walked up the cement steps on our way to school.

When we reached the corner of Lincoln and the Victory Parkway it was there, that for the very first time, I saw an older white male student wearing a white crisscrossed band that went over one shoulder and around his waist. There was a gleaming metal badge attached at the upper left portion of the band. This was the Crossing Guard. He stood, unsmiling, with a sign that had *STOP* printed on both sides and held at his side, while we waited for the traffic light to change. A cord was attached to a whistle that he held in his mouth.

When the traffic light turned red, he walked to the center of the street, held up his sign while simultaneously blowing his whistle. We walked safely across to the next corner while all traffic on Lincoln Avenue was halted. Then the same took place when it was time to cross the Victory Parkway. I was impressed by the Crossing Guard. I wondered how he got to our corner. There were no white people living in our area of Walnut Hills. The white people lived along Woodburn Avenue and the larger area behind Hoffman School.

Christine and I continued the walk to school along the Victory Parkway. On this day, everything that was familiar took on an exaggerated sense of proportion. The Parkway was wider and busier with more cars than I had ever seen before. The broad swath of green grass next to the sidewalk, that ran parallel to the Parkway, seemed broader and greener. The distance to Hoffman School seemed longer. Not even Christine's familiar smile and idle chatter could quiet my pounding heart. I was not apprehensive. I was scared.

I wanted to go back home, but then there would be no chance to know what the school was like inside or what my teacher was like. I swallowed hard and let myself just be scared. This wasn't like "monster scared," this was just "not knowing" scared. I turned my attention to the walk and the many large, green shrubs growing on the hillside near the sidewalk.

Springtime was the best time for walking along the Victory Parkway. Then, bright-colored tulips and yellow daffodils filled the green border for the few miles of the Parkway before that section met Gilbert Avenue. The flowers were not along the side where Christine, I, and other school children walked. The flowers were along the fence that separated the acres of the Gracelawn Cemetery on that side, hiding its identity from all passersby. This was across the Victory Parkway.

The fence along the cemetery was hidden by the tall green shrubs in front of it. We were forbidden, by law, to pick any of the tulips and daffodils. This assured their beauty until it faded when the last petals had fallen and only bare stems remained. Keeping the Victory Parkway beautiful was a full time job for gardeners who one saw when taking a walk there.

That side of the Parkway was the same area where my aunts picked the dandelion greens that Grandma cooked for supper. I did not like those greens. To me, they had a bitter taste. Granddaddy used the blossoms to make dandelion wine. He used a huge, white crock that he kept under the kitchen sink behind a dark, printed curtain that Grandma had made. The crock had a wooden lid which he removed to see if the wine was "ripe." The wine, like the dandelion greens, had a pungent smell. Granddaddy kept adding sugar. I thought this a very odd combination.

But this was not springtime. The air was cooler and the Victory Parkway flowers were gone. I was glad to hold Christine's hand. I did not like the idea of the Gracelawn Cemetery, and I was equally as glad to have it hidden from view so that we did not have to think about its existence.

Christine walked with me to the kindergarten room that was on the ground level in the back of the school. We walked through wooden doors with glass panels at the top half. Just inside, was my kindergarten classroom. Standing at the open door was, next to my Aunt Lockey Jane and my mother, the most beautiful young woman I had ever seen. She was my teacher, Miss Denman. Every fear, every apprehension, every feeling and all questions about my first day of school disappeared. Here stood a princess. Here stood a beautiful fairy. In front of me, smiling at me, bending down to greet me was Miss Denman. I entered heaven.

Christine returned to the outside cement yard where all the older students congregated to await the opening bell. Kindergarten children were not allowed to gather with the older children. They had to be safely in the room before the opening bell.

Miss Denman was very young, blonde and beautiful. Each morning, she met us outside the Kindergarten classroom and instructed us in the art of forming a line. Her voice was like music. She was always happy. What a change from listening to the complaints and unhappiness of Grandma. It was another world.

As my kindergarten days passed and my familiarity grew, the Hoffman School edifice might have been imposing, but once inside Miss Denman's room, it, too, was transformed as she ushered us in. When we entered the classroom, we were in a spacious, open rectangular space with gleaming, hard wood floors. The room had floor to ceiling windows on three sides, all facing the schoolyard outside.

150

Our restrooms were in an enclosed section in the back of the room. This section is where we hung sweaters and coats on a row of gleaming, brass hooks. Our galoshes, which were worn on rainy and snowy days, were placed on the linoleum floor beneath where the outer garments were hung. In this room, additional supplies were kept. It was lit by windows high above. It was also a room where we would spend time alone, if we became too rambunctious. Miss Denman rarely sent anyone here. This was our cloakroom. It had swinging doors that were woven cane at the bottom and solid wood on top.

I was learning so many new words and seeing many new things that my excitement grew every day.

The main room was divided into two areas; the largest had plain, hardwood floors where we sat for circle time. This room had one wall of blackboard above which large cards were visible displaying the upper and lower case letters of the alphabet. Next to the blackboard was a cork board where our artwork was displayed. Grandma's talk about a "blackboard" became a visible reality.

Rows of cubbyholes were on the wall beneath the blackboard. Just above the cubbies was the rim which held the chalk Miss Denman used. Each child was to bring an empty cigar box the second day of school. I had gotten mine from Rosen's Store on the corner. Our cigar boxes were stored in the cubbyholes marked with each student's name.

To the right of the entry door and closest to the outside play yard, was another large alcove. The floor in this area was covered with a plush carpet and held many child-sized tables and chairs. This is where we sat to do our "table work" and have quiet time.

I was in love with school. Our one room was larger than the four rooms in our apartment. Its spaces were open and it had lots of light. Colors sparkled in the room. There were pictures and books for children. All the items and activities were for us and Miss Denman was the beautiful, happy lady who would guide us. Here was true magic.

Except for four colored children, all others in my class were white. Although Anna Jackson looked white with her blonde, shoulder length, wavy hair, she was colored. Some people called her an "Albino," but Anna did not have pink around the rims of her eyes and her eyes were light brown.

Then, there was Cornelious Wilson. Cornelious was light-skinned as well and had very dark, short, wavy hair. He lived in a third floor apartment across the street from me. His mother never let him come down from the apartment to play because of the heavy traffic on Lincoln Avenue.

On rare occasions Cornelious' mother sat on the first floor steps and watched as he played. Most of the time he sat at their front window, staring down at other children playing and the traffic going by.

Kenneth Jackson and I were the only two who were brown. Kenneth was the darkest of all. He was almost a blue-brown. Kenneth lived in an apartment that was, like our apartment, steps down from the street. His apartment building had no basement beneath. He lived next door to Rosen's Grocery Store at the corner of Lincoln Avenue. Kenneth's mother walked him to school everyday. She was always dressed nicely and wore beautiful, large hats like ladies wore to church.

In kindergarten, we learned rhyming songs and finger games, the months of the years and the days of the week. We learned our ABC's and the difference between upper and lower case letters.

Miss Denman read stories which she had saved for the end of Circle Time. My favorite stories were about the adventures of Raggedy Ann and Andy. I loved these dolls with yarn hair and button eyes who had adventures as if they were real children.

One day during Circle Time, while he sat quietly listening to the story, Kenneth Jackson wet his pants.

"Kenneth, did you have an accident, dear?" Miss Denman asked gently.

None of us had noticed until then. We all stared at Kenneth, who did not blink an eye, nor move from his place on the floor. The other children snickered. I glowered at Kenneth. He did not answer

Miss Denman. He rolled his eyes up toward her, but did not open his mouth. Urine seeped from around the spot where Kenneth was sitting.

"Girls and boys, Kenneth has just had a slight accident. Let's not laugh at him," Miss Denman said.

She rose from her seat and took Kenneth by the hand and slowly led him, through the door marked "Boys."

Since the beginning of school Kenneth seemed to be a black shell of everyone else in our classroom. It was difficult to know whether he was very shy or not very intelligent. He got Miss Denman's loving attention. I envied him that, but, I would never commit the obscenity of wetting myself during the day to get it.

Each morning Kenneth was in a fog, as if he had not slept the night before. He did not participate in the guessing games and if Miss Denman called on him, he stared at her without answering. But, I couldn't forgive Kenneth for wetting his pants and reminding me of my own embarrassing, nocturnal bedwetting.

No one else had such accidents. Everyone walked far around Kenneth because he smelled of urine when he came to school. No one held his hand when we lined up by two's to go out for recess. I sat next to him to color during free time, but we didn't say anything to each other. When I did speak to Kenneth, he just stared at me and grinned.

Before the middle of the school year, I, along with Anna Jackson and Corneilious Wilson, was transferred to afternoon kindergarten. This class was also taught by Miss Denman. Our group was working with more advanced concepts. In the afternoon we were printing our names and doing pre-reading exercises. Our story time was held at the end of the day instead of at the beginning.

Grandma asked Kenneth's mother if she would take me to school on her way to pick up Kenneth from the morning session. She agreed and Christine took me home when school was out at three o'clock.

Although her pattern of speech was not as clear as Grandma's, Kenneth's mother was a warm, talkative woman. I enjoyed my trips to school with her. However, if Kenneth had the occasion to be with us, I made sure to keep my distance. He still had not learned to keep from wetting his pants.

Miss Denman put lots of gold stars on my papers, which I proudly took home to Granddaddy. He was full of praise and put my papers in the top dresser drawer with his other "treasures."

Just as Kenneth had his embarrassment, so did I. Grandma did not dress me like the other girls in my class. In the late fall and winter, I wore long, light brown, cotton, ribbed stockings with my white, high topped shoes. The other girls wore anklets and low cut shoes. The way I was dressed resembled the way my mother and aunts were dressed in the "old time days" of the past generation. Grandma said that I would catch my death of cold if I went to school with my legs bare.

At the end of the school year, I passed to First Grade. I took home my prized cigar box with its crayons and ruler. Kenneth flunked kindergarten and Miss Denman announced that she was getting married. The beautiful Fairy had found her Prince Charming. She told us that she would not be returning to Hoffman School the next year.

I had held onto the idea that I would pass her room each morning and at least be able to see and speak to her on my way to my first grade class; that would not be possible now.

After kindergarten and my love for school and Miss Denman, I decided that I was going to be a teacher when I grew up. I was going to be like Miss Denman.

MY FIRST SCHOOL
Hoffman ElementarySchool, Cincinnati, Ohio

2

A Prize Fight for Granddaddy

Joe Louis, the "Brown Bomber," was fighting Max Schmeling, the German. Granddaddy took his bath early and went into the living room to listen to the fight being broadcast on the radio.

It was late and past my bedtime, so I was already dressed and in my nightgown for bed. I was restless and could not go to sleep. During the week Granddaddy rarely listened to the radio at night. He read his paper after supper and went to bed. Granddaddy always said "Early to bed, early to rise makes a man healthy, wealthy and wise."

But, on this particular night his excitement showed. He sat on the hassock next to the table steadying the small, brown RCA Victor radio as he fiddled with the knobs. The radio's static drifted into my room. Then a loud voice could be heard. Wrong station. Finally, there was the sound of a roaring crowd and the clang of a ringside bell.

The electricity from the excited, cheering crowd invaded the apartment. It overtook Granddaddy. He sat, his ear planted against the wooden grill with a cloth that covered the speaker as if he couldn't hear very well.

There were two men, unseen, fighting each other for a boxing title, but Granddaddy kept saying, "Hit him, Joe! Don't let him get you! Hit him! Hit him!"

Never had I heard or seen Granddaddy so excited. There was a colored man and a white man fighting each other. I couldn't think of going to sleep. Then, I heard Granddaddy hitting his fist against his open hand. He laughed out loud.

"That's it, Joe. That's it, boy!"

When it was all over they announced Joe Louis the winner. I heard the soft spoken, invisible colored man's voice come through the radio.

"Hi, Mom. Glad we win."

156

Grandma called from the kitchen, "Why do you listen to that ignorant mess?"

"Because we got us one helluva, colored fighter. That's why!" Granddaddy said with a strength and pride in his voice, rarely heard.

Aunt Lockey Jane added a glossy picture of Joe Louis in his satin, boxing shorts to the wall in our bedroom. It was an autographed picture that she placed next to hers and Aunt Hookey's photo collection. Joe Louis had a boxer's stance. His prized boxing gloves covered his hands. He, the "Brown Bomber," was displayed with Chick Webb, orchestra leader, and Jimmie Lunceford, another band leader dressed in a tuxedo.

3

When School Ended

When school was over my Aunt Irene brought my cousins, Mitzi and Joan, with her when she came to visit Grandma. I used them as guinea pigs as I "practiced" being a teacher like Miss Denman. In preparation for their coming, I practiced printing on the back of Aunt Lockey Jane's used notebook paper and I practiced singing while playing at my "make believe piano." My make believe piano was a ladder back chair that I turned around, and while sitting in front of it in another chair, allowed my fingers to move lightly over imaginary keys.

Mitzi who was a year younger than me was eager to play "school." She did not mind my bossy, authoritative ways, but Cousin Joan, who was a year younger than Mitzi, was restless and whiney. She had her own ideas about what she wanted to do for her entertainment.

On other days it was difficult for Grandma to coax me from my play when lunchtime arrived. Playing "school" was so important to me that I never got hungry. I spent most of the day inside and was not distracted by Grandma's storytelling and the sadness that would overcome her.

Ohio summers were very hot and muggy. The least amount of time spent outside in the afternoon sun soon had me dripping with perspiration. Aunt Hookey and Aunt Lockey Jane bathed and dried me with a huge towel. Then, they sprinkled talcum powder over my back and chest. This was to keep me from getting a heat rash and to keep me cool, they said.

Those days after lunch and my bath, one or both of them made a pallet for the floor where I had to lie down for a nap. I waited patiently as my aunts each stood opposite each other holding the corners of a full-sized, winter blanket in their hands.

Then, they met each other in the middle with the blanket folded in half. They spread this on the floor, near the open, screened door in the bedroom where we slept. Next they repeated the folding process only this time with a clean white bed sheet.

When the sheet was spread over the blanket, Aunt Hookey said, "O.K., Sweetpea, lie down now. You'll be cooler on the floor."

I hated naptime. I had too much to do. I wanted to keep "practicing" being a teacher.

The last phase of their daily, summer ritual was to pull down the window shade next to our bed. This kept out the sunlight from the backyard, but the sun was shining brightly through the screen door and window on the front side of the apartment. This sunlight they could not shut out. They would have to close the door to the outside to accomplish this and that would keep out the air and any cross ventilation. It made it much more difficult to settle in for a nap

When I kept fidgeting because I couldn't settle down, Grandma would call from the kitchen, "Sweetpea, you get still in there and go to sleep."

I finally turned my back to the door where the light was coming in and stared into the bedroom. Eventually, I would doze off.

When I awakened from my nap, I was dressed in a "sun suit," a cute play outfit that had elastic, bloomer-type legs that fit like my underwear and a top part that covered my chest and was held up by thin straps. Grandma made several of these for me for summer. Not only were they cool, they were also easy to put on and left me lots of freedom to run.

After naptime I could play outside or inside, but I could not venture from the front of the apartment building. I had to be where someone could see me. This turned out to be our closest friends in the Helena Apartments, one of the Bells, Christine, Sister or Mrs. Bell, or Mrs. Robinson who had a small patch of grass in front of her apartment.

Sometimes on summer mornings, when I had wandered to the Bell's apartment, Christine and Sister Bell bathed me and put me to sleep in Mrs. Bell's big, comfortable bed. Their windows faced the eastern part of the apartment building, so at noon the sun was high in the sky and moving westward. This took away the bright glare of the sun and caused their apartment to be shady and cooler on this side. It was easier for me to fall asleep.

When I awakened, I was dressed in the same "sun suit" that I had on in the morning. My activity after my nap at the Bells was very different from after my nap at home with Grandma and one of my aunts.

Sister and Christine dressed up in their nicest clothes and took me with them on their walk to Mangrum's Drugstore. I skipped along in front of them, eager to get to Mangrum's. I knew that at Mangrum's they would buy me an ice cream cone or some candy. When I tired of skipping, I walked in front of the two teenagers. I hated walking in front because I couldn't walk fast enough for them. Their feet kept clipping the heels of my sandals or shoes. This irritated them.

They were constantly saying, "Walk up, Sweetpea. Walk up! You're going too slow."

Mangrum's was on a corner of Chapel Street, across from the Douglas School, which only colored children from that area attended. I envied the Douglas students one thing and that was being close enough to Mangrum's to get candy, ice cream and bubble gum after school when it was in session.

When we arrived at Mangrum's, Christine and Sister met two boys who were their friends. I was anxious to get ice cream, they were anxious to talk with the boys. This became one of my summer rituals when I was with Christine and Sister.

ME AT AGE 4 OR 5, WITH THE BELL SISTERS
TAKEN IN THE BACKYARD OF THE
HELENA APARTMENT BUILDING

L to R (Front): Lula "Sweetpea" Cooper, unknown boy. Holding my shoulders, Christine Bell. Behind Christine is her older sister, Elva Marie "Sister" Bell.

4

A Visit to Great Grandma Gabbitt

One summer my boredom was broken when Grandma announced, "We're going to see Grandma Gabbitt."

I knew that Great Grandma Gabbitt was Granddaddy's mother. I had heard Grandma and others talking about my mother staying with her before I was born and that my Great Grandma Gabbitt "just loves your mama."

I was excited and curious about going to see her. When I learned we were going on a train I was so excited that I could not sleep at night. This was to be my very first train ride.

"Grandma Gabbitt's getting old," Grandma said. "She wants to see you before she dies."

I was surprised that Grandma knew that Great Grandma Gabbitt was dying, and that she wanted to see me. I didn't know whether to be happy or sad. My excitement was tempered by this new revelation.

"She came up from Danville to see you once right after you were born," Grandma informed me.

I thought that I must be very important for Great Grandma Gabbitt to come from so far away to see me. Danville, Kentucky was where she lived and to me that must be far, far away since we had to travel by train.

There was another of our relatives, who I learned, wanted especially to see me. She was my Great Aunt Lula Dee who worked for a movie star. Margaret, on Granddaddy's side, told Grandma that if they named me after her I would never want for anything. That is when I was named Lula Delores after this other family member who had to travel far to visit family.

Grandma was busy preparing for our trip. She made an elaborate lunch to take with us on the train. She made deviled eggs, one of my favorite foods, and wrapped them in crisp Cut-Rite wax paper. The paper mashed the eggs so that the creamy yellow oozed over the white part. I could see the yellow through the opaque, wax paper.

Grandma made fried chicken and her yeast rolls that she usually made for Sunday dinner. Then she put in two bananas, one for each of us, and vanilla wafers for me. Our lunch was packed in an empty shoe box and the lid tied down with kitchen string. This was knotted and tied into a floppy bow that sat on the top of the lid. Lunch was put in the refrigerator to keep overnight.

Great Aunt Margaret drove us to downtown Cincinnati where we were to catch our train. It would leave from the Union Terminal, a gigantic arched roof building that looked like a cement rainbow. Train tracks moved in all directions, to and from the building, like spokes on a giant wheel.

Inside the terminal, magnificent murals of Gulliver-like giant men at work, and machines with cogs, were featured. These murals went around the high walls above the entrance to the terminal. I was in awe of so much color and the size of this historic edifice. Grandma had to take my hand and firmly pull me along so that we would not miss our train. People scurrying to train gates and out the front doors filled the building.

I watched the lights and colors of people and the red-capped, Pullman Porters, all of whom were colored. I saw a stand that had newspapers, magazines and candy for sale but I dared not ask for any. Then I heard the loud calls from the Station Master.

The colored red caps were rushing by pushing mounds of suitcases on their luggage carts. Grandma and I waited on the hard wooden bench, one of the many that sat in neat rows perpendicular to each gate from which people left to get to the lower area where they would board their trains.

When the Station Master announced our train we walked quickly towards the moving stairs that took us to the area below. There we mingled with the crowd that was catching the L&N train going south and to Danville, Kentucky where Great Grandma Gabbitt lived.

The lower level of the station, where the trains came in, was dark and less impressive than the colorful upper Station. The huge engine of the train was menacing.

I stood far back from the track's edge. Grandma had the porter help me up the high step, then we found our way to the car where we were to sit for our trip.

We sat on a long wooden bench that faced other passengers across the aisle. There were no other children in our car and passengers took a great interest in my excitement and curiosity about the train. Everybody in our car was colored. There were numerous whites who were waiting for this same train when it pulled in, but they were directed to other cars where only the whites were to sit.

As soon as the train left the station, I was suddenly very hungry.

"Can we eat now, Grandma?" I asked.

"Wait until we get a little farther along. We just got on the train," she said.

Some of the passengers laughed. But true to her word, when the train got out of the area where all the tracks were ending into the terminal and all the overhead wires got fewer and less intricately criss-crossed making the sky resemble some of my lines drawn abstractly on paper, Grandma untied the shoe box and opened it so that we could eat.

It was late afternoon when we got off the train in Danville, Kentucky where Great Grandma Gabbitt lived.

I don't remember how we got to her house, but I remember her house being a narrow, brown, frame structure. It was so low to the ground that I thought it would sink.

The road that passed in front of Great Grandma Gabbitt's house was not paved. Dirt abounded and the hot dry dust of Danville swirled around me in the light breeze that was blowing. I thought of my mother being here, carrying me inside her. It was too alien a place for me to feel happy and secure.

Great Grandma Gabbitt wore a long, full-length, cotton, print dress with a flowered apron over it. On her head, she wore a dust cap. This was a flowered, cotton covering with a small ruffle all around. It formed a soft gentle frame for her face.

164

Great Grandma Gabbitt did not look anything like Granddaddy. She was brown-complexioned, short, and bent over. She took me by the hand and walked me around her little house. I sensed that she worked hard and that she took great pride in her home. She also had a garden where she grew vegetables and flowers.

That night, Great Grandma Gabbitt prepared our dinner. She made apple pie for dessert.

"Your mama sure loved my apple pie when she was here with me," Great Grandma Gabbitt said.

I went to bed early that night. Never before had I known darkness the way darkness appeared at Great Grandma Gabbitt's. It was darker than the night darkness in our apartment. She had small kerosene lamps with tiny wicks to give off light. The light did not travel far and the shadows, even my own, took on ominous sizes that made me afraid to walk from one chair to another in the same room.

Great Grandma Gabbitt's screened-in porch went around the side of her small house. It was supposed to repel the mosquitoes. It didn't, and all night Great Grandma Gabbitt roamed the house, fly swatter in hand, attempting to assure that I was not bitten. I did not sleep much that first night. I absorbed the rural darkness and the loud night songs of the myriad of insects.

I loved being with my great grandmother. She was very kind to me. Her movements were slow and labored. She lived alone and I wondered if she was a lonely person. We had so many people in our apartment at times that no one was alone for very long.

A short time after Grandma and I returned home, we learned that Great Grandma Gabbitt had died. She had cancer of the stomach. I don't remember anyone leaving to go to her funeral, I just remembered my first ride on a train, visit to Great Grandma Gabbitt's country home, that she was a kind lady who had helped my mother, and that my mother loved her and her apple pies.

5

Tonsillectomy

I experienced a growing spurt between Kindergarten and First Grade. Granddaddy said that I "grew like Topsy." I did not know "Topsy." No longer was I "pretty hair" or "pretty, long hair." I became "skinny with legs like a Kildee." I did not know what a Kildee was either.

Grandma said that I now "ate like a bird." I understood that. But I soothed myself by thinking that at least I did *not* eat like my cousin, Joan. Joan ate only the tiny beans from inside the string beans that Aunt Irene cooked. She did not eat much of anything, but Aunt Irene did not "fuss" about it.

But, to *me*, Grandma and Granddaddy said, "Don't pick over your food like that."

If I left one tiny morsel on my plate, Granddaddy showed strong disapproval.

"You little Piss Pot, wastin' food."

Granddaddy did not eat large meals. He ate what probably were regular portions and mostly limited himself to single helpings. But he never left any food on his plate. If we had cabbage, cornbread and boiled potatoes, he even raised his plate to drink the "pot liquor." This was the juice left from cooking the cabbage and potatoes.

My feet grew, too, and from the talk I surmised that they grew abnormally large.

I became, "all feet with legs like a Kildee, grew like Topsy and pretty, long hair." When my legs hurt, which they often did during this period, I complained.

Granddaddy said, "Aw it ain't nothin' to gripe about. It's just growin' pains. You moan and groan as much as your, old, whiney Grandmammy."

166

But, Grandma and Hookey were worried. Grandma took me to General Hospital Clinic. The white, tiled floors and massive building gave an impersonal feeling to the hospital.

The doctors did not know what caused the pains in my legs, but they did notice that I should have my tonsils removed. At five years of age I did not know what that meant, either. I thought it was to be another routine visit to the clinic for a check up.

On the day of my tonsillectomy, Grandma and I arrived at the Hospital and were directed to a small, barren room. It had a high, padded table that stood near a wall. There was an odd assortment of instruments, but I did not believe they had anything to do with me.

I was greeted by a cheerful young nurse who began to undress me. Then she put me in a stiff, white gown. The room was very cool and I shivered. She took me under my arms and lifted me up onto the table. Next, I was told to lie down. I grew apprehensive.

It was then that one item out of the assortment of instruments was moved over me. The doctor came into the room and greeted me with a warm smile. I had not seen him before, so I was skeptical. He explained that he was going to use one of the instruments that was near the bed and that I would be just fine. He then asked my grandmother to leave the room. This bothered me more than anything else that had happened. It bothered me more than all the strange instruments and the coolness of the room. I pleaded with her not to leave, but Grandma did not disobey the doctor. She just looked back and said I would be fine. She left without another word.

The nurse came close and moved the instrument that looked like a strange mask with a hose attached so that it was positioned just above me. As I stared at it, the nurse brought it down and placed it over my nose and mouth.

Before everything turned black, I smelled the terrible, noxious odor of ether.

I was in a black world, aware of nothing. When I came to, I was in a large dormitory-type room with lots of other children who, like me, were in white beds with railings all around. They looked like baby cribs. My throat hurt and tears welled up in my eyes.

I didn't want to cry because even that would cause more pain.

Grandma, who was joined by Aunt Hookey, had been waiting for me to wake up.

I felt light-headed. My throat pained. I could still smell the odor of ether, but the mask was gone.

They came over to the bed smiling, as if glad to see me after a long absence.

"There's my precious," Grandma said, talking to me in baby talk.

I thought something must really be wrong. Didn't she know about the stabbing pain in my throat?

Aunt Hookey said, "Hi, my little, Sweetpea. How's my baby?"

I tried to talk but my throat was in such pain I stopped trying. I stood up in the bed, holding onto the railing. I waited for them to dress me and take me home. I didn't want to stay another minute. But they just stood there smiling at me and talking.

"Now, you won't have anymore old, nasty colds. Those bad tonsils are all gone," Grandma said.

I thought my throat and voice were what were "all gone" I did not know what tonsils were. Again, I tried to talk. Tears streamed down my face. Still, I tried to talk.

"Shhhhh," Aunt Hookey cautioned. "Don't try to talk. It'll be all right soon."

Finally, Grandma announced, "Hookey and I are leaving now. We have to get home for Daddy's supper. We will be back tomorrow."

I couldn't believe my ears. I wasn't going with them? I stood, staring in disbelief. I started to cry through the sharp pains. Grandma and Aunt Hookey bent over to hug and kiss me telling me not to cry.

As they walked away, I began screaming after them. The daggers in my throat tore away at the inside. Grandma and Aunt Hookey just kept smiling, blowing kisses to me as they turned and backed out the door. Then, they were gone.

The night nurse was surprised to see me wandering around the hallway trying to find Grandma. I wanted to go home.

"You can't be up," she said taking me by the hand leading me back to bed.

"I want my Grandma," I strained to speak. "I want to go home."

"They will be here in the morning. Now, don't cry. It will just make your throat hurt all the more." The nurse's warning was too late.

"Let's go back to your nice room," she said.

I did not smile, but let her take my hand. I went along with the nurse and the second one who had joined her, but as soon as they left I climbed out of bed again and cried for Grandma. This time the nurses put me back into bed, but to make sure that I stayed put they tied my arms to the side. I felt completely helpless and alarmed. I struggled, but to no avail.

I screamed into the darkened room setting off a riot among the other abandoned children. The night nurse came to quiet me. She stood by my bed saying, "Oh, look at these pretty bracelets."

I only grew more angry. Now, I definitely felt like a caged animal at the zoo.

The nurse stayed by my bed, holding her flashlight in one hand and stroking my head with the other. Exhausted, I finallyI drifted off to sleep.

I awakened to a hot morning and humidity. Grandma did not come by herself to get me. This time she brought Aunt Irene.

"Peasy, where'd you get those pretty bracelets?" Aunt Irene asked.

I looked at her as one betrayed.

"Here, Baby. Aunt Irene'll untie these so you can get out. We're going to take you home, now." She untied my cotton shackles.

My throat was sore for several days after my return home. I was brought lots of vanilla ice cream and cold drinks, but the trauma from the experience was deep. I felt a strangeness about my familiar surroundings. As night approached, I imagined the huge funnel being put over my face and the darkness of the room was the darkness of my being put to sleep.

When my Aunt Hookey finally came to bed, I scooted close to her, assuring myself that she was really there; she was not just a figment of my imagination and just my *wanting* her to be there.

After the tonsillectomy, night always brought with it the same fear of abandonment. I lost my feeling of having a grand adventure when a visit to General Hospital Clinic was on Grandma's agenda. I was never as compliant as I had been. Not even the ride on the bus held the same sense of fun and fascination as it once did.

A great deal changed for me after that first surgery. There were a lot of new words and treatment concepts that I had learned. I especially would remember ether and that it could render you helpless.

6

I Begin First Grade

The opening of school and my going to First grade could not come soon enough. Aunt Hookey bought my new dresses and my mother bought my new shoes.

Miss Nose, my First Grade teacher, was as homely as Miss Denman, my kindergarten teacher, was beautiful. But the biggest impression Miss Nose made was when she gave us homework. Homework was what Aunt Lockey Jane brought home from high school. Now I knew that I had arrived at a very important stage. I loved getting homework.

I bestowed upon myself a great importance at the beginning of this my second year at Hoffman. My own self importance came because I had learned about the "Dumb Class."

The "Dumb Class" was in a room on the second floor. It was a small room with French doors, like Papa Green's doors to his parlor. Children who could not learn in the regular classrooms were deposited in this room. It was a horrifying notion, being in the "Dumb Class." Those of us who were not were relieved. Some children snickered and rolled their eyes when the line from the "Dumb Class" passed us in the hallway. I did not participate in the mocking. I felt sorry for the ones labeled "Dumb."

Most of the time the children in this class just laughed if off, embarrassed, but on occasion they got angry and started fights on the playground. When this happened, the combatants were sent to Miss Rowe's office. She was the principal, short, plump and very stern. She had jet black hair and a round face. She walked around the hallways at times, looking mean and very officious.

Soon after the beginning of school, I was allowed to walk to and from unescorted. I no longer needed Christine, who had graduated and was attending Withrow High School. This was further testimony to my new "grown up" status.

In first grade, a runny nose began to plague me. It started in late September and developed into colds in the winter. I wondered why the tonsillectomy had not done its job; but I said nothing for fear that I would have another visit to the General Hospital. So, I learned to wipe my nose on the back of my hand or the sleeve of my dress.

Top priority was to be able to eat lunch in the school cafeteria. This was no easy accomplishment. It required twenty-six cents and eating at school. This could not be justified because I was in walking distance of my school.

"I don't have money for lunch," Grandma said, "You can come home."

She didn't just say this plainly and without emphasis, she said it with pain, as if I had injured her in some way just by my asking. But I really wanted to eat with my classmates. Eating in the lunchroom was a symbol, to me, of affluence and maturity. I needed both since Grandma insisted that I was "poor," and I insisted that I wasn't. Also, I was still treated like a baby at home, being the youngest in the apartment. But, not having to walk home in the rain or snow was also a good enough excuse, I thought.

When Aunt Hookey heard me ask for lunch money and heard Grandma almost in tears, she said angrily, "Here, Sweetpea. Take this and stop pestering Mama. And don't you lose it either."

She handed me the money. The twenty-six cents bought a round, silver colored, metal token with a hole in it. This token was then traded for lunch.

First graders were first in line and the upper classes followed. We walked slowly in front of the steam tables with hot food. My favorite school meal was meatloaf, mashed potatoes, gravy, carrots, buttered bread, a ginger cookie, and milk.

"I don't know why you'd give her money to eat at school. She won't eat what she's got here at home," Grandma told Aunt Hookey.

"Mama, I get tired of hearin' her mouth," Aunt Hookey answered.

"Well, now who's spoilin' her!? You're the one givin' in to her, not me! But no, I'm the one always givin' in to her to hear you tell it," Grandma insisted.

172

At school, I was free from such power struggles, guilt and anger. At school I learned phonics, vowel and consonant sounds. I practiced reading and I printed letters until each was perfect and my hands ached.

I learned to count and add, but numbers reminded me too much of money, which was in short supply at our house and when gotten, it was gone too soon.

Sometimes, Granddaddy gave me the twenty-six cents for lunch. I waited until he was comfortably settled in the living room with his paper, then I'd ask.

"Granddaddy, can I eat lunch at school tomorrow?"

"Sure you can," he said. "You can do anything you want if you got the money to pay for it," he said from behind his evening paper.

"But I don't have any money," I told him.

"You sound just like your Grandmammy," he said. As I turned, dejectedly towards my room, he added, "Here, you little shit pot. Here's your lunch money." He reached into his pocket, sorted through his loose change and gave me the quarter and penny that I needed.

When spring came that year, Hoffman School celebrated Arbor Day. This was a new occasion and a new word for me. It was one I could add to Christmas, Easter, Fourth of July and my birthday. We filed into the large auditorium where all major school programs were held. The fifth and sixth graders entertained that day. They were dressed up like trees in green and brown costumes they had made in Mr. Michael's art class.

One student stepped forward and recited the poem, *"Trees"* by Kilmer. One student read an original poem and another told a story of the forest and their importance to all of us living on earth.

At the end of the program each child was given a plant sprig wrapped and tied in a bag. The name of the plant and the instructions, for planting and its care, were stapled to the brown paper bag.

I had never been given something to grow like this little sprig. As it turned out, it was the sprig of the Forsythia bush. I was really excited when I arrived home with it. Granddaddy was happy too. That evening before supper he and I went into the back yard and planted my thin sprig on the hillside, directly opposite the cottonwood tree.

There it would get more of the sun and I could see it from my bedroom window.

My little Forsythia sprig looked pitiful beside the giant Cottonwood. I didn't think it had much of a chance to survive. But as it did grow, it spread out over the hillside. I watched as it filled with tiny yellow blossoms each spring and then green leaves took over when the blossoms had fallen away.

The Forsythia held wonder for me and I looked forward to spring, Arbor Day, and the blossoming of my own plant in the back yard.

7

Creating Adventures

Hoffman Elementary School was a grand, stately building. Large numbers of students of all colors entered as frightened, impressionable youngsters, and graduated from eighth grade a little more sophisticated. We were well-schooled in the basics. Ohio was a State known for its excellent schools. Hoffman was certainly one of these.

It had been a creative refuge for me. Each day I was eager for school to begin where I could be with a few friends, but more to be able to demonstrate my skills and receive the approval of my teachers.

The uneasiness I felt about and with myself presented itself in my acting out fantasies, and on occasion having bad dreams and nightmares. Grandma always talked about the bad dreams that she had. If she ever heard an owl hoot at night, she rushed to the living room closet and turned the shoes towards the wall. She said it was to ward off "bad luck."

One day Grandma was talking to me while she was sewing. She said," When I was a baby, my mother told me that I had been born blind. When I was five, they bought me glasses and I was able to see."

I thought this was a miracle.

Returning to school one afternoon after having lunch at home, I walked across the expansive cement walk that crossed the front of Hoffman School. As I descended the wide cement steps that led to the side play yard, I decided to find out what it would be like to be blind - like Grandma had been.

I closed my eyes and squeezed the lids so tight, not a line of light could get through. I groped my way to the side of the building with my arms extended in front of me. I walked ever so cautiously and slowly. No one was around. I had returned to school early, so now I could experiment in private.

I counted my steps. I had calculated the distance and sensed that I was ready to turn the corner. Unfortunately, I had miscounted. I bumped into the edge of the brick wall just at the edge of the play yard. A pain shot through my head. My eyes smarted as a lump formed in the center of my forehead. I immediately opened my eyes and felt my forehead. I not only had a lump, but there was blood from a minor scratch as well.

I had completely failed at being a blind person. I ran around the back of the school, through the doors and into the girl's bathroom. I got a paper towel and ran cold water over it to ease my throbbing head.

In some way, I wanted something serious to happen to me. Maybe I would break my arm like Maxine O'Brien. Maybe then, I could get a lot of attention. Maxine was in my class. She was a very tiny white girl with a face full of freckles. She was absent from school more times than she was present. She had some strange disease. When she was at school the teacher was very sympathetic and kind to her. When she was absent for a very long time her school work was sent home so she could study and keep up with the class.

Maxine was treated like a little princess when she returned. Then there was the time when she returned with her arm in a sling. I wanted to have a hurt that was as serious as Maxine's. Grandma's being blind was serious; that is why it was a miracle, to me, that she was able to see. But I could see and was not very good at pretending to be blind.

I never hurt myself really bad. I don't know what it would have taken to have a broken arm. I just had to be satisfied with getting colds in winter and skinning my knees in summer. It was a little boring.

176

8

"Wake Up Little Birdie"

In the morning and dressed to work, Granddaddy stood at my bedroom door.

"Wake up, little Birdie, wake up! The laziest bird is hopping about. You ought to be up with the rest."

How I hated being awakened like that. It was hard to get up some mornings no matter how much I loved school. At other times, he quoted Paul Lawrence Dunbar:

Liza, Liza, Bless de lawd, don you know de day's abroad? Get up from dere you scamp, else dere's g'wine be trouble in dis camp. Think I'se g'wine to let you sleep, while I make yo' board and keep. Get up from dere and comb yo' head. Looks jes' lak a featherbed.

"Granddaddy, who taught you that?" I asked.

"My brother Will," he said chuckling.

Then Granddaddy left the apartment, brown lunch sack in hand, to get his ride to work with Uncle Ben.

Granddaddy's brother Will had visited us on occasion with his wife, Mary. He was a minister in Lexington, Kentucky. His full name was William Proctor. He was not Corbin like Granddaddy because they each had different fathers. Great Uncle Will and Granddaddy were tall, big men. They said that Granddaddy had a "beer belly," but Great Uncle Will was a minister; he didn't have a "beer belly." He didn't look like granddaddy although they both had freckles. Granddaddy had finer features.

Great Uncle Will had a deep voice and a pleasant smile. The atmosphere in the apartment changed when he was there. Granddaddy was very nice to his older brother. You could tell that he looked up to him. Great Uncle Will's wife, Mary reminded me of my cousin Mitzi's grandmother "Mama Green." Both women were dark-skinned, fat, with large "backsides," and married to ministers. It seemed to me that all ministers' wives looked exactly the same.

Great Uncle Will was not one who did a lot of talking. He listened a lot. He knew his Bible. He got up each morning, long before any of us. He shaved and got dressed as if he was going to church. Then, he would go into the living room where Great Aunt Mary was still sleeping on the pull-out section of the sofa, sit quietly in the mohair chair where Granddaddy sat, and studied his Bible.

Granddaddy said that Great Uncle Will was the "good one" in the family, meaning that he and his half-sister, my Great Aunt Mae Georgia, left much to be desired in their behavior.

Granddaddy never visited his half-brother, Will, although every time Great Uncle Will was in Cincinnati, he always invited him. I wondered if Grandma and Granddaddy had visited him, would Grandma get even with Aunt Mary and try to out eat her?

As he was leaving after one of his visits, Great Uncle Will said, "Now, Foley, I'll be looking for you to come visit in the spring."

He was more like Granddaddy's father and Granddaddy acted as if he was Great Uncle Will's son. I thought this was because he was a preacher and Granddaddy was suspicious of preachers. But then, Great Uncle Will was Granddaddy's only brother.

"That's right, Will, I'll be down," Granddaddy said. Granddaddy grinned and nodded, as if he intended to keep his promise to visit Great Uncle Will. But, he never did.

Once Granddaddy had left Kentucky, he never went back, although he kept saying, "Goin' to take me a trip down to Lexington one of these days. Goin' fishin'."

Grandma's reply was always the same. "You ain't goin' to do no such thing so you might as well stop talkin' about it."

9

One Easter and One Saturday's Lunch

There was never a good time for having a cold, but the week before Easter was particularly bad. Grandma fussed, "That doctor didn't know what he was talkin' about when he said taking your tonsils out would keep you from getting colds."

She gave me a dose of Castor Oil, which I was more than just reluctant to take. I squirmed and turned my head away. Grandma had to grab my cheeks hard and force my mouth open. She said the Castor Oil would "work the cold out of me." This meant I would go to the bathroom a lot with "the runs," so I just had to swallow hard, forcing the thick oily, tasteless medicine down my throat.

"It's nasty," I told Grandma.

"How can it be nasty when it doesn't have any taste?" Grandma said.

"Yes, it does, too, Grandma. It tastes terrible. I don't like it."

"This will be the last dose," she assured me.

I looked forward to Easter, and most of all to the Easter Bunny's arrival. At school, we were making construction paper Easter baskets. I was having a terrible time with mine. I kept cutting the wrong part of the square that was to fold around to make the corner. I was managing the clips that held the handles on, but pasting the appropriate blocks was too complicated. I needed help and now I was going to be way behind due to an old cold.

Grandma bought the Easter egg dye and I was filled with anticipation as I looked forward to dying the eggs. The Easter Bunny would bring me a basket filled with artificial grass, marshmallow eggs, foil-covered chocolate eggs with white cream inside and little yellow marshmallow chicks with black dots for eyes.

Every Easter I got a new dress, shoes and spring coat. This Easter, when I was in first grade, Grandma bought me a beautiful, royal blue dress with box pleats all around. It had a fitted bodice and a neckline without a collar. This was the first dress that made me look like I had a "shape." No more "straight up and down beanpole" like Granddaddy said.

The dress was too long for me and needed altering. Grandma had just begun the alteration when I caught the cold. This was the most beautiful dress I had ever had and I was anxious to show it off.

Towards the end of my recuperation, Grandma came into my room to check on me. What she found was a pile of jumbled covers, crayons and paper in disarray and me half under and half on top of the pile I had made of the covers.

"Look at you! Just like some wiggle worm, covers all over the place."

She started to smooth the covers, but when some of my crayons fell behind the bed, she stopped.

"Well, you must be well enough for me to fit that dress on you, since you're not staying under the covers. I might as well get something done. Come on in the kitchen. "

I was happy to have an excuse to get out of bed. I walked into the kitchen and stepped onto the seat of one of the chairs near the open oven door. The heat felt good on my legs and would keep me warm during the fitting.

One by one, Grandma shut the kitchen doors that led to her room. She had removed the stitches of the dress's original hem in order to make a new one that would shorten the dress. She sat on the floor with her red, tomato-shaped pin cushion and began the measuring. She took several pins and placed them between her lips. Little by little I turned slowly, as instructed, while she placed the raw edge of the hem in place.

"Don't bend down!" Grandma told me through the pins she held tight in her lips. "The hem will be lopsided and I'll have to start all over."

"Stand up straight!" she said again when I had a lapse and looked down to see how long my dress was to be.

Then, I felt the hem as she placed it gingerly to just below my knees. It was going to be just the right length. I was truly excited.

"Thanks, Grandma," I said.

I climbed down from my perch and hurried back to my room and the array of covers. The pot-bellied stove was still giving off sufficient heat and Grandma did not need to add any more lumps of coal. I busied myself with an Easter picture, making a line of green grass across the bottom of the paper; a brown trunk of a tree with green ovals for the leaves and a blue line across the top for the sky. Finally I added some oval shapes of different colors to resemble Easter eggs. My picture looked like similar ones done by my classmates.

I had not forgotten about my unfinished basket at school, but the happy thoughts I had about my new dress and patent leather shoes made me believe that when I returned to school, I was just going to find a way to make a perfect Easter Basket out of construction paper.

Our kitchen walls had been freshly painted a deep, blue. I did not like the color they had chosen. It made the room dark. The corner near the sink, where Aunt Lockey Jane and I did the dishes was made even darker by this new color. The refrigerator blocked the light from one window so it did not matter that the paint was shiny, reflecting any light; it did not improve the darkness in the corner.

The kitchen seemed to have other problems in addition to being dark. I thought the corner under the sink was sinking. Granddaddy said it was just my imagination because I didn't want to do the dishes. Grandma thought the floor was sinking, too. She kept watching it from her chair when she sat at the table eating.

One Saturday, before Granddaddy left for work, Grandma said, "I think the floor is sinking in that corner."

"Uhnhuh," Granddaddy muttered.

He drank his coffee and said nothing further.

"You'd think Sudduth would do something about this place for all the rent he charges. Roof leakin' all over the place. It's so cold and damp in here, my arthritis keeps actin' up. My hands ache all the time and my knuckles are numb." Grandma catalogued her ailments.

"You're just gettin' old. Not a young chicken like you used to be," Granddaddy teased.

He took the last piece of his toast and sopped up the remaining egg yolk from his plate.

Granddaddy did not complain much. He said that Grandma had enough complaints for the both of them. On Saturdays Granddaddy only worked a half day so he did not take a lunch. As he was leaving, Grandma reminded him that she was going to Kroger's to do the weekly grocery shopping.

"What do you want for lunch today?"

"Whatever you get, Sister," he said

"Well, do you want Limburger cheese?"

"Yep! That sounds good."

"You want some pickled herring and hogshead cheese," Grandma continued.

"Yep!"

"Anything else?"

"Nope."

"Don't be fussin' at me, then if I don't get everything you want to snack on."

"I ain't goin' to be fussin', gal. I got hot peppers still in the jar-- red hot, too. And I got me some souse from the other day, and crackers, dill pickles, onions and mustard." Granddaddy rattled off his supply of Saturday lunch food. Then he added, "Oh, I forgot. Get me some sardines. We ain't had sardines in awhile."

"You want sardines *and* pickled herring?" Grandma asked.

"Why not?" Granddaddy said.

"Just wondered."

Granddaddy left for work. Grandma got dressed to go to the store. She rolled the stockings down to the foot, crossed one bare leg

182

over the other, slid the stocking, carefully over her toenails, to keep from snagging them, and then flexed her leg outward. The stockings came just above her knees where she secured them with a fat, round, garter. She knotted the stocking, tucked it under the garter, rolled it down a turn or two and prepared to repeat the process with her other leg.

She had begun her shopping list on Friday and completed it early Saturday morning after she had gotten Granddaddy's input. Saturday morning was when she did the weekly shopping at Kroger's, a large supermarket chain which carried everything one needed to stock their cupboards at home.

One of Kroger's main stores was several blocks away at a busy intersection of Woodburn Avenue and the main thoroughfare that ran all the way to the streetcar line that ended in Obriensville and Madisonville. Woodburn Avenue was where people transferred from the streetcars coming from downtown Cincinnati if they wanted to go in the opposite direction towards Lincoln Avenue and to Gilbert Avenue.

If Grandma ran out of anything that she needed during the week, I had the chance to go to Rosen's, the corner store, to get it for her. I really liked going to Rosen's. They had the best dill pickles and large, peppermint sticks. Grandma liked their calves' liver and bought that from Rosen's rather than Kroger's.

The only problem with Rosen's was that Mr. and Mrs. Rosen and their oldest son, David always asked lots of questions about our family. Grandma said they were "nosey."

But she still sent me there for the calves' liver and other items.

Kroger's was big and impersonal. You didn't really get to know the clerks and butchers there like you did at Rosen's. Both sons, David the oldest and Ivan the youngest, spent time working in the store and were very smart in school. Ivan was six going on seven; my age.

Kroger's was several blocks from our house. Grandma walked this distance pulling a wire shopping cart which she kept, in a collapsed state, in the corner near the kitchen sink. She never took the bus or streetcar to Kroger's not even in winter when Cincinnati and Walnut Hills were cold and damp.

That Saturday, Grandma finished her shopping and came home with her cart loaded with large bags of flour, sugar, canned goods and other items. I was only interested in the cookies, especially the vanilla wafers she got to make the banana pudding that Granddaddy and I took to Longview State Hospital on our Sunday visits to Uncle Bobby.

Grandma put away her groceries and made me a bologna sandwich on Taystee Bread with Miracle Whip salad dressing. In the summer, I had Kool Aid with my sandwich, but in winter I had milk tea made with milk, hot water and sugar.

Then, Grandma prepared the table for the time when Granddaddy would arrive and they could sit down to their lunch together. Every Saturday, in preparation for their lunch, Granddaddy stopped at the liquor store and bought a pint bottle of gin and three quarts of Hudepohl beer. Hudepohl was a Cincinnati beer company. Cincinnati was known for its beer making.

The Saturday lunch menu never suited me. I liked Sunday dinner when we had fried chicken with milk gravy or roast beef with carrot, potatoes and coleslaw. On Sunday, the kitchen smelled liked a banquet room; but on Saturdays, it smelled like a garbage can. I always left the kitchen when Grandma and Granddaddy got ready for their lunch.

Granddaddy liked Hudepohl beer. Grandma liked gin. It looked like water. After Grandma took a "swig" of gin, she and Granddaddy laughed and ate until the "swigs" took charge and the brown quart bottles of beer were in empty disarray among the slick, white wrapping paper that held the hogshead and the foul smelling limburger cheeses. The dill pickles, hot peppers and mustard were in their open jars on the table alongside the red and white Zesta cracker box and lemon wedges.

While Grandma and Granddaddy ate their lunch, I spent my time quietly coloring the last tulip and putting the pink inside of my reasonable facsimile of an Easter Bunny. Crayons and paper lay spread over the top of my covers.

I had been making pictures of bright tulips, which I had learned to make in school. The colored eggs lay hidden in that very tall, green grass that I had made with high and low patches along the bottom of my paper. No perspective, no sense of distance was evident in my work at this stage. The sky was still a thick blue line with a cloud or two floating beneath.

I heard Grandma's chair scrape against the linoleum floor as she got up to use the bathroom. When she returned, her voice drifted towards me then faded as she turned to go back into the kitchen.

"That bathroom window needs fixin'. It's cold in there," she told Granddaddy.

The bathroom window had frosted glass on the bottom so no one could see in or out. Clear glass was in the top window so that more light could enter. When anyone went in, stinking up the bathroom, they lifted up the frosted window and placed a small, empty Miracle Whip Salad Dressing jar beneath to hold it in place. This allowed air to flow into the bathroom and rid the inside air of any odor.

There had been a rope that once made it possible to raise the window without any prop, but it had been broken and Grandma worried that the window would fall, breaking the frosted glass.

"Well, I ain't fixin' it today," Granddaddy said.

"I didn't say you had to fix it today. I just said it needs fixin'. It's been broke three weeks now," Grandma told him.

"It can stay broke for another three for all I care, Sister." Granddaddy's laugh was tinged with sarcasm.

"I can't say nothin' to you without you getting' smart-alecky with me," Grandma whined. "The cold air just about freezes my bottom every time I use the toilet."

"Well, don't go in there then, Sister," Granddaddy joked.

"What'm I goin' to use for a toilet then? You sound so ignorant with that stupid talk." Grandma's tone turned angry.

"Use a pot like you're used to," Granddaddy laughed even harder this time.

"I ain't goin' to use no pot! We don't have no pot around here to use, you old fool!" Grandma shouted now as her anger increased.

"Well, go down in the cellar, then," Granddaddy offered.

I could not see Grandma going to the toilet in the dark cellar under our apartment. She never went near the cellar. Only Granddaddy, Aunt Hookey and I went into the cellar and that was when we put in the coal for the winter and took it out when needed for the fire in the pot-bellied stove in my bedroom.

"You're just drunk," Grandma said. "Who's drunk?" Granddaddy asked. He sounded surprised at Grandma's accusation.

"You're drunk. That's who! Drinking three whole quarts of beer and a pint of gin."

"I drank the bottle of gin? What about you, Sister? You're the one who drank all the gin. Besides, I put one bottle of Hudepohl in the refrigerator. That's how much you know."

"I drank all the gin? I drank all the gin!?" Grandma repeated in haughty disbelief. "You drank more gin than me. I just had one little drink."

"One little drink! I just had one little drink!" Granddaddy mimicked Grandma.

"I did! That's all I had," Grandma defended herself.

"Well, who ate up all the Limburger cheese, then?" Granddaddy asked.

I heard the slick, white wrapping paper crackle. It was Granddaddy wrapping the souse.

"Who went to the store and bought it?" Grandma asked.

"Who paid for it, Sister?" Granddaddy retorted. "You may have gone to the store and brought it home, but I'm the guy who paid for it! I'm the guy payin' for things around here, Sister!"

"Well, what about me!? I made twenty-five dollars this week on those slip covers and I don't have a penny to show for it."

"That ain't nothin' new, Sister. I been workin' all my life and don't have nothin' to show for it. Not even a pot to piss in."

"Whose fault is that? Workin' for that old, Mayor Reed for nothin'. You love him better'n you do me. Do anything he tells you to

186

do. You'd walk out in the middle of the ocean and drown if he told you to, you old dumb bunny."

"It ain't the boss, Sister. He ain't the one spendin' every penny I make."

"You ain't makin' nothin' to spend. Grinnin' and "yes mannin'" those old peckerwoods."

"That's all you know, Sister. You was nothin' but a snotty-nosed, spoiled brat? That mammy of yours just spoiled you rotten!"

"I wasn't poor trash like you," Grandma said coldly.

"I wasn't poor trash, no such thing, Sister." Granddaddy became defensive.

"If it wasn't for my daddy," Grandma continued, "you never would've even had a trade to earn a livin' at all. Your old, white daddy sure didn't think nothin' of you."

"That's all right, Sister. I didn't think nothin' of him neither. My mama took care of me."

"Huh!" Grandma retorted. "You was so mean, I don't call knockin' you in the fireplace takin' care of you. My mama never treated me or my brothers that mean."

"You'd've turned out a damned sight better if she had. You was just a spoiled little brat, that's all. And don't you forget, I'm the one who made somethin' out of myself. I wasn't born with no silver spoon in my mouth like you. And your old, drunken half-white daddy didn't teach me nothin'. I taught myself."

"Taught yourself!? You didn't learn what my Daddy was teachin' you, you old, fool. My daddy never worked for no man. He had his own business, and if he had, he sure wouldn't 've worked for nothin' like you're doin'. If it wasn't for my daddy, you never would've been nothin'."

"Ain't nothin' now, Sister. He didn't do a damn thing for me!"

Granddaddy had a laugh that was a low, sarcastic chuckle, a motor running down, out of gas.

"I know one thing!" Grandma continued, "I'm poorer now than I was when I was little. My mama didn't bring me up to be like this, without nothin'. She brought me up to be a lady."

"Lady!? She should see you now, you old, drunken sot."

Granddaddy's words were vicious.

"Mama told me that she wanted me to marry Fred Day. He's been a fine doctor for years. His wife has plenty of money."

"I wish you'd've married him too, Sister. Would've saved me a peck of trouble. I'd have somethin' by now."

"Like hell you would!" Grandma spat back at Granddaddy. "Everything I make from sewin' goes into this house. I sure don't spend nothin' on myself. I don't have one decent pair of shoes to show for twenty-five years of marriage."

"You got more out of it than me, Sister. All I got is hand-me-downs from the Boss."

"Nobody told you to wear those old, beat up things. They're too small anyway. Even if you had new ones, you wouldn't wear 'em. You'd still be wearin' those hand-me-downs because you just luuuuuuuvvvvvvv your old, Boss." Grandma teased Granddaddy.

"That's all right. I ain't no spendthrift like you, Sister."

"Spendthrift? Ain't nothin' to spend. I never should've married, at least not you anyway." Grandma began to whine again.

"I wish you hadn't, Sister. I'd been a damned sight better off than I am."

"You old ignorant fool. If it hadn't been for Daddy, you'd still be tendin' bar down in Lexington."

"If I hadn't met that old, crazy, half-white Daddy of yours, I wouldn't be in the fix I'm in now. That was my mistake!"

"Mistake! Mistake!" Grandma shouted. She started to cry. "I'm the one who made the mistake. Mama told me I'd regret it every day I lived if I married a no account like you."

188

"You should've stayed with that old mammy of yours. She made you so you're not worth a dime."

"I was somethin' when you met me. I had my life then. You took the best years of my life and now treat me like some old dish rag."

"That's what you say, Sister. That ain't the way I see it."

"You're just an evil, old bastard. You don't know nothin' about nothin' decent 'cause you didn't come from nothin' decent."

Grandma blew her nose, loudly and with force.

"Aw, shut up, you old drunken woman."

"Drunk!? Drunk!? How'm I gonna' be drunk when I ain't had but one drink?"

"That's the biggest lie I heard all day." Granddaddy laughed again.

I wanted them to stop the endless arguing. I wanted them to stop saying such terrible things to each other. I wanted them to stop, but they didn't.

"Oh, so now I'm a liar. Why, oh why did I have to marry and be so unhappy-make my life so miserable." Grandma was crying harder.

"I gave you the best years I had. Now that I'm old and decrepit you just want to downgrade me."

"You said it, Sister, I didn't."

Grandma got up from the table, the gray metal chair legs scraping across the linoleum floor. I lay still. I had escaped under the covers listening as their earlier laughter and joy had turned to arguing, tears and sarcasm swirling around them, a whirlpool dragging their day down into the depths, into the empty parts of themselves.

"I was good enough to have all those babies by you. I know that!" Grandma emphasized through her tears.

I heard her steps as she stomped out of the kitchen. I heard their bedroom door being slammed behind her.

"That's it, Sister. Break the damned door down," Granddaddy shouted behind her.

Grandma didn't reply. She didn't hear him over the noise of the door slamming. Granddaddy remained at the table, hovering over the sardines, pickled herring, Limburger cheese, the hot mustard and red hot peppers.

He laughed again. "Took the best years of your life? Who took the best years of mine?" He asked aloud.

The question hung in the air unanswered. Grandma must have fallen asleep on top of her good, chenille bedspread as she always did after Saturday lunch.

The apartment was quiet. Granddaddy got up from the table. Slowly, he began cleaning up. He put the food away until another Saturday. I heard the hollowness of empty beer bottles as Granddaddy tossed them in the trash can under the sink where the floor was sinking.

I heard the slick, white, butcher's wrapping paper being carefully wrapped around the remaining hogshead cheese and souse. I heard Granddaddy as he replaced the lids on the dill pickle and pickled herring jars. I heard the sound of the jars as they were pushed against each other as he made room for them in the refrigerator, now full, after Grandma's morning of shopping at Kroger's.

I lay under the covers, listening. The pot-bellied stove still warmed my room. A lump of coal broke into embers and settled, trapped at the bottom.

"Just like her old, crazy Daddy," Granddaddy muttered to himself. "Never could take a drink without getting drunk…never could appreciate nothin'."

When he finished in the kitchen, Granddaddy came into my bedroom. The metal door of the pot-bellied stove creaked as he opened it to check on the fire. I stayed under the covers pretending to be asleep. I heard him poke the coals with the long black-handled metal

190

poker. I heard him throw in a new lump of coal. I heard the sparks flare up and the thud of the coal as it landed securely in place.

"There, Sweetpea!" my grandfather said. "Now, it'll be nice and warm in here for you, girlie."

I didn't answer. Granddaddy went into the living room, settled in his favorite chair and picked up the evening paper. Before long he was asleep like Grandma. The paper that he had once held before his face now rested on his chest. Only the crackling sound of the fire in the pot-bellied stove could be heard. Saturday lunch was over. My grandparents slept. I could not.

10

The Ducklings Arrive

The Easter when I was six, I got the ducks. The Saturday evening before the holiday, I had my bath and my hair washed and put into Shirley Temple curls. I was clean and smelled like pure Ivory Soap.

A fire roared in the black pot-bellied stove which would soon be shut down for the warmer season. I was restless. It was too early to go to bed and too late to do anything but be anxious about Easter, and the arrival of the Easter Bunny. I stood in the corner of my room near the stove. I was keeping warm and idly melting broken crayons on the hot stove pipe. Rivulets of waxy color ran down the sides.

Granddaddy sat in the living room reading his paper, the *Cincinnati Times Star*, while Grandma was in the bathroom finishing her bath. The corner was cozy but I knew that a few feet from where I stood, I could quickly and easily get chilled.

Granddaddy heard them first.

"Somebody's comin'," he called, snapping one side of his evening paper down to peer out the window opposite his chair. Granddaddy always read the *Cincinnati Times Star*, the evening paper, and the *Cincinnati Inquirer* on Sunday morning.

I scampered from my corner and hurriedly closed the door to my bedroom. I did not wish to be caught in night clothes. I could not make out the muffled voices, neither could Granddaddy who was frozen in position, squinting at the door.

It was my mother and stepfather. Mama knocked and opened the door to come in at the same time.

"Eckey! Here's Eckey." Granddaddy erupted into smiles.

He got up from the chair to give my mother a big hug.

"How's my girl doin'? Hi there, Neil. How're you doin'?"

Granddaddy shifted his attention to our second guest. Neil is what the family called my stepfather. His real name was Cornelious. Mama answered first.

"Bless your heart, Honey. I'm doin' just fine," Mama said hugging and patting Granddaddy on the back.

As soon as I heard Granddaddy say "Eckey," I opened the door and scooted into the living room to greet my mother. It was such a surprise to see both of them visiting, and at night. My stepfather just smiled. He was a man of few words, but very kind and gentle. He was holding a small container the size of a shoe box. His eyes danced with delight.

"Hi, Sweetie," he said. "How're you doin'?"

Mama said, "Awwww, look at my baby with those beautiful curls. Come here, Honey. Just look how Mama's baby has grown."

My mother laughed her loud, happy laugh as I hugged her.

"We brought you somethin' for Easter," she said. "Look at this!"

My stepfather, whom I called, "Daddy," took a seat on the brown, mohair sofa while still holding the box. I heard movement from inside and knew that something alive was in there. He lifted the lid. Inside were two frightened, yellow ducklings with black beads for eyes and small, creamy orange-colored beaks. I was overwhelmed with joy and surprise. I looked at the little ducklings almost unable to breathe.

"Oh, look at the little things," I said in a whisper. "They're so cute."

"Here! You hold them," Daddy said.

I eased carefully on the seat next to him so that my back would be supported by the back of the sofa. When I was securely seated my stepfather put the box on my lap. I could feel it shift as the ducks were moving and fluttering back and forth, fearful of the uncertain motion of the box. I was in awe. I thought to myself: *Ducks. Baby ducks, just for me.*

I had never owned a live pet before. I had dolls with crisp pastel dresses. I had been given books, crayons and a tin tea set. I didn't have soft stuffed animals like a Teddy Bear. The only thing soft that I could remember were the brown cotton-ribbed stockings stuffed with candies and oranges at Christmas. I usually worried that they would be stuffed with cinders, ashes and switches. I was always so sure that Santa Claus would never leave me anything good. But Mama and Daddy had brought me two of the softest, cutest ducklings ever.

How did my mother know what to get me? How did my mother know that I would love these little yellow ducklings? I didn't really know my mother. I knew her from brief visits I made before she moved away and the ones when she came to visit me but left crying because of Grandma's harsh words.

My stepfather was never with her at those times. I knew my mother through the stories Grandma told about her. These were all bad. Then there were times when I saw pictures of her as a little girl with a huge floppy bow in her hair and when she was older, standing with Aunt Hookey in the backyard.

I had seen these pictures in the tin box that Granddaddy kept in his top dresser drawer. There was one picture of Mama sitting in a row boat with newly bobbed, beautiful, silky, black hair. What a smile she had that day. "This is your mama's plait," Granddaddy had said, showing me the long braid with a red bow tied on the end. Granddaddy kept the plait that he had cut off tied with a red ribbon, in the same tin box. I held it. I felt it. This was my mother's hair. It was like my own. From the items in Granddaddy's tin box, I got a different, softer view of Mama. But these photos and other things only gave me glimpses of her. They weren't like Grandma's stories. But none of these things let me know my mother. She was more like a distant aunt coming to visit me.

I adored the ducklings. My child's soul went out from me and into that small box and joined with the two, vulnerable, frightened little creatures that my mother had brought me.

When Mama and Daddy left, Granddaddy went down to the dark cellar and found an empty box that had once held bananas. This box had large air holes. He and I very carefully put the ducklings inside and slid the box that held them under my bed where they were to stay. This would be their new home.

When the house was quiet, I leaned over the edge of the bed and whispered to my first pets, "Goodnight, little ducks. I'll see you in the morning."

I slept little that night, awakening at any peep, any motion from inside the box beneath my bed. I wondered what I would name my ducklings. I wanted to be original. I wanted to give them special names. I was thinking hard about this.

In the morning, when I pulled the banana box from beneath the bed, one of my ducklings had died during the night. I was very upset, but I couldn't cry. Now, I had one duckling remaining. It was the little female that had died and the male duckling had lived. I named him "Donald."

The Monday after Easter, Donald wandered beyond the bedroom and got into the kitchen. I was in the bathroom when I heard Grandma squeal and heard Donald's frantic peeps.

"Sweetpea!" Grandma yelled. "Come in here and get this thing. I just stepped on it."

Horror gripped me with such profoundness that I saw all the pictures instantaneously. I saw Grandma's foot stomping on the yellow down of my little duck and all his insides oozing onto the faded patterns of the kitchen linoleum. I saw Donald's eyes close, a white skin over them announcing his death. I saw myself standing, too hurt to cry, silent, as Donald was buried in the backyard where the wash was hung. I saw sheets flapping over Donald's grave.

I rushed out of the bathroom and into the kitchen. There was no squashed Donald. I was surprised when instead, I saw Grandma, her back turned, stirring the Cream of Wheat she was making me for breakfast. Donald, more scared than ever, scurried helter-skelter past me, out of the kitchen, through the hallway and into the safety of the bedroom.

"I was fixin' your breakfast and didn't know he was in here. When I stepped back, I stepped on him. You just can't let him run loose like that," Grandma said angrily.

"You have to keep him in his box. I don't know why your mother gave you those ducks. This ain't the country like where she lives."

I barely heard Grandma. I was so relieved that Donald was alive that I followed him into the bedroom and retrieved him from under the bed. He had headed there to hide. I sat on the edge of the bed cradling him in my arms. I felt his little heart pounding like a jack hammer. He peeped, then proceeded to mess on my night gown.

I put Donald in his banana box so that he could quiet down. As he scurried away in the small shelter, I noticed that his right wing dragged. It had been damaged in his encounter with Grandma.

As Donald grew, he lost all his beautiful, soft, yellow down. This was replaced by white feathers. His tiny webbed feet were replaced by monstrous pads and his damaged wing remained a handicap which kept him from flying.

The banana box was replaced by a wire pen that Granddaddy made for the backyard. Sometimes Donald got out. When I chased after him, he tried to flap his wings, but the damaged one would always end up on the ground and I could easily capture him. When Granddaddy went out to feed the squirrels, he fed Donald too.

I loved Donald, but then his desire for independence became annoying. I was constantly chasing him to return him to his pen. My playmate and school classmate, Cornelious Wilson, was the only one who liked Donald as much as I did. His mother allowed him to come to play and help me feed Donald.

In the summer, Cornelious and I decided to make a "house" in the backyard for just the two of us and Donald. The "house" would be in the empty space where the shed that Mr. Tate had fallen on top of once stood. Cornelious and I worked at scraping dirt away using Granddaddy's shovel from the cellar. We worked like little beavers.

Grandma said, "What on earth are you two working so hard on?"

"We're making a house for us and Donald," I answered.

Grandma said, "You're not going to be playin' no "house" with that boy!" She told Cornelious that he had to go home and I had to go inside for the rest of the day. I was dumbfounded. What was wrong with our making a "house?"

Donald was kept in his pen. One day at the end of summer, Minnie Payden, Aunt Hookey and Aunt Crystal's best friend, came for a visit. At the time I was playing with Ann Butler at the Tate house next door.

In the late afternoon, I was seated at the dining room window in Ann Tate's house. I saw Minnie leaving. She was standing in front of our apartment building saying goodbye to Aunt Lockey Jane. In her hand she was holding the handles of a brown shopping bag. I saw Donald's head as he peered out over the edge. He was just looking around.

Before I could get outside Minnie's ride arrived and she got in the car and was gone.

Donald had been given away without a word being said to me.

Later, Aunt Lockey Jane told me that Minnie was going to cook and eat Donald for her Sunday dinner. I never heard if that was true. I did not protest much because Donald was getting me into a lot of trouble. I thought that because Minnie lived in the country she would let Donald roam free with her chickens.

11

A Sisters' Weekend

It was Aunt Hookey's weekend to have off from her job with the Freulands. Aunt Lockey Jane was happy to have her home. She had missed her closest sister. She did not have many girl friends at school except for her closest friend Minnie, who at this time lived across the street. Minnie was a year younger and a grade behind Aunt Lockey Jane. Both of my aunts liked Minnie. But on Aunt Hookey's first weekend home, only she and Aunt Lockey Jane went out on Saturday night.

Very late that night or early morning, I was awakened by my two, giggling aunts, shoving each other against the door in their effort to see who could get in the house and to the toilet first. I knew something was wrong.

"Be quiet, Hookey," Aunt Lockey Jane said. "Don't wake up Mama."

"You're the one making all the noise, not me," Aunt Hookey said. "Let me go first, Lockey Jane. My stomach's really upset."

"No, Hookey. If I don't get in there, I'll wet all over myself."

The door from the outside flew open and hit against the wall. It's knob banged into the side of the dresser that stood next to the door. The glass shook but did not break.

Aunt Crystal froze in the doorway. Neither of my aunts had taken the first step into the apartment. By now, I was sitting straight up in bed wondering about all the commotion.

"Hookey, do you think we woke up Mama?" Lockey Jane asked. She sounded scared.

"How'n the hell do I know?" Aunt Hookey replied.

No sound came from Grandma's room. Grandma and Granddaddy's bedroom door was closed and they were sleeping soundly after their Saturday lunch.

"I'm going to be sick," Aunt Hookey managed to say just before vomit spewed out like an oil gusher.

It went all over the wall just opposite the bed. It startled me as I stared into the dark trying to make out their images. Aunt Crystal's form could be made out. She was feeling her way, hoping to avoid Aunt Hookey's vomit. In a matter of seconds the room reeked of the smell of vomit. Aunt Hookey made her way into the bathroom. The commotion awakened Grandma who got out of bed and headed for the source of the commotion.

She flipped on the light switch as she stumbled into our room, her nightgown straps falling down revealing the nipples of her sagging breasts. The sudden flash spotlighted the vomit on the floor and on the wall. Aunt Crystal was supporting herself by holding onto the metal foot board of our bed.

"Look at this! What a mess! What do you call yourselves doin', gettin' drunk and pukin' all over the place?" Grandma was very angry.

"You can just get yourselves a bucket and clean up your own mess. I'm tellin' you that right now!" Grandma glared at Lockey Jane, something that she had never done before.

"I didn't do it, Mama. It was Hookey. She's the one who drank some old, bad whiskey."

"I don't care who it was! Goin' out drinkin' and galavantin' around like some common streetwalkers. I never thought the day would come when you'd carry on like this. Now, you have the nerve to come in this house drunk! I don't put nothin' past Hookey, but you, Lockey Jane, ought to know better."

Grandma gave her strongest, accusatory glance at Aunt Lockey Jane who stared down at the floor.

Aunt Hookey stumbled out of the bathroom. She had not heard Grandma as she continued vomiting. Her face was as white as her Cashmere Bouquet body powder. Her freckles stood out like neon lights.

I looked at the vomit that was on the wall oozing down in slow moving rivulets, white, foamy, pink with flecks of brown like Aunt Hookey's freckles. I lay back down and pulled the covers up under my chin. Grandma pulled her nightgown up and readied herself for a long, drawn out confrontation. She had already forgotten the one she and Granddaddy had engaged in earlier in the day.

"What do you call yourselves doin' comin' in here drunk?"

"Aw, go on back to bed, Mama," Aunt Hookey directed. "I'm goin' to clean it up."

"I'm not talkin' about cleaning it up. I'm talkin' about you comin' home drunk in the first place. Out carousin' all hours of the night."

Aunt Hookey was barely able to remove her coat. She examined it to see if she had soiled it with the vomit. Aunt Lockey Jane slipped into the living room to make down the sofa bed and escape Grandma's ire.

"This'll have to go back to the cleaners," Aunt Hookey said. A spattering of vomit covered the front of her coat. "Another dollar down the drain."

"Serves you right!" Grandma was not sympathetic. She was mad.

"Aw, shut up and come on back to bed," Granddaddy called from their bedroom. "And stop all that fussin' this time of night."

"It ain't night. It's mornin'," Grandma argued back. "I know you don't care about how they live, but I do! I didn't bring them up to be drunkards."

"I ain't no drunkard, Mama. This is the first time in my life that I ever got drunk." Aunt Hookey's voice was weak and tired.

"And it better be your last if you intend to live in this house!"

"I just had one drink too many and it made me sick."

"Well, what's that if it ain't bein' a drunkard? You sure ain't no example for Lockey Jane. Teachin' her bad habits."

200

"Mama, Lockey Jane ain't no baby. I didn't force her to go nowhere with me."

Aunt Lockey Jane had removed her clothes in the living room, slipped into the hallway behind Grandma and into the bathroom without being noticed.

Granddaddy came in from the bedroom, the rope belt from his fading, flannel robe dangling in the front.

"Leave her alone," Granddaddy defended Aunt Hookey. "A little drink never hurt nobody."

"That's what you'd say. Can't expect nothin' better out of you. You'd just let them carry on any old kind of way."

"Well, I don't know what all the fuss is about. She's cleanin' up after herself. What more do you want except somethin' to stand around and fuss about at all hours of the mornin'?"

"She'll fuss at me, but she won't fuss at Lockey Jane." Aunt Hookey scrubbed up the vomit.

Grandma turned away and finally made her way back to her room, muttering as she went, "Comin' in here all hours of the night drunk. I never carried on like that when I was their age. I never would disgrace my mother's home like that. I had more respect for my mother."

Granddaddy now stood in Grandma's vacated spot quietly watching Aunt Hookey and laughing. "What'd you have to drink there, Hookey, my gal?"

"I had some old, bad whiskey at the Wine Bar."

"You'd better learn how to hold your liquor, girlie. If you're goin' to be drinkin', don't be drinkin' no cheap whiskey. That's the worst kind. It'll make you sicker'n a dog."

Aunt Hookey did not reply. Granddaddy yawned and went back to bed.

After Grandma and Granddaddy were once again settled in their bed, Aunt Lockey Jane came out of the bathroom. Aunt Hookey sloshed and jerked the bucket over the floor. I heard her moaning as she dumped the waste into the toilet where I heard it being flushed down. Then I heard her run water in the sink. I thought she was cleaning herself up before coming to bed.

Aunt Lockey Jane, already dressed for bed, came into the room whispering, "Hookey, Mama shouldn't be fussin' at you. You work so hard and you're away so much. It was only a little drink. It's not like you drink all the time"

"Shhhhhh," Aunt Hookey said.

"Don't worry about Sweetpea, Hookey. She's asleep," Lockey Jane said. "If she wasn't, she'd be talking."

"I ain't payin' Mama no attention," Aunt Hookey said, her voice like a frog's croak. "That's all she knows to do is fuss."

I heard the dresser drawer being opened and shut. I felt Aunt Hookey collapse on the bed. I was scared, but didn't want them to know I was awake.

Aunt Lockey Jane was quiet for a minute then she whispered, "You know that dark-skinned fellow who kept watchin' you? You were talkin' to Paul Jones and didn't pay him any attention. I think he made Paul jealous."

Aunt Hookey groaned again, turned on her side and put the pillow over her head.

Aunt Lockey Jane kept talking.

"I think Paul really likes you, Hookey. But, he's so quiet. Good thing he has a car and can drive down from Dayton."

Aunt Hookey pushed the pillow over to the side just enough to allow her nose and mouth some air. Exasperated she said, "Lockey Jane, I'm too sick…Just go to bed, please and stop talkin'!"

12

The Bell Family and the Helena Apartments

There were many things about the Helena Apartment left in disrepair. The old shed that had broken Mr. Tate's fall lay in a heap of rubble next to its cinderblock retaining wall. I could easily see it from my bedroom window.

The shed, like the rotting downspouts, no one bothered to repair while torrential rains came through the roof's downspouts cascading down onto our heads as we scurried into our apartment. All of these things stood like a broken person, bent out of shape with no one caring.

The back stairs, too, just got more and more dangerous in their disrepair. Every Monday morning, when the weather was good, the women of the Helena Apartments complained as they picked their way over rotting risers to take their wet laundry down to the backyard to be hung up to dry. Mrs. Bell was one who especially complained.

The Bell's apartment was my second home. Mr. and Mrs. Bell were a hard-working couple and Mr. Bell was rarely home. He was well-dressed and very handsome, with a fair complexion and even features. Mrs. Bell thought that their son, Frank, looked like him. Christine and Elva Marie, called" Sister," were his color but they had broad noses like Mrs. Bell's.

Under Mr. Bell's hard-working exterior was a restless personality. Eventually he left his wife and almost grown children for another woman. He never returned. Mrs. Bell voiced her belief that it was a temporary separation, since they had been married for so many years. She continued working seven days a week making canapés for the Mayo's Catering Service. This was a convenient and steady workplace for her as it was within a half-block's walking distance.

Walter, the eldest of the children, was a cook in the Navy. His photograph in his Naval uniform was kept on Mrs. Bell's "what not" shelf in the living room. Frank, Jr. was a year younger than Sister. He was a free-spirit and often played with me outside when the weather was warm.

203

From the time I was six, he and I had foot races from the front of the apartment building to Rosen's Store, a full block away. Frank always won and laughed at me for losing. He pulled my braids and said, "Think you'll ever get those big feet of yours off the ground?"

"I'm going to beat you. Just wait and see," I retorted. I did not like being teased by Frank.

Mrs. Taylor, who lived across the street, was my friend Ruth's grandmother. She was watching us from her front porch. She gripped her flyswatter and frowned. Frank just looked at her and said aloud, "Good Morning, Mrs. Taylor."

Mrs. Taylor thought we were both wild and lacking in manners and decorum. Frank's greeting was so straight forward that Mrs. Taylor was taken by surprise. Frank laughed again.

He laughed a lot at himself and most everybody else, except his father. Frank grew more restless, more handsome and more daring. On his way to work he would leap over the banister of the second floor making it a short cut from his apartment to the yard below. I envied his daring. The first time I saw him jump from the second floor I was playing "Jacks," with my friend Cornelious on the splintered, wooden, first floor porch. I heard a loud thud as Frank landed on the patch of grass near the stairs. Cornelious sat with his mouth open and his eyes as wide as saucers.

"See me do that, Miss Sweetpea? Now don't you go tryin' that! You're too little," Frank warned.

I thought Mrs. Bell had chased him out of the apartment as she usually did when Frank started telling "ornery jokes." His sisters, Christine and Sister, enjoyed these raucous stories, but Mrs. Bell said she wasn't going to have any of that. Usually Frank escaped by running out the screen door of their apartment, taking two and three steps at a time, down the inside staircase and through the main door to the outside.

When he got outside, Frank yelled, "Hey Mama!" and then he would start re-telling his jokes. Mrs. Bell came to the porch pleading with him not to tell those awful stories because we children might hear him. Frank would blow her a kiss and go on his way down Lincoln

Avenue. Mrs. Taylor would sit shaking her head at this uncouth neighbor.

My goal was to beat Frank. My chance came in the form of a pair of hand-me-down, high-topped, boy's gym shoes that Granddaddy brought from one of his roofing jobs. The white lady he worked for that day gave him a small box of children's old clothing.

When I put on the gym shoes, they were more than a little tight. They bound my feet with the firmness of a straight jacket. My big feet were not only daintier looking, bound by these shoes, but were also "non-existent." I could feel nothing but a faint throbbing sensation in the tips of my toes.

I practiced running in my "hand-me-down" shoes. It was as if my feet were not touching earth but had transported me, magically, into space. I felt like I was flying through the air. Never had I run so fast.

I ran from our apartment to Rosen's store and back several times a day preparing with my new secret weapon. Each time, I would return home sweaty and grimy from the exercise. Grandma told me to go in and wash up because I smelled like someone's dog. I never told Grandma about the race I was planning.

When Mrs. Rosen saw me practicing, she said, "Sweetpea, what are you doing now?"

When business was slow, Mrs. Rosen stood with the screen door to her store open, looking out at the traffic going by and waiting for her chance to see people as they passed. Mr. Rosen rarely came outside no matter how hot it got or how empty the store. He told Mrs. Rosen she was letting in flies. Mrs. Rosen pretended she didn't hear him.

In the summer the Rosen's two sons, Ivan and Davy, worked in the store. Davy was as old as Frank, but fatter and quieter. His parents said that he was brilliant. I thought they were telling the truth because he had attended Walnut Hills High School and you had to be very smart and pass a special test to qualify. My friend Ruth's brother, George, Jr., attended Walnut Hills. We called him a genius.

Ivan was closer to my age and was delicate in appearance. I thought he was also stuck up and superior acting. When I went in to buy a large dill pickle and peppermint sticks, he talked down his nose to me like he was more grown up. I liked Davy better. As I was leaving the store, I stuck my tongue out at Ivan.

All of the Rosens wore white butcher aprons that were always dirty in the front from wiping their hands.

I told Mrs. Rosen, "I'm running. Getting ready for a race."

"A race where?"

"Just here. I'm going to race Frank Bell."

"But, he's too big for you to race."

"I don't care," I said taking off towards home.

I caught Frank as he came from his job at a laundry.

"Hey, Frank. I'll race ya!"

"Naw. You're not good enough. I beat you too much," he teased.

'That's okay. I'll race you anyway."

"All right, I'll give you a head start to help you out…poor little thing."

"Unhuh. I don't want a head start."

"Oh, ho! Just listen to that. That's big talk for a skinny runt. Just let me set my stuff down," Frank said.

He put his bag of work clothes on the apartment steps. We lined up at the telephone pole next to Mr. Tate's driveway. Frank called, "On the mark! Get Set! Go!"

I headed into the wind. My high-topped, boys' gym shoes, swept me across two of the scored, cement blocks that made up Lincoln Avenue. I was two of them ahead of Frank.

I ran past Mr. Tate's house, past Papa and Mama Green's, past the Glenn's and headed for Rosen's Store that loomed ahead. If I could keep up the pace, I would win. I never glanced back. I heard Frank's laughter behind me. When I reached the corner, I had won. I had beaten Frank Bell. He rubbed the top of my head laughing.

"I was just too tired today," he said. "But for that, I'll buy you some candy. You were really fast. You got those big feet up there this time."

It was the greatest triumph of my life. It was even greater than making it to the third seat, front row of Mr. Talmadge's Math Class.

I learned that pretty and clean white, low-cut, girl's gym shoes were fine for Mr. Bischoff's Gym Class at school but they didn't help you win impossible races as I had just done against Frank Bell.

My feet pained so badly after the race that I hobbled down the cement steps, anxious to shed my second hand wonders. I never told Frank what it took to beat him.

But I awakened early on this particular Monday morning to hear irregular footsteps as Mrs. Bell, loaded with her laundry basket, carefully descended the broken stairs. I held my breath hoping she would not fall.

Mrs. Bell was the first one out with her wash as she had to leave for her job at Mayo's early each day. If she had to leave at five in the morning instead of eight, her daughters, Sister and Christine came down the stairs with the wash before leaving for school.

Sister and Christine weren't like Mrs. Bell who carefully and quietly came down the steps. Sister and Christine came down carefully and cursing.

"These danmed steps. Somebody's going to break their damned ass. It sure ain't goin' to be me!"

Grandma yelled at them from the kitchen, "Sister Bell, you and Christine stop that cussin'."

Sister put her hand over her mouth and whispered to Christine, "Shit, I forgot about Mrs. Corbin being in there." Then, to Grandma she yelled, "I'm sorry Mrs. Corbin."

Sister and Christine giggled as they hauled the laundry basket up the stone steps to the weed infested backyard plateau.

The Bell's sheets were as white as Grandma's. Clothes were on the line sorted by categories. Colors together, sheets all together next to the pillowcases and white shirts, underwear and last the women's delicate items - bloomers and brassiers. Aunt Hookey called bloomers, "drawers."

The clothes hanging on the line were like a painting come to life and blowing in the wind. At the end of the day the teenaged girls or their mother gathered to unpin their work. They folded each item neatly with the tenderness of a mother with a child. They reveled in the odor of clean clothes.

"Smell this, Christine. I told you that powder would make these smell good," and, "I told you bluing would make Mama's old sheet look just like new." Sister held the sheet out for Christine's inspection.

I listened to them and watched from my bedroom window as they gathered the clean, dry clothes like flowers.

I liked visiting the Bells. When they lived in one of the two back apartments on the second floor all of their four rooms were in a single line. There was one entry door and this took you directly into the kitchen off the hallway that separated the apartments.

When Mrs. Bell was at home she spent most of her time in the kitchen cooking.

The rest of the time she was away working for the Mayos.

Mrs. Bell always had the pretty iced cakes called petit fours that she brought home from the Mayo parties. I loved sitting at the kitchen table eating these beautiful cakes with an icing flower and green, icing stem on top. Sometimes Mrs. Bell would let me sit in the living room eating a petit four. This is how I learned to be very careful as I held a saucer on my lap with one or two cakes to eat.

I was in awe as I surveyed our backyard from the Bells' apartment. Never had I stood in a place that was so high up that in looking down I could get such a different view of the yard, and what it really looked like from above.

Many times, Sister and Christine Bell took me for walks to get ice cream from Mangrum's Drugstore. One of the fascinating stories that I heard when I was little came from my Aunt Lockey Jane.

She said, "Do you know how you got your nickname, "Sweet-pea Well, when you were a tiny baby, you were baldheaded except for one, little curl in the middle of your head. Sister and Christine said you looked just like Popeye's Sweetpea in the funny papers. So, from then on we started calling you "Sweetpea."

That day, I watched Aunt Lockey Jane as she brushed her shiny hair while getting ready for school. I tried to picture myself a *Popeye's Sweetpea* in the funny papers. I wondered "what are funny papers?"

"You didn't smile at all when you were little. You just looked mean," she added.

I got lost in her words, remembering only that Sister and Christine Bell had given me a name that everyone called me. I was never called by my real name, Lula Delores.

The Bells were like my second family. I felt closer to them than any other family living in the Helena Apartments, except maybe the Robinsons.

Our home's backstairs continued to deteriorate. Horace Sud-duth, the owner, rather than repair the stairs, closed the back entrance so no one could use them. He gave no thought to the inconvenience this imposed on the tenants in the upper apartments. As owner, he neglected his responsibility to keep repairs updated, but he did not neglect collecting their rent.

His collector came weekly to get the money. He listened to the tenants' complaints, even experienced the waterfall from the leaky downspouts and gutters when he collected the rent on rainy days. He agreed with the tenants, promised to have Mr. Sudduth correct the problems, then left. This ritual was repeated each collection day and still there was no follow-up to the complaints.

Horace Sudduth was one of those elite, fair complexioned Negro men who had accumulated enough money from his business to live a very comfortable life. He lived in a large, stately home only a few blocks from Lincoln Avenue. He did not mind the fact that his building was the only one on our street that was run-down. It was an eye sore for all the other homeowners. He never saw it. The street on which he lived, was considered one of the most prestigious places for Negroes to live. He preferred being called "Negro" to being called "colored."

Mr. Sudduth was a lucky man. The families in the Helena were hard-working, responsible people. There was little or none of the transient in them although they were of very modest means. They were stable and dependable.

Regardless of the dependability of his tenants in paying their rent on time, this did not help them make Mr. Sudduth change his attitude towards them and his building, the Helena Apartment.

The Bells and other women from upstairs were forced to use the long way to get to the backyard with their wash. They went down the front hallway stairs, out the front door, around the side of the building and down the same, cracked cement stairs that we used to get into our apartment.

This was a hardship and very time consuming. Mr. Sudduth didn't care.

13

Aunt Hookey Leaves Home
and Returns

Paul Jones, the fellow Aunt Lockey Jane said liked Aunt Hookey, lived with his mother in Dayton, Ohio. He and Aunt Hookey had a weekend romance whenever she was off from work at the Freulands. She and Paul always met at the Wine Bar, a favorite place for most of the young people, and old ones as well, to socialize. It was in the busy section of Gilbert Avenue that ran perpendicular to Lincoln Avenue, the street where we lived.

My cousins, Mitzi and Joan, and I liked sections of Gilbert Avenue. The corner of Lincoln and Gilbert was a long four blocks from my apartment building. But we gladly took the walk with Aunt Irene because there, on that one corner was the best hamburger place in all of Cincinnati. It was Bay Joe's. Only White Castles came close in popularity. White Castles were cheaper and smaller. Bay Joe's made hamburgers that looked like they were the size of a dinner plate. At least that's how they appeared to us. Mustard, catsup, dill pickles and thick slices of onion were what we added. Nothing tasted as good as a hot Bay Joe's hamburger.

Bay Joe himself stood behind the hot grill with hamburger turner in hand, flipping his burgers. His white apron was as dirty in front as the one worn by the Rosens in their little corner store. But Bay Joe added a white hat that sat jauntily on his head, one end to the front and one to the back. Then, the hat spread out on each side to make for a snug fit. Whenever Aunt Irene let us stop for a Bay Joe's hamburger, we were in heaven.

The Wine Bar was further down on Gilbert Avenue. You had to pass a large brick apartment building, the Harriet Beecher Stowe House on the next corner, and in that same section, but on the opposite side of the street, a convenience store and the pool hall.

The Harriett Beecher Stowe House sat on a small hill above Gilbert. There were stories that the Underground Railroad tunnels ran beneath the house. There were never any people seen at the Harriett Beecher Stowe House. In those days we knew little about the Underground Railroad which helped enslaved people flee the south to freedom.

Another of our favorite places located on a street just off of Gilbert was the Beecher theater. My cousins and I went there on Saturdays to see the cowboy and Indian movies with Gene Autry, Gabbie Hayes, Roy Rogers and Trigger. We were allowed to go to the afternoon shows that were shown as serials that ran twenty minutes each, with the sequel appearing the next week.

Our children's entertainment and places to get candy, comic books and bubble gum were interspersed with the areas for adult entertainment. The Wine Bar was in the last block on Gilbert, before that street turned down the hill towards the Victory Parkway.

It was a quiet section of Gilbert that veered into a small side street and residential area. The Wine Bar was very popular. You couldn't see in or out. The outside brick wall went all the way up to a row of small windows that were covered with blinds from the inside, and neon lights in front of the blinds. The large wooden door had just a circle of glass in the top center from which people could peer out.

Sometimes when we passed the Wine Bar on our way to my cousins' apartment, we could see inside when the door was opened. It just looked dark and uninviting to us. I wondered why Aunt Hookey, Aunt Irene and Aunt Lockey Jane spent any time at all inside such a dreary place.

But, this is where they went for entertainment, and this is where Aunt Hookey rendezvoused with Paul Jones. After a year, they married. Aunt Hookey quit her job with the Freulands. She told us that the Freuland children cried because their "Cottie" was leaving. "Cottie" was the nickname the children had given Aunt Hookey because they couldn't pronounce, Catherine, her real name

Aunt Hookey and Paul were married in a civil ceremony at the Court House in downtown Cincinnati. Afterwards, she packed all the things she had at home and moved to Dayton to live with Paul and his mother in his mother's house.

I felt a deep loss and emptiness when Aunt Hookey left. She was like a mother to me. Whenever she was at home, she took care of me, even more than Grandma. She washed me in the basin by the kitchen stove. I did not like Aunt Hookey's scrubbing my face as hard as she did, but I had gotten accustomed to it. Aunt Hookey also helped me with my school work and was good with numbers. She used some of the money she made at the Freulands to buy new clothes for me when the school year began, but most important, she and Granddaddy were the ones who paid attention and seemed interested in what I was doing in school. It was Aunt Hookey who paid for my subscription to the *Wee Wisdom* magazine that arrived weekly in our classroom. I loved *Wee Wisdom*.

I hated being left in the house with Grandma and wanted to be away or outside, but I was very dependent on her. It was during these early years between six and seven when Aunt Hookey left, that I began the habit of rubbing my eyes.

In the mornings when there was a crusty residue around my eyes, that everyone called "sleep," I began removing this with my fingers instead of the washcloth. Over a period of time, there was more than a crusty residue following my vigorous rubbing, but pieces of gelatinous tissue that began to appear in the corners of my eyes.

During idle moments I rubbed my eyes continuously until they became red and swollen. In the morning there were puffy bags under my eyes and I was embarrassed to have anyone notice them. Most of this rubbing was done at home. I never rubbed my eyes at school. Granddaddy worried about me.

"Stop rubbing your eyes," he said irritated. "Wanna make yourself blind?"

Still, I continued the habit. Granddaddy asked my aunt, "Lockey Jane, can't you get her to stop digging at her eyes that way? She's goin' to make herself blind."

"I can't get her to quit and neither can Mama," she answered.

No one had any influence on me and the habit continued. It became so bad that in order to ease the swelling, I had to resort to using a very warm, wash cloth which I held over my eyes for several minutes at a time.

Aunt Lockey Jane was the only aunt remaining at home; and with her I felt competitive, even though she was thirteen years older.

She did not like me getting into her things, putting on her good smelling perfume and powder. She did not like me bothering her school books. To her, I was a nuisance.

She and I had a running feud over the dishes. We alternated washing and drying.

One day she dried and I washed. The next day I dried and she washed. But no matter how fast I worked, she always finished before me. I hated that. It made me feel "little," and not like a big girl.

One time I thought I had found a way to slow her down. I held back a knife, fork and a plate to keep her at the sink, towel in hand, waiting to complete the drying.

"You're just fooling around and I'm not waiting for you to finish."

Then, she put her towel on the wooden towel rack that hung from the wall, and left.

"Grandma!" I called out in frustration, "Lockey Jane won't dry the dishes."

My aunt explained what was happening. It was Granddaddy who responded.

"Just hurry up and finish up in there, Sweetpea! Fussin' over a few dishes. You sound just like your Grandmammy."

"Now what did I do?" Grandma asked.

I was frustrated. Now, not only did I have to dry the remaining dishes, which I felt were Aunt Lockey Jane's responsibility, but I had to be in the kitchen all alone finishing up while Grandma and Granddaddy were in the living room and my aunt prepared to go out.

Lockey Jane did not become more motherly towards me because Aunt Hookey was gone. She was more distant. I missed Aunt Hookey.

This same year, Aunt Lockey Jane finished Withrow High School and started work with the Mayo's Catering Service where Mrs. Bell, our upstairs neighbor, worked. Mayo's was a half- block from

214

our apartment so she did not have to go far. She had to buy a uniform like Mrs. Bell's, and the two of them often walked to work together. This was my aunt's first real job.

The Mayos were highly respected people on our block. Mr. Mayo was an attorney. He was a dignified, quiet man with a face full of freckles. He had more freckles than Granddaddy. He was tall but not heavy. Mrs. Mayo, on the other hand, was short, quite plump, very aggressive and determined. The Mayos had a pet English bulldog. It looked like Mrs. Mayo.

I was deathly afraid of their bulldog. After my aunt began working for Mayo's, I ventured to the Mayo back door to see if I could get some of the little cakes or something good to eat. The first face at the screen door was that of the Mayo bulldog, barking ferociously. I never went inside no matter how many times Mrs. Mayo invited me. The Mayos were very nice to me and never sent me away empty handed.

Otto was the only child of Mr. and Mrs. Mayo. He, like his father, had a face saturated with freckles. He was attending college to be a lawyer and was only home in the summer months. Otto was infatuated with Aunt Lockey Jane. She was beautiful, even when she was wearing her work uniform. She knew that Otto was interested in her and that he was highly intelligent, but she did not seem to hold the least bit of interest in him.

There had been a time when my aunt was still going to high school and Otto was home on a break. He offered and she accepted a ride to school. Otto drove his own car. Almost no one we knew on Lincoln Avenue had their own cars except Mangrums, Thatchers and Hulls.

On that morning Otto had an accident and Aunt Lockey Jane came back home, blood streaming down her face from a gash she had received on her forehead. She did not go to school because of the accident.

I don't remember if she went to the hospital. I just remember Grandma's alarm and her cleaning the blood from the wound. My aunt had a scar near the center of her forehead for a very long time after the accident.

She liked working for the Mayos. We loved it when she brought home lots of canapés, the little tiny sandwiches some open-faced, and my favorite petit fours. I adored those beautifully decorated little cakes. Now, I could get cakes from Mrs. Bell, Aunt Lockey Jane and Mrs. Mayo.

Dayton was forty-two miles away, and rarely did we hear from Aunt Hookey. It might just as well have been a million miles. Then one day to our great surprise, Aunt Hookey walked into the apartment with her suitcase in hand. She had left Paul Jones.

I heard her telling Grandma, Granddaddy and Aunt Lockey Jane that Paul Jones had not been working and was content to let his mother take care of him. Aunt Hookey said that Paul and his mother did the food shopping each week and she was given thirty-five cents a week spending money.

Grandma was shocked and kept asking Aunt Hookey a lot of questions.

Aunt Lockey Jane said, "But the Jones own their home. I thought you were in love with Paul. Why would you want to leave? You didn't have to work. I don't understand."

"I'm not used to sittin' around. I've been workin' since I was sixteen and I have had my own money. Paul was too lazy to work. I didn't have a pot to piss in living with him and his mother," Aunt Hookey replied.

She said that she saved ten cents out of the thirty-five cents allowance, until she had enough for bus fare to get home. She said that when Paul and his mother were shopping, she packed her suitcase, walked to the bus depot and headed for Cincinnati.

Aunt Hookey got her divorce from Paul Jones. We never saw or heard from him again. Granddaddy hugged her and was genuinely glad she was back. She immediately settled in and went about job hunting. Meanwhile, she took over many of the household duties from Grandma, and fussed with Grandma about her having neglected my upbringing.

216

"You don't make her do none of the things we had to do," she chastised Grandma.

"Now, don't start on me. I do the best I can with her. She just won't mind. Just hard-headed like her mother. I never could get her to do her work."

"That's because you were always sick and it all was left for Robert and Irene to do."

"I couldn't help it if I was sick," Grandma whined.

"Aw, Mama. I don't want to hear all that old stuff."

"Listen to that. Just because you fell out with Paul Jones, don't come into my house and take it out on me."

"My situation with Paul Jones doesn't have a thing to do with this, Mama. I'm tallkin' about bringing Sweetpea up to be responsible and to learn how to do things."

"Oh, so now I'm the bad guy! Not that Mammy of hers. Oh, no, not her! She never gets blamed for all the trouble she brought me. I took Sweetpea because I knew Eckey couldn't raise her right. What do I get but a lot of heartache and criticism? Well, if you're so good, see what you can do! See if you can make her mind!"

Grandma was working at her sewing machine while she was arguing with Aunt Hookey. She was making a slipcover for another client's sofa. It was made of a beautiful, shiny fabric with large, colorful flowers. She and Aunt Hookey were able to argue back and forth between the two rooms. I sat on the bed in our bedroom listening. Aunt Hookey was doing the dishes.

"You should've let Eckey have her to raise." Aunt Hookey put the black, cast iron skillet in the drain.

This statement surprised me, coming from her. I was confused. Didn't Aunt Hookey think I should live with her, Grandma and Granddaddy?

"Eckey's too wild. She never would've raised this child right. She ain't raisin' the others right," Grandma said haughtily.

"Mama," Aunt Hookey said turning from the sink and staring at Grandma's back.

"That's just not the truth. You took Sweetpea because you lost your last baby. You and Daddy were too old to be having any more children, anyway."

"You don't know what you're talkin' about, Hookey! You act like I'm the only one it took to have a baby. That was a change-of-life baby - a blue baby."

I continued listening and coloring in my coloring book. I knew about this baby that Grandma and Aunt Hookey were talking about. At times, Grandma would talk about her "blue baby" and how she had died. Her name was Beverly. When Grandma was mad at me she said that if her little girl had lived, she would not have grown up to be like me. I always wondered what a "blue baby" was. I envisioned a baby colored blue, like one of my Crayola crayons. Maybe it was the pretty blue-green I liked so much.

While Aunt Hookey and Grandma's verbal battle raged, I tried very carefully not to go outside of the lines of any of the pictures I was coloring. I didn't want Aunt Hookey to say I was messy. Whenever I did go outside the lines of a picture, I would leave it and start a new one, determined not to make the same mistake. Then, Granddaddy would fuss at me saying that I "never finished what I started."

"It don't make a difference what the baby was, Mama. If that baby had lived, you never would've taken Sweetpea from Eckey," Aunt Hookey was insistent.

"I didn't take Sweetpea no such thing! She gave Sweetpea to me! She knew I was right." Grandma turned from her machine, geared for battle.

"Sweetpea's got a better home here than she would've had with Eckey. Goin' 'round to those Beer Gardens every night."

"That was a long time ago, Mama and you know it. Eckey's been in the church since then and has changed her life."

"That's what you say! She's still the same liar to me."

218

I heard the legs of Grandma's chair screech as she forced them back across the linoleum floor. The linoleum in Grandma and Grand-daddy's bedroom where she did all of her sewing, was maroon with a large leaf pattern all over the area that was under the bed. Some of it showed in the small amount of space left around the bed and dresser.

There was a band of two smaller, leaf patterns which made up the border hidden under the dresser and across the doorways into the room. The linoleum was so cold on my feet that for me to step any-where, but on the scatter rugs, sent chills and shock waves through my body.

"Mama, you're always criticizing Eckey. She was too young to marry in the first place. If you hadn't fussed so much at her for having Sweetpea and forced her to marry, maybe she wouldn't have been so wild." Aunt Hookey was relentless in her defense of my mother.

"There you go actin' like I'm the bad guy. I'm not the cause of the problem. I never could tell Eckey nothin'. She was just so bull-headed, she got herself into trouble. If she had listened to me, none of this would've happened," Grandma said.

I left my coloring to go to the kitchen. Maybe they would stop arguing if I went in to get something, maybe vanilla wafers.

"You still didn't have no business havin' another baby. Us poor as piss and Daddy not having steady work and you havin' babies." Aunt Hookey rolled her eyes and shook her head.

Grandma started to cry, saying that she got blamed for everything. Aunt Hookey looked at me, "What do you want?" She sounded angry with me.

"Can I have some vanilla wafers?"

She went to the cupboard and pulled down the box of Vanilla Wafers and gave me a handful. I retreated to the bedroom.

Aunt Hookey didn't say any more to Grandma after Grandma started crying.

I hoped the arguing was over. Aunt Hookey and Grandma rarely had any good conversations. Grandma was more like a child who Aunt Hookey scolded. Only Granddaddy and Aunt Hookey got along and found things to laugh about. The two of them together laughed at Grandma.

Aunt Hookey cleaned, cooked, washed and ironed. With Aunt Hookey back home and taking over the chores, Grandma could sew without stopping. My aunt read *True Confession* magazines when she wasn't doing housework or fussing with Grandma.

———————

I was back sleeping with Aunt Hookey. She said, "Sweetpea, if you don't stop peeing in the bed, I'm going to feed you a dead rat. That'll make you stop."

As guilty as I felt about wetting the bed, and as terrified I was at the possibility of eating a rat, I could not stop wetting the bed.

Aunt Hookey dutifully changed the bedding and washed the sheets every morning. She had long before put rubber sheeting on the bed to protect the mattress.

Sometimes, my bed wetting caught Aunt Hookey by surprise. I would slide close to her where I could feel secure that the monsters would not get me.

When I relaxed in this security, the urine just flowed out and Aunt Hookey woke up cursing. She changed herself and yanked the wet clothes off of me. I sat shivering, in winter or early spring, waiting for a dry gown.

Then, sitting in dazed silence, I watched as Aunt Hookey changed the sheets. I formed a picture in my mind of me sitting at the breakfast table, with a dead rat on the plate before me. I wondered how eating a dead rat would stop me from wetting the bed.

Both Grandma and Granddaddy were scared of little mice. I wondered who would be brave enough to catch a rat. I knew they would have to go to the cellar to find one. But nothing ever happened. No one ever caught a rat and Aunt Hookey just kept repeating the threat.

Finally, Aunt Hookey thought of a solution.

"Mama, don't give Sweetpea anything to drink before she goes to bed tonight."

"I can't stop her from drinkin'," Grandma whined. "I'm not the one causing her to wet the bed. You can blame that one on your daddy. He's the one always slipping her stuff to drink. Get on him about it."

"Mama, you know you give in to Sweetpea all the time. We never got away with the things you let her get away with. When we were her age, we were doing everything for ourselves."

Fortunately, Aunt Hookey had to tend to the clothes. There was a buzz that let her know the sheets were finished in the washer. Now she had to stop arguing with Grandma. She had to get the sheets outside on the clothesline so they could dry.

Before she married Paul Jones, Aunt Hookey was always serious and unsmiling. She only had fun when Aunt Irene came for a visit or when she and Granddaddy were joking or teasing about something.

Since she left Paul Jones, Aunt Hookey was even more unhappy than she had been before. Each day seemed the same as she and Grandma had more run-ins than ever. I hoped that she would find work soon.

"You always were mean, just like your Daddy. You're two peas in a pod when one is enough. No wonder you two are thick as thieves," Grandma told Aunt Hookey one day.

For once Aunt Hookey didn't say anything. She just walked out with the laundry basket full of wet sheets.

14

Andrew Fant

Aunt Lockey Jane was dating a young man named Andrew Fant. He was the first cousin of her best friend, Minnie Payden. No matter how hard Otto Mayo tried to convince her that he was the person for her, Aunt Lockey Jane was nice to him, but would not go out with him. Andrew Fant was the new person in whom she had a serious interest.

He was never called by his first name. He was known as "Fant" by friends and enemies alike. Fant drew attention as he was extremely handsome with beautiful, reddish-brown skin, an engaging smile and soft voice. He knew how to dress and was never seen without being in a suit, shirt and tie. His hat was the crown of glory. Adding to his attractiveness was the fact that he was one of the few young men who owned his own car, and always had wads of dollar bills in his pocket.

Fant's story, which he did not tell, came from those in his family, like Minnie, who was close to our family. Fant's father was married to Minnie's aunt. The Fant family lived in the rural area, called the sub-division, fifteen miles from Cincinnati. When Fant's father was a young man, he left rural South Carolina to move to Ohio. He was known to be a brutal man who beat Fant's mother and beat the children as well.

Fant loved his mother and hated his father. At age thirteen, when he could no longer bear to see his mother being beaten nor endure the beatings that he had suffered, he ran away from home. They said that Andrew Fant was a self-made man..

He left the rural sub-division and the Lockland area to move to the Walnut Hills section of Cincinnati. Fant began work at the Kahn's Meat Packing Company in Cincinnati, earning enough money to take care of himself, buy good clothes and a car. He was a hard worker, which made him different from Paul Jones, Aunt Hookey's first husband.

Fant worked from six in the morning until four each afternoon. Work at the Kahn's Meat Packing Company meant butchering carcasses and making sausages and hot dogs. During the butchering process they said that Fant wore thigh-high, rubber boots and stood knee high in animal blood all day. At the grocery stores Grandma always bought Kahn's Bologna and Franks. They were the best.

Andrew Fant had an entrepreneurial side. After work, he cleaned up and dressed in his best clothes. It was said that he had a "loan shark" business on the side. He spent his time at the Pool Hall and Wine Bar on Gilbert Avenue, lending money and charging interest. He avoided the one "colored" policeman the city of Cincinnati kept stationed at this trouble spot outside of downtown. The policeman's name was Tony but my aunts called him "Tony the gorilla." They said that Tony was black and looked like Susie, the famous gorilla at the Cincinnati Zoo. On any given Saturday night, if he caught any wrong doer he would beat them over the head with his billy club before kicking them into the paddy wagon to be hauled off to jail. No one messed with Tony.

Fant was able to avoid Tony as he conducted his loan-sharking business in the dark side streets or back rooms of the Pool Hall and Wine Bar. He ran quite a successful enterprise.

Grandma was very unhappy when she heard that Lockey Jane was "courting" Andrew Fant. He had been married before and Grandma heard that he had beaten his wife and was so jealous that he kept her locked in their apartment while he was at work.

There was nothing in his outward demeanor that would indicate that Fant was a person with violent tendencies towards women or had a questionable reputation.

Divorced, he now was going out with Aunt Lockey Jane. People said that Fant liked pretty women and Lockey Jane, now nineteen, was more than pretty, she was beautiful, sweet and innocent. Although she was seen at the Wine Bar with Aunt Hookey, she was never known to respond to the flirtatious mannerisms of many of the men gathering there. Most felt her "stand-offish" and "stuck-up."

Fant, however, had won her over and no matter how much Grandma cried and cautioned her not to marry Fant, Aunt Lockey Jane continued dating him.

She kept working at Mayos and Otto Mayo was finishing up Law School. He still hoped that Aunt Lockey Jane would reconsider, but she did not.

Whenever Fant came to visit, he always had a lot of change that jingled in his pockets. His car was shiny and clean without a scratch on it, and I never saw him when he wasn't wearing a hat and suit. My aunts had a word for men as good looking as Andrew Fant. It was "sharp!"

He was extremely kind to me and never left without giving me a few nickels or quarters. I thought he was rich and wondered why Grandma didn't like him.

I believed that Grandma was relieved to have Aunt Hookey back home, even with all her meanness. The two sisters were like they had been before. They went out together. Aunt Lockey Jane postponed any early wedding plans, but there was no doubt that her main interest was Andrew Fant.

He played up to Granddaddy and the two seemed to like each other; but Grandma never smiled when he came to pick up Aunt Lockey Jane. Grandma was happy when she thought that their relationship had cooled off.

PHOTOGRAPH DURING HER COURTSHIP
WITH ANDREW FANT

AUNT LOCKEY JANE, AGE 19

Crystal Lucretia Corbin

15

Bed-wetting

Aunt Hookey still had no job. She and Grandma returned to their days of verbal sparring. I was happy to be away in first grade learning new words. The longest words were insulation and porcelain which we had to sound out phonetically. I felt like I had just captured the greatest prize of all, learning that I could spell such big words.

We began to read out of our first books, *Dick and Jane*. I loved reading aloud.

I loved practicing at home. Aunt Hookey paid for my subscription to *Wee Wisdom Magazine*. I looked forward to getting each new issue.

No matter my success in school, I still had not mastered the bed wetting problem. I had learned to outsmart Aunt Hookey, or so I thought. If I wet the bed at night, I carefully removed my wet underpants and dropped them on the side of the bed near the wall. I was sure that Aunt Hookey wouldn't discover them. I was wrong, and that's when the discussions would begin anew.

Aunt Hookey told Grandma about my hiding my wet underwear. She discovered several pairs when she was changing the sheets and again told Grandma to stop letting me have anything to drink at night.

I sat at the kitchen table while I waited for Aunt Hookey to finish washing the breakfast dishes. She was going to walk me to school.

Grandma said, "You weren't a bed wetter, Hookey. Eckey was the only one of all of you who kept wetting the bed."

She had begun her work for the day on the large slip cover for a sofa.

"I don't care," Aunt Hookey raised her voice. "You'd beat Eckey's behind if she wet the bed. You're too easy on Sweetpea."

"There you go blaming me for everything," Grandma said.

Grandma got up from her sewing machine and slammed the door so she didn't have to hear Aunt Hookey's talk. I wanted to get out of there. I wanted to go to school where the talk was different. I wanted to go to school so I could run and play with my classmates.

Aunt Hookey washed the extra sheets caused by my having accidents. Her wash was the whitest on the clotheslines. Grandma did not have to do the wash and clean house while Aunt Hookey was back home.

One morning Aunt Hookey said, "Sweetpea did you wet the bed?"

She felt the sheet on my side. Once the damp spot was discovered, she pulled the bed out from the wall and retrieved my wet underpants.

"Now this is ridiculous!" she said. "Anybody who can wake themselves up to throw wet pants behind the bed ought to wake up and go to the toilet. That just makes me madder'n hell when you're just too lazy to get up. You ought to be ashamed of yourself!"

I never argued back with Aunt Hookey, but the idea of getting up in the dark and going to the bathroom by myself was much more horrifying than thinking about eating the dead rat that Aunt Hookey threatened to cook for me.

On Saturday nights Aunt Hookey bathed me. She scrubbed my neck and ears so hard I thought the skin was coming off. My neck stayed red for a long time afterward. She said that her scrubbing my neck like that would keep it from getting dirt-filled rings and creases.

"Hold still," she said grabbing me by my arm.

"Don't be so rough," Grandma called out to her.

"Hookey ain't hurtin' that little shit pot," Granddaddy said.

I couldn't help but think that Aunt Hookey carried her anger at my bedwetting over to the time she gave me my bath; and that the harsh scrubbing was my punishment since Grandma didn't let her whip me for wetting the bed.

Aunt Hookey lifted me out of the tub and dried me off with a large towel. She used the same vigor drying me off that she had when she washed me. She stooped down to my level. I watched her face with the freckles. She had freckles like Granddaddy. Everybody had freckles like Granddaddy except Uncle Bobby and Aunt Irene. I discovered that even I had freckles. In this way, we were alike. Aunt Hookey rarely smiled.

16

Second Grade

My second grade class was divided into two groups. One group was the "X" Group and the other was the "Y" Group. If you were placed in the "X" Group it meant that you were an advanced learner working above second grade level. If you were placed in the "Y" Class you were working at or a little below grade level.

I was assigned to the X Class along with Anna Jackson and Cornelious Wilson, with whom I had formed close friendships. Our white X Group classmates were Barbara Reichart, a short, very plump Jewish girl with long, wavy, blonde hair, Jon Campbell, a tall, frail, white boy with delicate hands, and several others whose names I can't remember. Both Barbara and Jon were arithmetic whizzes. They also competed for the top grades in science. I scored highest in reading, spelling and penmanship and got B's and C's in Arithmetic.

Both Barbara and Jon wore glasses and were non-athletic. I got along very well with them and we became close friends. We socialized a lot at recess. At other times I played kickball and hop scotch with the other classmates. Cornelious lived across the street and had been a playmate since we were old enough to visit. Anna Jackson lived too far away for us to become close friends, but we did get along well. Anna resembled an Albino, but she wasn't. Her hair was more blonde and wavier than Barbara Reichart's, but she was considered "colored."

Barbara's father had a friend who worked for a playing card company. She brought shiny new cards with different landscape and animal scenes. These were used as "trading" cards. This was a new hobby that I learned from Barbara. She gave me a stack of these beautiful cards from all of her extra copies. There were pictures of Vermont winter scenes, Rocky Mountain areas with placid, blue lakes and tall, green pine trees reaching up and into the sky. These were my favorites. Most of the trading card enthusiasts favored pictures of black Scotty dogs and little white kittens with blue eyes and pink tongues.

"I'll give you the little kitten and the two mountain scenes."

"How about one mountain scene and one kitten…and I'll throw in one river card."

"Okay."

This was our trading card language. It was very different from playing "War," the card game where the highest card gobbled up all the lower numbered ones.

Every recess and every free moment after lunch was spent in a corner of the cemented play yard or on the hillside near the baseball field, trading cards. Barbara had given me my starter stack and it grew. I searched at home for cards that I could turn into trading cards, but only found the kind with black or red spades on a white background on the front. These were fine for Granddaddy and Aunt Hookey who liked playing cards, but were not suitable for "trading."

In our enthusiasm to have a stack of trading cards too thick to hold in one hand, bartering continued between aisles in class. Our teacher, calmly, but firmly reminded us to, "Put the cards away, children. If I see them out during class, I will be forced to take them away."

We never allowed things to go that far because we did not want our stacks to diminish. The goal was to get the largest stack with the most variety of pictures.

Penmanship was a major area of practice in second grade and I was the best in the class. We graduated from the "hills" and "circles" that we made on the lined, practice paper we had in first grade. Now a hill and circle became an "s" and "m." We were well on our way to writing in cursive.

Hoffman School was becoming ever more intriguing as we were exposed to so many new things and my days as the class spelling whiz were launched in those early grades.

When Granddaddy and I made our Sunday visit to see Uncle Bobby at Longview State Hospital, I told him all about the new words I had learned and about being in the "X" group which meant I was in the "smart" class. Uncle Bobby was impressed with my progress and told me that he always knew that I was going to be smart in school.

On that particular Sunday visit, the three of us walked to the Commissary where patients and visitors could get snacks and other items. Every so often, Granddaddy or Grandma left a certain amount of money in the Commissary Bank so that during the week Uncle Bobby could go to the Commissary and get something that he liked. That day Uncle Bobby bought me an ice cream cone.

"Here, Sweetie. This is for being so smart in school," he said.

17

Thanksgiving for All But One

Our Thanksgiving celebration began with Aunt Irene arriving early in the morning with my cousins, Mitzi and Joan. Uncle Francis, Aunt Irene's husband was always welcome, but he chose to spend the day with his sister and parents. It was customary for Aunt Irene to come in time to help with the dinner preparations. The day before, Aunt Hookey and Lockey Jane did the housecleaning while Grandma completed the grocery shopping and making home-made yeast rolls.

Grandma was still in her nightgown when Aunt Irene and my cousins arrived. Granddaddy wore his stocking cap to keep his hair in place after he had washed it the night before. He put Vaseline on his hair and pulled the stocking cap over it. Granddaddy's hair would be slicked down to his scalp and as shiny as a new penny.

The stocking cap was made from one of Grandma's stockings that could no longer be worn because they had flaws or "runs" in them. One of the stockings was cut off and a knot tied in it to make it small enough for Granddaddy to fit tight on his head.

Aunt Hookey and Lockey Jane had gotten up well before Grandma and Granddaddy and were working in the kitchen.

"Here's my little Corn," Granddaddy called from the living room as he opened the door for my aunt.

"Hi Mitzi! Hi, Joanie! How're my little babies?" He said patting them on top of their heads.

I didn't like Granddaddy being so nice to my cousins. I waited in my room. Aunt Irene had brought a shopping bag with a change of clothes for my cousins and another bag with food for dinner.

"Corn Green, what have you been up to, Chick?" Aunt Hookey laughed. I was happy that she was in a happy mood for a change.

"Nothin', Honey," Aunt Irene answered. "Ain't nothin' shakin' but the leaves on the trees," she laughed. "Look at Lockey Jane.

Where'd you get that "vine?" Aunt Irene commented on Aunt Lockey Jane's dress.

"Wait, Corn. I'll be there soon as I get my clothes on," Grandma called from her bedroom anxious to join her three daughters.

Aunt Hookey whispered, "She's been sayin' that all morning. She'd be dressed by now if she wasn't so busy meddlin' with me and Lockey Jane and runnin' her mouth."

"You shut up, Hookey. I'm not lettin' you spoil my Thanksgivin'. Always bossin' me around like you're the mother and I'm the child," Grandma shouted back.

Aunt Hookey busied herself with the turkey. She put the stuffing that she had made from stale bread, cornbread, onions, celery and sage, into the large cavity in the turkey. She took Oleo margarine and spread it over the legs and breast of the turkey and sprinkled salt and pepper on top. Last, she lifted it into Grandma's big, roasting pan, covered it with the lid and shoved it into the pre-heated oven.

Each Thanksgiving and Christmas, mayor Reed, Granddaddy's boss and Lockland's mayor, gave Granddaddy twenty-five dollars and a turkey. Grandma said that he should have given Granddaddy more money and she could buy the turkey herself.

Aunt Lockey Jane was becoming a good cook since working at Mayo's. She prided herself on the macaroni and cheese and candied sweet potatoes that she made.

This Thanksgiving, Aunt Irene made the cole slaw while Grandma prepared the rolls and greens.

My cousins and I played at our games but were always preoccupied listening to the talk and activity going on in the kitchen. There was lots of laughter as my aunts spoke to each other in Pig Latin to keep us from knowing what they were saying.

Each of the aunts called the other by their nick name.

"Orncay, avehay, ouyay eensay arveyhay?" Aunt Hookey asked. This was Pig Latin for, *"Corn, have you seen Harvey?"*

Harvey was a friend of Aunt Irene's. He was always picking her up and taking her places she needed to go. Uncle Francis did not own a car.

"Onay, oneyhay. Iway ain't tay eensay imhay inay eekway," Aunt Irene answered , *"No, Honey. I haven't seen him in a week."*

"Corn, you're lyin'," Aunt Hookey laughed.

"Ask Lockey Jane. She knows I'm tellin' the truth."

Lockey Jane said, "Nooooo, Corn Green. Don't get me into that."

On Saturday nights, Aunt Irene and Aunt Hookey sometimes went out together when Lockey Jane was working late for Mayo's. When she was off, Lockey Jane went out with them.

To Mitzi, Joan and me, Gilbert Avenue loomed big in our minds as the hub of all their Saturday night activity. Aunt Irene and Uncle Francis each had a night when they went out alone. Uncle Francis went out on Friday nights, after work and Aunt Irene went out on Saturday nights. They never went out together. There were times when they took Mitzie, Joan and me to the Beecher to see a scary movie, but the two of them did not seem to enjoy each other's company although they had been married for a number of years.

Aunt Irene didn't want Uncle Francis to join us for Thanksgiving. We just thought he wanted to be with his own family. My mother, stepfather, half-brothers and sister didn't come for dinner either. Grandma never invited them.

"Mama, how come you didn't ask Eckey, Neil and the kids?" Aunt Irene asked.

"I don't want those wild, younguns runnin' around here tearin' up my things. You know they're not used to nothing," Grandma answered defensively.

Later, I heard Aunt Irene whisper that she thought it was a shame that Grandma didn't invite Eckey. Thanksgiving would be another time when I would feel sorry for my mother and how she was treated so different from her sisters. It was as if Grandma hated her.

234

While the women prepared the dinner, Granddaddy dressed to go get Uncle Bobby who was allowed to come home for the day when he was well. If he had been a disturbance at Longview, then Granddaddy would go to pick him up only to return home without him. But when he could come home, Uncle Bobby was very happy to see the family. On some holidays he was very quiet and mostly sat in the living room just watching us play. Aunt Irene thought they had given him some sort of medication to make him quiet.

Thanksgiving dinner was the best dinner ever. The grown ups ate at the kitchen table while a card table was set up in the living room for me and my cousins. We liked sitting by ourselves. That way we could eat any way we wanted without being corrected.

We loved the turkey and dressing, but especially the cranberry sauce that was sweet like a dessert. Our next favorite was Grandma's yeast rolls with lots of butter and jelly, and last, the macaroni and cheese and candied sweet potatoes with oven browned, marshmallows on top. We ate and giggled and it never failed that one of us would knock over our water glass, drenching our table cloth. Then Aunt Irene would come and clean up without fussing at us. She would just laugh and tell us to be more careful the next time. Aunt Irene was nothing like Grandma and Aunt Hookey.

We would be too stuffed to eat dessert right away and Uncle Bobby fell asleep on the living room sofa when he finished. After that, my aunts would clean up the dishes and store the food away, but Aunt Irene was able to pack turkey on Grandma's rolls for them to eat later, when they got home. She said that late at night, Grandma's rolls made the best tasting turkey sandwiches.

Dessert was Grandma's apple or pumpkin pie. Mitzi was the only one of us children who liked pumpkin pie. When we ate the apple pie, we sometimes had vanilla ice cream on top and at other times we had sweetened whipped cream. We preferred the ice cream.

At four o'clock Granddaddy had to awaken Uncle Bobby so that he could get him back to the Longview State Hospital on time. Then Aunt Irene had my cousins change into their "good" clothes so that they could prepare for their walk home.

Thanksgiving was my favorite holiday, that is after Christmas and Easter.

But there was a gnawing feeling - a piece that was missing. It was the part of our family that wasn't there; the part that wasn't invited because Grandma didn't want them.

18

A New Awareness

I couldn't remember when thoughts or notions about sexuality began. It seemed that the notions and ideas were always floating about in the thoughts and actions, in some physical form or by innuendo, among my relatives. When much younger, I felt that I was in love with Uncle Francis. This was before all the negative talk took hold and I took sides with my Aunt Irene.

I can remember feeling deep, warm feelings for Uncle Francis and when he came to visit, Grandma and Granddaddy teased me about "loving Uncle Francis." When they said this in front of Uncle Francis, he just smiled and laughed. He thought it was funny.

I was so embarrassed that I would run into Grandma's room to hide until he left. I certainly didn't know what it was about. I just really liked Uncle Francis.

Real feelings of sexuality swirled around my adult relatives. These were like invisible whirlwinds at times blowing them together. Sometimes, Granddaddy seemed blown by his invisible whirlwind. When he came through the front door, home from his day at work, he was swept straight into the kitchen where Grandma, with her back to him, was stirring a pot with supper.

Granddaddy's whirlwind swept one of his arms up to take hold of one of Grandma's shoulders and the other arm, mischievously guided the other hand down the dividing line of Grandma's buttocks and up and under her house dress. Granddaddy's sexuality collided with Grandma's pristine self.

"Stop that! You know I hate you doin' that," she fumed.

Granddaddy laughed, removing his hand. "I was just teasin' the old gal. Wanted to see if you still had some life in you."

On rare occasions, Grandma's whirlwind swirled around her and she was in a good mood when Granddaddy came home from work. In the summer, he often came in perspiring from his day in the sun. He would sit down in a kitchen chair, remove his beat up, Panama hat and fan himself. Grandma sauntered over to him smiling.

"How's my Poppie, today?" she cooed as she leaned over to kiss him.

"Hot and tired, Sister," Granddaddy barked.

I thought these different adult responses were sometimes funny and very peculiar indeed.

19

Cousins and the Son of a Minister

When my Aunt Irene, her husband, Uncle Francis and my cousins, Mitzi and Joan, lived with "Papa and Mama" Green and their daughter, Naomi, it was easy for me to visit them. The Green's house belonged to the First Baptist Church, and since "Papa Green" was the minister, this is where they lived. His real name was Francis P. Green, Sr. Uncle Francis was his only son. I don't remember "Mama" Green's first name.

The house where they lived was called the Manse and was one of the large, three-story, Victorian-style homes on Lincoln Avenue. It sat on a hill with cement steps leading from the street to the front door. There was a front porch where "Papa Green" sat in a rocking chair during the week and on warm days when there were no church services. The walk, leading from the cement stairs to the porch, was lined with Holly Hock and Hydrangea bushes. Dodging the bees that flew in and out of the flowers was no easy task.

I could easily run the half-block down the street to reach their house. My cousins and their parents lived on the second floor and the rest of the Greens lived in all the other areas.

Aunt Irene was firm about our not venturing out of the second floor apartment.

Papa and Mama Green were old and grumpy.

"I don't want you playin' downstairs havin' Mama Green fussin'," she warned.

"I'll be glad when we move away from here. I get tired of hearin' her grumpy mouth."

Aunt Irene worked very hard in their section. It was spotless although sparsely furnished. She was so great to be around. She let us play uninterrupted unless we got in to fights.

When Uncle Francis was at home he was quiet. He looked a lot like Mama Green. He was short, brown-skinned with a large belly. He consumed a lot of food, like the Greens, sat in chairs a lot like the Greens and espoused their air of aloof inertia. Uncle Francis wanted us to be quiet while he ate and read his *True Detective* magazines.

There was an eerie feeling about the Green's house. It was always dark inside lending itself to our childish flights of imagination. We had monsters lurking in the dark hallways and behind the beveled, glass doors. Mitzi and I, being older than Joan, loved to slide down the front staircase banister from the second to the first floor. This we did on rare occasions when we need not fear the sudden appearance of Mama and Papa Green.

In the parlor was Aunt Naomi's piano. She was the church choir director and was an accomplished musician. She was a graduate of Wilberforce University and had majored in music. She could be heard practicing in preparation for Sunday's services.

Aunt Naomi was taller than Uncle Francis. She was brown-skinned, knock- kneed and fat. She was not married. Like the rest of the Greens, she loved to cook and eat. They were not, however, fond of cleaning the house or themselves. Yet, they were fastidious dressers. Papa Green was always seen wearing a three-piece, black suit with a gold watch chain dangling from the vest pocket. Mama Green loved flowing, flowered dresses. They used a lot of powder and perfume, "to cover up the stink," Aunt Irene said.

If the Greens weren't at home, we were free to play as we wished.

"Make us some fudge, Mama," Mitzi asked Aunt Irene as we rested from our play.

"No. Make us malted milks," Joan pleaded.

As was usually the case, Joan won. We sat at the kitchen table watching as Aunt Irene took the bottle of milk and a pint box of vanilla ice cream from the ice box. She put the contents into a large, glass mixing bowl, and using the egg beater, blended the ingredients.

She kept a large jar of malted milk in a tall, wooden cabinet that stood in the corner near the back door. This tall, narrow cabinet with several shelves was used to store canned goods and utensils.

240

Next, Aunt Irene spooned heaping amounts of the chocolate malted milk into the ice cream and milk mixture, and then beat the ingredients until a thick layer of foam formed on top. Her entire body moved in motion with the beater and the skirt portion of her dressed danced back and forth across her hips.

Aunt Irene was pretty. She had a cream-colored, narrow face with bright, flashing eyes. She had a thin nose and lips, like Granddaddy. Her hair was black, long and wavy. This she wore out and down to her shoulders. When they described Aunt Irene's shape, they laughed and said that she had a bottom that was" flat as a pancake." As we watched her mixing the malted milk drink, her dress did move back and forth and her bottom was flat like they said.

Joan, who was on her knees in the chair, leaned over and scooped some of the foam off the top of the drink with her finger.

"Stop, Joan!" Mitzi said.

"Leave her alone, Mitzi," Aunt Irene said. "Here, Shingy," she purred, giving Joan a spoonful of the mix.

Aunt Irene's nickname for Joan was "Little Shingy" or sometimes just "Shingy."

"I want some, too, Mama," Mitzi pleaded.

"Get the glasses and I'll pour you some," Aunt Irene instructed.

I watched, envious of Joan. I wanted to ask for some of the foam, but didn't.

"Give me the foam, Mama," Joan whined.

Aunt Irene spooned the malted milk into our glasses, saving the foam for Joan. Mitzi and I were angry, but said nothing. We drank our malts with relish, watching Joan out of the corner of our eyes. She always got her way.

When we finished I asked Mitzi, "Wanna play house?"

"Yeah," she said.

We rushed away from the table leaving our empty glasses.

"Me, too," Joan called, hurriedly trying to finish her foam.

Mitzi and I ran down the long, linoleum covered hallway and away from Joan. We didn't stop until we got to my cousins' bedroom.

The ceilings in all the rooms were extremely high. The hallway angled near the bay window which jutted out over the driveway below. These angles provided privacy and a barrier that muted the sound while we played.

When we got to the room, we made the area for play on Mitzi's side of the room. Joan soon followed us out of breath.

"Why didn't you wait for me? I wanna play, too," Joan whined. We ignored her.

"I'm ready to play house," she announced.

"We're not playin' house," Mitzi said to my surprise.

"We're playin' Movie Stars," she looked at me. "I'm going to be Deanna Durbin," she stated.

"Then, I'll be Barbara Stanwyck," I responded.

Joan looked at us puzzled, then quickly recovered saying she was "going to be Sabu's wife."

Sabu, the elephant boy, was the rage of our grade school set. He was a fresh star from India, brown with a magnificent smile, turban-headed and riding on the back of an elephant. He represented a handsome relief from Tarzan and the African Natives, forever the load bearers whose only utterances were, "Bwana, Bwana" and "Simba, Simba." We got mad every time we saw the parts of the Tarzan movies when the natives said these phrases. It was as if they were stupid. But, Sabu was a little older than we were. We might just have a chance to marry Sabu.

"No you won't," Mitzie said to Joan.

"Why not?"

"Because you're not playing with us," Mitzi answered as she dragged one of Aunt Irene's old dresses out of the chest that stood at the foot of their bed.

242

"Why?" Joan persisted, staring at us with her cherub face and big eyes.

" Simply because," Mitzi said.

"Because, why?" Joan implored.

"Just because," Mitzi said. "Just because we say so!"

Mitzi remained calm and resolute. Joan's bottom lip quivered. Then, she began to squeeze her eye lids closed. She did this until tears formed. Still we ignored her.

Mitzi picked up her doll, Betsy. It was a pink, plump doll with rosy cheeks and a little red mouth. "Betsy Wetsy" was the latest in dolls and actually drank from a tiny bottle and wet her pants.

Aunt Irene always bought Mitzi and Joan the latest toys and games. My cousins also liked card games like Old Maid and War. Grandma said that good little girls did not play cards so I could only play cards when I visited my cousins.

Joan turned defiant after this last dismissal.

"I'm gonna tell Mama that you won't let me play."

"We don't care," Mitzi answered unconcerned.

"MaaaaaMaaaaa!" Joan cried out. Aunt Irene did not answer.

"Maaaaaaaa! Maaaaaaaa!" She yelled louder and her voice quivered. "I'm gonna tell Mama on you."

"We don't care," Mitzi said. Then she pulled Aunt Irene's old dress over her head. She was ready to portray Deanna Durbin.

Whenever Aunt Irene talked about Mitzi, she said that she looked more like the Greens than she did the Corbin side of the family. Mitzi had knock-knees like Aunt Irene, but she was fat and was shaped like her Aunt Naomi. Sometimes when they were visiting us and Grandma used Mitzi's full name, you knew there was trouble.

"Sylvia Naomi Green, where on earth did you get that odd shape?" Grandma laughed. Mitzi didn't.

I got mad and cried when Grandma said things criticizing me; but not Mitzi. She never cried, only grew very still. Then Grandma laughed again saying, "Now look at you swellin' up like an old toad."

Now, Joan goaded Mitzi. She boldly got into Mitzi's face saying, "And you're knock-kneed and out of shape just like Aunt Naomi. Nahh, nahh, nahh!" She stuck her tongue out at Mitzi.

Mitzi stared at her as if she was crazy. Mitzi knew that she was her Aunt Naomi's favorite because she had inherited the Green look and their aptitude for music. She knew her aunt had taken her under her wing because she could see that her mother gave most of the attention to Joan. Mitzi was a little brown-skinned and Joan was very fair-complexioned. In fact we told her she was so fair that she looked like Milk of Magnesia.

Grandma thought that Joan was cute with her large eyes and her "rosebud" mouth.

She said that Joan had a mouth like hers when she was a little girl. *"Little Shingey,"* Grandma called Joan, *"you have a mouth just like me when I was little."*

Joan had hay fever and was constantly sneezing and rubbing her eyes and nose. She also had asthma attacks like her Aunt Naomi. She walked around with a roll of toilet paper. *"Poor little Shingey,"* Aunt Irene would say, *"Come sit on Mama's lap, baby."*

When Joan stuck her tongue out at Mitzi, I grew very tense. Aunt Irene had told us to "play nice." Just as Mitzi raised her hand to hit Joan, Aunt Irene appeared in the doorway.

"I'm going to the store. Who wants to come?" she asked.

"I do. I do, Mama," Joan said, forgetting her anger.

My aunt stroked her hair and took her by the hand. That settled it. I was relieved. We had escaped trouble.

"Can we stay here, Mama?" Mitzi asked.

"If you promise not to go downstairs and get into anything while I'm gone."

"Can we go down and play the piano?" Mitzi inquired. She took piano lessons from Aunt Naomi and knew how to play Swans on the Lake, her first two-handed piece.

She tried to teach me, but I was terrible at any attempt to learn and was jealous of Mitzi's ability, after all, I was older and should be better at things than Mitzi and Joan, so I thought.

"No!" My aunt was emphatic. "Not until I get back. I don't want Mama Green yellin' at you. I will be so glad when we move away from here," she repeated.

Aunt Irene and Joan left for the store and Mitzi and I had the luxury of being alone. We decided to pretend to ice skate like Sonja Henie. It was Mitzi and Joan who first introduced me to her. They had been to the movies and seen her. Later, I saw the same movie and was mesmerized.

Mitzi was the sophisticated one at her school, knowing about the latest movie stars and movies. I assimilated their sophistication and experiences by osmosis. First came Sabu. Joan talked about him incessantly; then I started dreaming about him. Then, came Roy Rogers with his slanted eyes and Gene Autry, singing, "*I'm back in the saddle again*" I learned all the latest from my cousins and was thereby able to keep up with my peers.

Now, we played "Sonja Henie." We got towels from the closet and tied one on each foot. The linoleum covered hallway was converted into the ice skating rink; and although the linoleum was faded with holes in certain spots, we avoided these. Aunt Irene's mopping and putting two or three coats of wax on it made the floor slippery and shiny. Now, it was Sonja Henie's world made ours as we slid first one towel covered foot forward then the next.

When we finished "skating," we were exhausted and hungry. We headed down the back stairs to the kitchen.

"Let's have mayonnaise sandwiches," I suggested.

"Unhuh, I want apple butter," Mitzi said.

"I want mayonnaise anyway."

The fresh loaf of Tastee bread was in the metal bread box on top of the ice box. We opened the package and pulled all the slices down until we got to the middle where we knew we could find the softest ones. Mitzi put a huge pat of Oleo on her bread then heaping tablespoons of apple butter. I got the small jar of Miracle Whip and spread globs of it on my slices. Then I put the two slices together for my sandwich. We sat eating like famished pigs.

"Beat you to the front room," I challenged Mitzi when we finished. We dashed up the back stairs with me way ahead of my cousin.

The front room was their living room. I was very fast and always beat Mitzi any time we raced. She attributed this not to my skill as a runner, but to my being tall and skinny. Aunt Irene said that my mother was always a fast runner and could beat all the children on their street when they were growing up. Aunt Irene had fun things to tell me about my mother.

I waited for Mitzi in the doorway to the front room. This room seemed to belong to Uncle Francis more than to anyone else. Near the window was his big, easy chair which due to excessive use had taken on Uncle Francis' shape. It had a huge, greasy spot on the back where Uncle Francis rested his head. The greasy spot came from the pomade he used to slick his hair down.

During the day, Aunt Irene covered this with an embroidered strip that she had made and removed it in the evening before Uncle Francis got home.

"When're you going to learn to run faster?" I asked my cousin. "You're slower than a turtle." I laughed.

"I don't care," she said, sauntering over to the magazine rack that sat next to Uncle Francis' chair.

She sat down and pulled out several of his *True Detective* magazines. These magazines frightened me. The covers of each one had a picture of a man or woman, white and in some state of partial dress, who had been brutally murdered. On one cover, a knife, the murder weapon dripped with blood that ran down to the bottom of the picture.

"Let's do something else," I pleaded.

"I want to look at the pictures," Mitzi insisted. I was beginning to tire of playing with Mitzi.

"I'm going," I announced.

"Don't go. Don't leave me by myself."

"You're not by yourself. Mama Green's downstairs," I said moving towards the door.

Mitzi jumped up blocking my way.

"I don't want to go down there," Mitzi said.

"Well, stay up here, then. I'm tired and Grandma will fuss if I don't get home."

"Awww, Sweetie, please. Just 'til Mama gets back."

Here was my cousin Mitzi, lover of monster movies and admirer of gruesome pictures in *True Detective* magazines, scared to be by herself, just like me. I relished my moment of power. She needed me.

"Welllllll, maybe," I said.

"Please. Pretty please," she begged. Then, her eyes lit up. "I know. Come on. I want to show you something. It's a big secret."

She grabbed me by the hand and dragged me towards the door.

"But, you have to promise not to tell anyone."

I thought for a second. My interest was piqued.

"What is it?" I asked. I was curious.

"Be quiet. Just come on."

"I want to show you what Daddy keeps in his drawer."

She led me down the hall into Aunt Irene's and Uncle Francis' bedroom. I was hoping she wasn't going to show me any more gruesome, detective books.

I got scared. I knew how angry Uncle Francis could get over his food being eaten without his permission. Once Mitzi got into his ice cream and he knocked her away from the table, bloodying her mouth just for that. Aunt Irene was livid. She called him a "fat-butted, rusty, tightwad" and told him: *"If you ever lay another hand on my child, I'll kick your ass. Hitting that child over some damn ice cream."*

"Mitzi," I said to her. I was breathing hard. "You better not get into Uncle Francis' things. You know how he is," I cautioned.

"Shhh. He won't know it. He keeps dirty books in his drawer."

"Dirty Books?" I exclaimed. Now I really was scared. What if Grandma found out? "Uncle Francis has dirty books?"

Mitzi did not answer she was too engrossed in rooting around in the drawers, pushing aside underwear and undershirts in search of the books.

I had never seen a "dirty book." A few kids at school drew what we called dirty pictures and wrote dirty words like "dick" and "pussy" but I could not conceive of these in an entire book. Mitzi lifted up the last few undershirts and came away empty handed.

"Where'd they go?" she asked. "They were here the other day. I bet he took them to work with him," she muttered to herself.

"Come on, then" I said relieved. "Let's go. I'll stay with you until Aunt Irene gets back."

"I know!" Mitzi exclaimed, "I'll look in the big drawer."

She bent over and pulled open the larger, bottom drawer. This is where Uncle Francis kept his clean dress shirts. Mitzi reached further to the back of the drawer. Then, she pulled out a large brown bottle, carefully wrapped in a sleeveless undershirt, the kind Uncle Francis wore in the summer. She stripped the shirt from the bottle. We looked at each other in disbelief and said loudly, "Hadacol?"

We could not believe that Uncle Francis was taking Hadacol. The advertisement on the radio for Hadacol had people saying things like, *"I used to be so dumb, I couldn't read. After taking a bottle of Hadacol I can read like a college graduate."*

Everybody laughed at the Hadacol commercials, even Uncle Francis. But he must have believed those ridiculous radio ads. We couldn't stop laughing.

"It's almost gone, too," Mitzi said. She rewrapped the bottle and put it back. Mitzi closed the drawer then opened the one above.

"Here's one," she said grinning from her success. "What happened to the others?" She asked herself with a quizzical look on her face.

The book she found was very small. It was perhaps four inches square. At first I thought it was a copy of *The Daily Word*, the religious book Grandma got in the mail each month. But the book had a cover made of flimsy, brown paper, with black lettering.

"What's it say?" I asked.

"Shhhh! Not so loud."

The house took on renewed eeriness. Mitzi tiptoed over to the edge of the bed. I closed the door. I was so scared I could hardly breathe. The title of the book was *Joe E. Brown and Barbara Stanwyck*.

"Barbara Stanwyck? I just played Barbara Stanwyck. Let me see that!"

I snatched the book from Mitzi. On the first page was a caricature of Barbara Stanwyck, nude, with a bushy crop of hair around what Grandma called her "pocketbook." Joe E. Brown, the comedian with the huge mouth had bulging eyes, ogling her. He was removing his clothes. Excited, we hurried to the next page.

"I haven't seen this one before," Mitzi said. It was obvious that she had gotten into Uncle Francis' dirty books before. Our eyes grew bigger.

The next page showed Joe E. Brown with a huge "dick" drawn with exclamation marks all around it. Barbara Stanwyck was standing up holding a douche bag. At first glance, I thought it was a regular, hot water bottle. My cousin thought so, too.

"What're they going to do with a hot water bottle," Mitzi asked.

I looked again. Now I could see that the bag was like the one Grandma kept hidden in the bottom drawer of her dresser. At times, she removed it and took it into the bathroom with her; usually on Saturday night.

Once, I had gone into the bathroom after she had used the bag. It was still hanging from the nail over the toilet where she had left it to finish draining. I wondered what the long, black apparatus on the end was used for. It had a lot of holes in it and looked like one part of the sprinkling unit that the Taylors used on their lawn in the summer.

Mitzi hurried to the next page where Barbara Stanwyck was displayed lying on the floor with Joe E. Brown putting the "black sprinkler" in her "pocketbook." His enormous mouth, broad enough to swallow a donut whole, was stretched wider in a monstrous grin. His gigantic penis again had exclamation marks around it that made it look like the rising sun that we drew on our pictures in school. This made no sense to us.

I had not forgotten the beating I had taken when Ann Butler wanted me to stick the umbrella rib into her "pocketbook." We were stopped by Grandma. The shame from that had not left me.

"That looks so dumb!" my cousin said.

It was "dirty" like the secret dirty pictures drawn by some kids and passed around at school, and all the while praying that the teachers would not catch them. But, as excited and scared as I was to see the dirty book in the secrecy of my cousin's house, I found myself more confused. Moreover, it belonged to my Uncle Francis who rarely said a word about anything.

"Let's go on," my cousin said, "Maybe we'll find out something on the next page.

We didn't get to the "next page." Aunt Irene opened the door just as Mitzi started to turn to it. She and Joan had returned from shopping and we had not heard them because the door was closed.

"Mitzi Green!" my aunt said, "You know better than to be in my bedroom. Give me that!"

She snatched the dirty book from my cousin and angrily threw it back into the dresser drawer slamming it shut.

"You know better than to get in your daddy's dresser!"

I wanted to crawl under the bed. Mitzi just stared with fear written all over her face.

"I was looking for some drawing paper," she lied.

"You know good and well, there's no paper kept in here."

Then, as if to some invisible spirit, my aunt said, "I don't know why Francis Green keeps those old, nasty books around here in the first place. All that ornery mess! Come on out of here and don't go into his things anymore. Do you hear!?"

We both vigorously shook our heads.

"He'll be mad as the devil if he finds out you were in here."

"And Peasy," she turned to me, "You know Mama won't let you come to play if she knows you've been reading bad books. I sure don't want her blamin' me for Francis' old, nasty stuff. I'd never hear the end of it."

I was ashamed and mortified. I did not want to cause any trouble for my aunt. I knew she was right. If Grandma heard this, no one would ever hear the last of it. I wasn't going to say a word.

"Goody, Goody, Goody," Joan stood mocking us from the hallway. "You-u-u-u-u got-t-t-t-t caught-t-t-t-t," she said in a sing-song voice.

Mitzi and I were too engrossed in our own feelings to care. We rushed out of the room, relieved that Aunt Irene did not mete out any harsher punishment. She and I sat on the sofa without saying a word or looking at each other.

Finally, I broke the silence, "I told you not to go in there."

"You did not!" Mitzi said glaring at me.

251

"I did, too."

"Well, you looked anyway, asking me all those stupid questions."

"Well, I really didn't want to!" I said.

"You did just the same!"

Aunt Irene was not angry with us. She was angry at Uncle Francis for having the books in the house. She put the groceries away then put out some Windmill cookies. These we had with milk. Everything settled down.

I decided that if we ever played "Movie Stars" again, I would never, ever be Barbara Stanwyck. I'd be Maria Montez instead.

Exhausted from the events of the day, I got my things and went home.

20

Granddaddy's Cousin Ike

As I made my runs back and forth to Rosen's Store, I could see that most of the colored people on Lincoln Avenue were so white and near white that it was hard to figure out why they were called colored. The neighbors were fiercely independent people who respected each other and kept up with each other's families, yet they remained to themselves.

I decided very early that old Mr. Tate was just plain mean. He kept his white face in a perpetual frown and when he talked to Ann, he growled. He called his wife, "Mama." She was white like him. Both had silver hair. Grandma never visited with any of her neighbors and only occasionally spoke with Mrs. Tate if they were both in the back-yard at the same time. She had no close friends living on our street.

I could count the people who were really brown or black. I fell into the brown category along with Aunt Margaret, Uncle Ben, the Glenns, the funeral directors, Mama and Papa Green, Aunt Naomi and Uncle Francis. Mrs. Bell was brown, but her husband and children were not. Aunt Mae Georgia, Uncle Doodlum and Delaney were brown, but their daughter Cleo was so white she was called "high yellow." Color gradation was very important in the community and in many instances; your status was determined by it.

The majority of the families on Lincoln Avenue were in the professional category. The Hulls, Hunters, Miss Helene, Ann's mother and Mrs. Mangrum were all teachers. Mr. Mangrum was a pharmacist and ran the drugstore. In addition to teaching, Mrs. Mangrum played the organ for the Presbyterian Church. Everyone was hard-working. Only the older people like the Tates and Taylors, Mrs. Robinson and the ladies in the Home for Aged Colored Women were porch sitters. Mrs. Taylor was the neighborhood gossip. What I observed was that even most of the women at the Home for Aged Colored Women were light-skinned, and almost white.

But when Grandma's Cousin Ike, Great Aunt Margaret's sister's child, came up from Kentucky, he stood out like a sore thumb. Of all the people I knew on Lincoln Avenue, Cousin Ike was the tallest and the blackest. He was rangy and handsome, and he had the most beautiful, even, white teeth.

Great Aunt Margaret took him in, giving him a temporary place to live. Before I was born, she had taken Grandma, Granddaddy, my mother, aunts and uncle in when they had no place to go. Cousin Ike spent a lot of time wandering up and down Lincoln Avenue. His comings and goings were carefully monitored by Mrs. Taylor.

One afternoon Cousin Ike came by our apartment. Grandma seemed suspicious of Cousin Ike because he was taking his time getting a job; and she said he was too old not to be working. He was, at the time, in his thirties. Grandma told Granddaddy that Cousin Ike was a "no account." Granddaddy said that Grandma "didn't know nothin'."

On this occasion, Cousin Ike said he was "just stoppin' by." Grandma stopped sewing, but in a few minutes, she picked up her sewing again. Cousin Ike did not stay long when he saw that Grandma had no time for him.

One evening after dark, Cousin Ike came by. He was talking to Grandma and Granddaddy in the living room. I was doing the supper dishes and heard their conversation.

Cousin Ike said, "I got myself a job. I'm taking Numbers now and just wondered if you'd like to play them with me?"

What Cousin Ike explained was that he was running numbers, a grass-roots form of gambling. After he started collecting the money for the "numbers," Cousin Ike didn't sit down when he came by, and he always came after dark. He stood by the living room window constantly peeking through the curtains.

Grandma said, "Ike, why don't you sit down and stop being so fidgety?"

Cousin Ike said, "No thanks, Cousin Lillian. I'm just fine."

"Do you want something to eat?" Grandma was much more cordial on this occasion.

"No, M'am. I ate at Margaret's. I just came by to see if you wanted to play the numbers."

Cousin Ike was breathing hard and peeking out the curtains. Granddaddy went back to reading his newspaper ignoring Ike's question. For some reason Grandma became adventuresome.

"Ike I might try the Numbers just this one time."

Grandma knew that Aunt Irene and Uncle Francis played the Numbers, and that Aunt Irene had been lucky and "hit" for twenty dollars.

Grandma never played Numbers or Bingo. She did play Pokeno with Granddaddy and Aunt Hookey and from time to time they played for pennies. But, just as Grandma did not read much, neither did she play many games. I was taken aback by Grandma's decision to play the numbers.

As I washed the meat platter, I saw a set of numbers on the back. I had not paid attention to the back of plates and platters before, but this time I saw the numbers 486. I took this as a sign of good fortune. I went to the living room and whispered the numbers in Grandma's ear. She gave these numbers to Cousin Ike.

"Do you want to box it or play it straight?" Cousin Ike asked.

"What do you mean?" Grandma said.

"If you play it straight that means if it comes out 486, just as you played it, then you win. If you box it you will win if any combination of the numbers come out," Cousin Ike explained. He seemed very knowledgeable.

"I'll play it straight," Grandma said giving Cousin Ike a quarter.

"Grandma," I said, "You should box it."

"Be quiet! You don't know nothin' about Numbers," Granddaddy said looking surprised at my involvement.

"Yes, I do, Granddaddy. Aunt Irene plays the numbers and wins all the time. She's lucky. It's better to box it," I said with juvenile authority.

I felt as sophisticated as Mitzi and Joan at this moment. I was excited that Grandma was displaying a degree of "worldliness." But, it cost fifty cents to box it. Grandma said that was too much money.

The following night when Granddaddy's evening paper, the *Times Star* came, Granddaddy checked the numbers. These numbers appeared in a part of the newspaper people, who played the Numbers, knew where to look and decipher the code. The number came out 864. If Grandma had boxed it, she would have won two hundred and fifty dollars.

Cousin Ike felt that Grandma had come so close to winning that this was his opportunity to make her a regular customer, and maybe convince Granddaddy as well.

To Cousin Ike's disappointment, Grandma never played another number.

I came in after school one day with Grandma's Cousin Ike following right on my heels. He practically knocked me down getting into our apartment.

Grandma was in her room sewing and thought that Cousin Ike was me. She yelled, "Sweetpea, don't come bustin' in the house like somebody crazy."

Cousin Ike rushed to the back room scaring Grandma.

"Cousin Lillian, can you hide me?" He breathed rapidly.

"Hide you? What on earth for, Ike?" Grandma asked.

"The police are after me."

Cousin Ike looked back over his shoulder to see if the police were behind him. Grandma slowly turned around in her chair facing Cousin Ike like she was calmly entertaining company. Cousin Ike was frantic. He started hopping up and down, then going to the door, then back to Grandma.

"Why would the police be after you?" she queried.

"Can you hide me?" Cousin Ike pleaded.

"Ike I can't do nothin' like that! What're you doin' to be in trouble with the law?"

"I got me some moonshine from down in Kentucky last weekend and I been sellin' it."

Cousin Ike's face was a picture of excruciating pain, like someone needing to go to the toilet but couldn't and had to "hold it."

Finally, he bolted for the door and made a run for it up the rickety, back steps. He must have had a sixth sense for the uniformed Cincinnati police were right behind him.

They caught Cousin Ike out in front of the Helena Apartments. He was taken away in the dark blue, patrol wagon with Cincinnati Police Department blazoned on each side. Mrs. Taylor and all those porch sitters were out of their seats, standing on the edge of their steps staring at the commotion transpiring in front of the Helena Apartments.

We didn't see Cousin Ike after that. He went to the County Workhouse for several months. When he was released, he returned to Lexington.

Grandma said to Granddaddy, "I told you he was a no account."

"Well, you're the one gamblin' with him, Sister, not me," Granddaddy answered.

Indignant, Grandma said, "I wasn't gamblin' with Ike no such thing."

"What'd you call playin' the Numbers, if that ain't gamblin'?" Granddaddy asked.

Grandma sat with her mouth open. She was speechless.

My Cousins Move Away

When Aunt Irene finally got her wish and they moved out of the Green's house, this posed some difficulty. She, Uncle Francis and my cousins moved many, many blocks away to an apartment on Fredonia Avenue.

Aunt Irene wanted Mitzi, Joan and me to grow up as if we were sisters. When they lived on Lincoln Avenue with the Greens it was easy for us to visit and play together.

Fredonia was a short walking distance from Gilbert Avenue where Saturday entertainment took place for the adults, and it was within walking distance to the Beecher Theater where we went to the Saturday matinees to see cowboy and monster movies. Although the greater distance made it difficult for us to see each other during the week, I could spend entire weekends with my cousins.

Since my cousins were the only grandchildren of a very prominent minister, the Reverend Francis P. Green, Sr., they attended Sunday School and the Children's Band at First Baptist, their grandfather's church. Neither Aunt Irene nor Uncle Francis ever attended church.

No one in my apartment attended First Baptist either, but Grandma let me attend Sunday school and the Children's Band. I did not like to hear Papa Green preach. He was getting so old that it was difficult to understand what he was saying. His voice was weak because of his age. But I did like playing with my cousins in the huge, ornate, red brick building, before church services.

At home, Papa Green sat in a rocking chair in a three-piece black suit. At church, he did not walk across the floor, he scooted and he needed help getting up the steps to the carved, high-backed, wooden "throne" that was his seat behind the pulpit.

A picture of Jesus was painted on the expanse of wall behind the choir loft. It looked out over Papa Green sitting on his throne. Here was Papa Green. Here sat this little, black man, with graying hair and rimless glasses, who could not get himself up the stairs, who sat at

258

home being waited on hand and foot, who was grumpy with his grand-children and whose wife worked in order to have spending money be-cause he, who was the messenger of Jesus Christ, was so stingy with his money. His parishioners adored him. Baptist leaders across the country knew and admired him. He, Mama Green and Aunt Naomi were church royalty.

Papa Green could not spread his arms out with strength like the Jesus in the painting. When he did, his hands trembled. I sat in the last pew with my cousins, snickering.

First Baptist Church was the largest colored church in Cincin-nati. Papa Green had been its minister for more than forty years. For me and my cousins Sunday was a time to get extra money from our re-latives to put in Sunday school and church collection plates. Half made it the other half was spent at Mangrum's Drugstore after church where we bought ice cream or candy. Mangrum's was a block from the church.

Church parishioners hesitated to correct my cousins, but Aunt Naomi frowned at us from her bench at the organ. She had a mirror over her seat from where she directed the church choir and could see out over the church audience.

Grandma read the *Daily Word*. It was the only thing I ever saw her read except her sewing patterns. Grandma tried to talk Granddaddy into going to church, but he told her, "I ain't givin' my hard-earned money to no jack-legged preacher." Grandma argued with him saying "It ain't for the preacher," but Granddaddy insisted, "like hell it ain't."

Granddaddy's Brother Will was a preacher and I wondered how he could be so nice to him when he came to visit and yet so harsh in his assessment of other ministers, calling them jack-legged preach-ers. That made no sense. Was Papa Green not being able to walk caused by being "jack-legged?"

Mitzi, Joan and I always made it a point to be at church on the Sunday of baptisms. That was when the pulpit and Papa Greens "throne" were moved, and the flooring raised to expose a large baptis-mal pool filled with water.

Papa Green wore a long, white robe on Baptismal Sunday. Again, he had to be helped down into the pool. An Assistant Minister, who was younger and stronger, laid the person being baptized, straight back into the water and immersed him or her. The person held his nose but always came up choking. I was amazed that Papa Green could stand up in the water so long.

At one baptism the director of our Children's Band, Mrs. Adams, was immersed. She came to First Baptist from the south and moved to O'Briensville. She had attended the Wednesday prayer meetings and Sunday services for more than a year when she was baptized.

On Baptismal Day she wore a long white flannel gown and a heavy rubber, swimming cap to keep her hair from "going home." "Going Home" occurred when a woman got her hair straightened only to get it wet and it went back to the naturally curly state of many colored people's hair. Straightening made the hair more like white peoples' hair.

Papa Green must have told Mrs. Adams that she had to remove her swimming cap because she did just before being laid back and submerged in the water. She had shiny, straight hair before she was submerged, but as soon as she was brought up, her hair went home fast. Mitzi snickered. Mrs. Adams hurriedly covered her head with her hands.

I looked over at Mitzi and wondered why she was snickering at Mrs. Adams. She had her hair straightened and when she and Joan had water fights, her hair "went back" just like Mrs. Adams'. Grandma said that Aunt Irene should not straighten Mitzi's hair - that she was ruining it by using that hot iron on her at so young an age.

Mrs. Adams left the Baptismal pool through the curtained door at the back of the pulpit, while the next person took his turn at being submerged "in the name of the Father, the Son and the Holy Ghost."

First Baptist Church occupied a third of the block near Mangrums's Drugstore. The parishioners prided themselves on their education, their fine way of dressing and their superiority over other churches in the area. They were the "Hill" Baptist, short for Walnut Hills. This, they thought, set them apart and above the "Downtown" Baptist and the "Lockland" Baptist.

They were the elite. As such they did not allow themselves the same frenzied excitation as did their brothers and sisters in the other

260

branches. There was a modicum of "Amens." Shouting with religious fervor was treated with condescension. If any member understood enough of what Papa Green said in his sermon to make them shout, finely veiled hats swirled around with such suddenness as to create a refreshing breeze. The culprit received stony stares to mark their disapproval. For us, First Baptist was entertainment equal to the Early Bird movies at the Beecher movie theater.

After Mrs. Adams' Baptism, she became an even more tireless worker in the church. In addition to her Wednesday night prayer meetings, through which Papa Green was known to sleep while a Deacon took over, she added the Children's Band to her responsibilities. Children's Band was Sunday school held on Monday after school.

We went in through the side door facing Lincoln Avenue and into the basement of the church were our group met. Mrs. Adams was the primary teacher. She had one assistant who was extremely quiet, while Mrs. Adams talked incessantly. She called us "chillerings" instead of "children" and she split her verbs.

"Now chillerings, I wants you to be good chillerings and get in line. We has lots of things to do."

She pursed her lips and held herself as straight as a soldier. Her white uniform was starched to perfection. She wore white shoes and stockings as well. Mrs. Adams looked more like a nurse than the leader of the Children's Band.

We tried not to laugh. We had never had a teacher who spoke like Mrs. Adams. It was dangerous to laugh at Mrs. Adams. She could be very mean and very quick. She maintained a sweet Christ-like smile on her face. It was her "*suffer little children to come unto me*" smile that could change instantaneously if anyone got too rambunctious or became inattentive. This person would find herself slammed into one of the wooden folding chairs kept in the basement for the extra church gatherings. You could be slammed in the chair so hard that the imprint of the slats could be left on your bottom.

We needed extra light in the room for Children's Band. There was only the light that came in through the small, frosted windows on the street side of the room. Lights were turned on and folding chairs were placed to form a large circle. Once we were in line, Mrs. Adams had us march around the room singing:

> *Jesus loves me this I know,*
>
> *for the Bible tells me so.*
>
> *Little ones to Him belong.*
>
> *They are weak but He is strong.*
>
> *Yes, Jesus loves me.*
>
> *Yes, Jesus loves me.*
>
> *Yes, Jesus loves me*
>
> *for the Bible tells me so.*

Next, we sat in a circle to learn the Books of the Bible or had Bible stories read to us. No one was allowed to speak. We had to sit perfectly still.

Mrs. Adams' favorite Children's Band member was a girl named Martha Ann. She was tall, thin and wore glasses. She was given the privilege of passing the plate around to collect our dues. Her glasses slipped down on her nose as she did this and she had to constantly readjust them. Martha Ann was very intelligent. This followed her from Douglas School, where she was a student and only colored children attended.

We learned the Beatitudes, a word that took several Mondays for the entire group to be able to pronounce correctly. For all of Mrs. Adams' verb splitting and calling us "chillerings," she never had any trouble with her Bible pronunciations.

Each week, we had to memorize one Beatitude and be prepared to recite it at our Monday session.

"Blessed are the meek for they shall inherit the earth."

"Blessed are the pure in heart, for they shall see God" and so it went until we had completed them all.

Every Monday we went home with homework for the next week just like regular school. Mrs. Adams said that the first one to

262

learn the names of all sixty-six books of the Bible would get an ice cream cone from Mangrum's Drugstore as a prize. Martha Ann won. She stood in the middle of the circle of chairs, glasses sliding down her nose and created a miracle. She pronounced those exotic names, Zaccharia, Malachia and all the remaining sixty-four Books as if she had known them all of her young life. We were in awe.

Mitzi, Joan and I often forgot our Children's Band homework until the day of Children's Band. Joan was too little to be a serious attendee, but Aunt Irene wanted us always to be together. It took me five or six Mondays to master the names of the Books of the Bible, one week to learn the Ten Commandments, and another week to learn the Twenty-Third Psalm which I thought the most beautiful piece that I had learned at First Baptist Church's Children's Band.

22

First Baptist and the Chautauqua

At Easter and Christmas, the Children's Band presented a program before the Sunday school classes. When regular school was out for the summer, we continued to attend Church Bible School and Children's Band. One summer we prepared for the largest convention for children called "The Chautauqua."

"The Chautauqua" was held at the Hamilton County Fair Grounds near Hartwell, Ohio. This was a special convention bringing all of the colored Baptist Sunday school children together to represent their individual churches. This is where the elite, First Baptist "Hill" children met with children from downtown and the rural communities where colored people lived and attended Baptist Churches.

Each Monday in the muggy basement of First Baptist, Mrs. Adams drilled us as we learned to march, not in a single file but in groups of four. We marched with the precision of an Army Drill Team. We learned songs that every Sunday school would learn to sing together, and we had individual selections chosen by each Church. A few of us were given special pieces to recite. I was one of those selected, along with Martha Ann, to give an individual recitation.

Mrs. Adams, who earned her living doing "Day Work" for white people, wore her white uniform to Children's Band. For the Chautauqua, the girls were to wear white dresses and the boys were to wear white shirts, ties and long, dark pants.

"Now, chillerings, be sure you be ready to wear nice white dresses and socks. Boys, you wear dark pants, white shirts and ties. Tell your mothers," she said cheerfully.

Aunt Irene was at Grandma's waiting for us to return from Children's Band. As soon as Grandma heard our news about The Chautauqua and that we were going to be with children from all over the County, Grandma said, "Sweetpea, you'll probably see that ol' black grandmother of yours, Molly Martin, with her important self. She's a big shot in the Church."

"Hush, Mama!" Aunt Irene said. She looked shocked.

"Hush! What for? She might as well know old black Molly'll be there showing off her big rusty self."

Molly Martin was my natural father, Goodie's, mother. I had not expected to ever see either of them in person. She had been a figure in Grandma's sad, angry stories. She was a mean person who wouldn't let my father marry my mother. She was a person who talked down to Grandma because my mother got pregnant.

Grandma continued, "Callin' your mama a common street walker."

Aunt Irene said, "Peasy doesn't need to hear all that, Mama."

She smiled at me as she patted my head. Grandma kept talking. Aunt Irene didn't know that I had heard this about the Martins many times before.

At our next Children's Band meeting Mrs. Adams said that we would march around a viewing stand; and that Mrs. Molly Martin, Head of the Sunday School Association, would make a speech to all of us. I wanted to disappear. I didn't want to go to Chautauqua. I did not want Molly Martin to see me. I did not want to recite anything before her.

Then, just before our trip to Chautauqua, Grandma was talking about my father having gotten another young girl pregnant when he left college; but this time, he had marry the mother and that he had another daughter just a little younger than me. Grandma said that she would probably be at Chautauqua, too, since Molly Martin demanded her children and grandchildren be active in the church. There was nothing I could do. With much trepidation, and dressed in a lovely white dress that Grandma had made, I rode the church bus to the County Fair Grounds where The Chautauqua was held.

We children stood in groups in front of a large viewing stand. We stood where, during the regular County Fair, prized pigs, goats and sheep were housed in pens awaiting the results of the judges. The track where there were horse races formed an oval that went around in front of the viewing stand. I was overwhelmed by the size of the event and the size of the Fair Grounds.

It was as Grandma and Mrs. Adams had said. Molly Martin, my other grandmother, stood before us dressed in her finest white dress with a huge corsage on her shoulder; and like Grandma also had said, she was black as coal. She was a large woman with a deep voice that resonated out over the crowd as she gave her address to our large group of children.

When Molly Martin had finished, each unit gave its presentation. I recited my piece, wondering if Molly Martin knew who I was. I decided that she couldn't know me and by distracting myself with this thought, I almost forgot the last lines of my piece. Mrs. Adams prompted me and I was able to complete my recitation.

I stepped back into a sea of white dresses as Molly Martin took the podium and introduced all of her grandchildren. There was Mary Martin who was my age with her father, Joe, who was a teacher and coach at Lockland Wayne School. There were others, but it all became a blur to me as there was loud applause after each introduction.

Then, Mike Martin's daughter, my father's other child, was introduced and I saw my half-sister for the first time. She had a much lighter complexion than me. Where I was brown-skinned, she was a cream-color like my mother, grandmother and aunts.

The sun beat down on us. The heat was suffocating. We had picnic lunches and cold drinks. Chautauqua lasted the entire day and when the buses appeared, we were all too happy to board them for our trip back.

I had now seen the Martins. Molly was a big shot in the Church like Grandma had said. Her grandchildren were important because they were her grandchildren!

Alone in my room at home, I was glad to be out of the scorching heat and away from the source of the searing insecurity that seeing the Martins and knowing that I had been rejected by Molly and my father, had presented. I did not like participating in Children's Band and The Chautauqua. Martha Ann could have all the honors.

I did not like seeing Molly Martin at this church activity. She did not *"suffer all her little children to come unto her,"* and she was head of all the Sunday Schools. No one knew how I felt.

Mitzi and Joan enjoyed Chautauqua. They were the most important young children there because they were the only grandchildren of the Reverend Francis P. Green, Sr., the most important colored, Baptist minister in Hamilton County. As a result, they, like the Martins, received special treatment.

23

Mrs. Adams Dies

The Monday after Chatauqua, Mrs. Adams praised us for our performances.

"You chillerings wuz jus' the sweetest and the bes' little things there. God knows I wuz so proud of you, I could've jus' busted wide open."

I remember Joan being carried by Mrs. Adams because she got tired walking around the Fair Grounds race track. Mitzi swore that she had stepped in horse manure and kept scraping her foot on the post near the viewing stand where Molly Martin sat.

"Jus' for bein' so good and 'cause God jus' loves you little chillerings so much, we're goin' to have us a nice party next meetin'."

Our chorus of joyful squeals erupted, lightening the drab atmosphere of the basement room.

"So when you come next Monday, I want each of you to memorize a Bible verse."

We groaned, "Awww, Mrs. Adams, do we have to?"

Mrs. Adams' face turned dark like a gathering storm. She folded her eyebrows into a ferocious frown and pointed her finger, like Moses'staff, straight out at us. Her eyes spewed fire.

"Now, you all jus' hush up! Hush up. Do you hear me!? You ought to be ashamed of yo'selves groanin' and complainin' like a pack of whiny brats. God don't like ugly," she said. "He gives you all the best of everything. A place to live, a mama and a daddy and food for yo' bellies, and what do y'all give Him in return!? A few pennies on Mondays."

Mrs. Adams sounded like a preacher. The veins in her temples popped out and throbbed. I decided that she wasn't talking to me since I didn't have a "Daddy." Mitzi poked me in the sides waiting to see if I was going to laugh at Mrs. Adams. I quickly looked away. I did not dare laugh. Mrs. Adams was angrier than I had ever seen her.

"I wants you chillerings to remember how good the Good Lord has been to you and don't you ever forget it. Do you hear me?"

There was a chorus of "Yes, Mams."

"Well, I be all right now," Mrs. Adams announced as she calmed herself.

She removed a linen fan-like folded handkerchief from her uniform's pocket and wiped the perspiration from her forehead. Then, she fanned herself with it.

"God forgive us all our weaknesses and I knows he understands that you little chillerings jus' don't know no better yet."

We smiled at Mrs. Adams. "Thank you Mrs. Adams," we said. "We won't do that anymore."

Mrs. Adams smiled. She had no children of her own. We were her church children.

With the success of the Chautauqua, First Baptist Church and Mrs. Adams were given written praises for the outstanding work done by the Children's Band. The Church rewarded Mrs. Adams by making her head of the Female Benevolent Society and Treasurer of the Church Choir in addition to her duties with the Sunday school and Children's Band.

On Sundays, we watched Mrs. Adams race from one class to another getting materials, making sure teachers were prepared, and kissing and hugging those of us in her Monday group. Then, she met with the Benevolent Society after church. On Sunday, she was one of the last ones to leave the ornate church building.

A few weeks later Mitzi told me that Mrs. Adams had died. Papa Green got the call from her husband. Mitzi overheard him telling her Aunt Naomi. We had not had anyone so close to us children die before. Death was what waited around the next corner in scary movies. Death meant graveyards and stillness. It meant Zombies, the living dead, Frankenstein, and the Wolfman.

Mrs. Adams' death frightened those of us in the Children's Band. For several days after hearing the news, I slept under the covers breathing hard and sweating. I had nightmares of the Headless Horseman coming after me and awakened shaking with fear. I looked out the window into the backyard and seeing the early morning mist knew, for sure, that the Headless Horseman was going to get me. I pulled the covers up over my head so hard that they came loose from the bottom where Aunt Hookey had tucked them.

She awakened fussing, "What's the matter with you? Stop jerking the covers like that."

I was happy that Aunt Hookey was awake and that she was real and not a ghost. I moved closer to her hoping to be able to sleep.

At the next Children's Band, Papa Green came to break the news. Shuffling in wearing his black, three-piece suit, he slowly sat in one of the wooden chairs and told us: "Mrs. Adams has gone on to Heaven." His voice was weak and barely audible.

"The Good Lord came with His angels and summoned her to come with Him. She will not be with you at Children's Band anymore. Mrs. Beulah, here, will take charge for Mrs. Adams. She loved you children and wanted you to be good."

Papa Green said no more, just got up and shuffled out. I pictured God in flowing robes with hundreds of angels coming to get Mrs. Adams. I imagined it was like the picture of Jesus with his outstretched arms that was on the wall over the choir loft and pulpit. I imagined that Mrs. Adams had a nice peaceful smile on her face and she was walking up pearly white slabs of marble stairs leading into a blue cloudless heaven.

Mrs. Adams would have said that she had gone to meet her Maker.

The older members of the Children's Band were asked to stand at the foot and head of Mrs. Adams' casket during the funeral service. We took turns in twos for fifteen minutes at a time.

Flowers filled the church and people came from all over Hamilton County to pay their respects. Martha Ann, Mrs. Adams' favorite, went up first. Tears streamed down her cheeks. When Martha Ann took her seat after standing at the casket, it was mine and Mitzi's turn. Mitzi stood at the foot and I stood at the casket's head. It was a gleaming, bronze casket. The faces in the pews were a blur; the fans were going rapidly as the Female Benevolent Society Members kept fanning themselves.

The Church had a yellowish-pink glow to it from the electric candles, that graced the front of the pulpit just behind Mrs. Adams' casket. I had never stood so close to the dead before. My head felt light and my chest heavy. Perspiration poured down my armpits and my mouth became excessively dry. Mrs. Adams' face looked like the ashes Granddaddy removed from the pot-bellied stove in the winter. Her hair was straight and shiny. Mrs. Adams would have been proud of that.

The Choir sang a mournful, *"Going Home. Going Home. I'm just going Home. Quiet like, some still day, I'm just going Home."*

One woman shouted out loud, "Lord, Lord, why'd you have to take my sister."

Tears welled up in my eyes. My head felt like a balloon filled with water. I swallowed hard to fight back the tears, but without success. They washed down my face and onto the bodice of my dress. I tried to imagine Mrs. Adams, not in the casket, but in the air, above the church somewhere.

I was angry that I had to stand by that horrible casket with the body of Mrs. Adams. Mrs. Adams wasn't there. She was gone. I looked off into the space above the pews. I watched the hands on the clock on the wall opposite the pulpit and counted the minutes until I could sit down.

They took Mrs. Adams' body to the cemetery in a large black hearse followed by a long line of cars. We did not linger at the church. Mitzi and I walked as fast as we could to Mangrum's Drugstore and got a double dip cone of ice cream. I imagined Mrs. Adams up in the blue sky in a long white robe looking down on us and smiling.

24

A Luncheon Invitation

When Mrs. Bell saw me sitting on the second floor porch banister watching the activity taking place at Ruth's house across the street, she thought that I was getting up the nerve to make a Frank Bell leap. Nothing could have been further from my mind. It was summer and I was wondering why Ruth had not wanted to play with me lately. Now there was a car that had pulled up in front of her house and I was puzzled.

Ruth's mother and father were teachers and I knew that they were above those of us living in the Helena Apartments, but I never let it stop me from trying to get as many chances as I could to play with Ruth.

When we played inside Ruth's house we often played in the attic. It was very dusty and hot up there, but Ruth had so many things with which to play that we never minded the heat. She had a doll house that had belonged to her older sister, Mary Betty, who was away at college and hadn't returned home yet. It was in the attic that Ruth and her brother, George, Jr., kept many comic books. George, Jr. and Ruth liked *Flash Gordan*. I did not. I preferred *Batman* and *Superman* of all the comics. *Wonder Woman* came in a distant third behind those two.

Ruth was exactly my age with long, reddish-brown hair. All of the Hulls and Taylors were very light-skinned colored people, and being that color as well as having been well-educated, they were held in high esteem in the community. Ruth's mother taught at the Douglas Elementary School attended by Ruth. It was the school that had only colored children in attendance and Grandma said it wasn't as good a school as Hoffman, where I went, with its children of different races.

Mr. Hull, Ruth's father, taught mathematics at a high school in downtown Cincinnati. During the summer he worked as a Pullman porter on the railroad. Ruth's grandfather had worked as a Pullman porter before he retired. In his day, being a Pullman porter was a very prestigious position for a colored man. Mrs. Hull taught summer school when school was out for the regular season.

272

I watched from Mrs. Bell's porch as Mrs. Taylor, Ruth's maternal grandmother, left their front porch and went to the car that had parked on the side of their house. I had never seen her with such a broad smile on her face. As two girls emerged from the car, she embraced them, flyswatter still in her hand. Mr. Taylor, too, came to life. He broke his tradition of being a quiet, somber elderly man who sat on the porch swing saying very little, but just observed the activity on the street. He moved rapidly from his seat and was all smiles.

Ruth came to the door slowly. She was dressed in a crisp, plaid pinafore and white blouse. She looked like Raggedy Ann but with real hair. There was a round of stiff greetings between the girls. Ruth was subdued. This was very curious as Ruth always took charge when we played together. She had mentioned that she was expecting her cousins to visit and that they were coming from Washington, D.C. where they lived.

I knew that the two girls were her cousins. They were tall and very slim. I was called skinny, but there was a difference with these two girls. They were older and dainty looking. They wore black patent leather shoes that had a little heel. They were not children but teenagers approaching womanhood. Their look of refinement was intimidating. I suppose that was why Ruth was so subdued. Ruth was not dainty like these cousins. She was plump, but not fat and at times she was a little clumsy.

The shorter of the two cousins had Shirley Temple curls and the tallest had her hair in a page boy. This style required very straight hair that was turned under all around. She had a wide ribbon tied around her head to hold her hair back behind her ears. Each girl had dresses with matching jackets. They wore white gloves, carried purses and, to show the ultimate status symbol, they wore silk stockings.

Ruth looked over and saw me watching them. I waved to her but she just gave me a faint smile and looked away. The entourage disappeared into the house. I sat mesmerized. Ruth's cousins were like the girls in the movies. They were like icing on elaborate cakes. They were the petit fours served at Mrs. Mayo's rich white people's parties.

I envisioned myself looking like Ruth's cousins. I gracefully descended the apartment stairs. Gone were the hand-me-down, high-topped, boy's sneakers. Gone was the impulse to make a Frank Bell leap. I wanted to be like the ladies descending the staircase of a Fred Astair and Ginger Rogers' movie. I imagined myself a Ziegfield Follies girl.

For the week after Ruth's cousins arrived I made myself visible in the front of our apartment building, hoping that I would have a chance to play with them. I jumped the hopscotch squares alone, thinking that Ruth might come out and talk to me without saying a word, but with exaggerated movement of her lips "mouthing" the question, "Can you come over to play?"

The more days that passed the more curious I became about these young ladies.

I entertained myself playing Jacks and Cars. Cars required only that a player know the makes of the cars that were passing. If you played with others, the first one to miss the name of a car lost the game. We only counted Fords, Buicks, De Sotos, Packards and Cadillacs. We didn't count "rattletraps."

To my disappointment Ruth and her cousins rarely appeared. I did see them once, sitting on the front porch on the glider quietly chatting and reading. They avoided the sun to keep from getting brown. This day, they had on sun dresses.

I missed playing with Ruth and felt more isolated as one of the "poor people" who lived on the street. Mrs. Taylor made me very aware of where she placed us on the social ladder.

Ruth's mother was different. She was a very kind lady who was interested in what I was doing. Once, when I was visiting, she had me sit next to her in their living room. She asked what I liked to do and when I told her I liked to write, she asked me what type of writing. I told her that I liked writing stories. She said she would very much like to read some of my stories.

I was so thrilled that an adult was interested in what I was doing, especially Ruth's mother, I decided to write a play about our group of girls. I had gotten a new composition book and, priding myself on my penmanship, I began to write. It was my first attempt at writing a play. I was hoping for an opportunity to return to Ruth's and show Mrs. Hull what I had written, but this seemed like a far off dream now that Ruth's cousins had arrived.

274

The Friday before the cousins were to leave I received an invitation in the mail. It was an invitation to a luncheon. This was really something. I had received invitations to birthday parties before but never an invitation to a luncheon.

"Grandma, Mrs. Hull and Ruth have invited me to a luncheon for Ruth's cousins."

"A what!?" Grandma asked. "Let me see."

She took the pale yellow and white card. After studying the invitation for a minute she said, "My, you'll have to dress up. This is something very special. Ummm. I hope you'll know how to mind your manners," she added.

This made me very scared. Maybe I wouldn't know how to mind my manners. Maybe you had to have special manners.

Ruth was learning special manners in an elocution class that she and some of my other school age friends attended on Mondays. Their parents paid a lady to school their girls in manners appropriate for being considered "lady-like." When they became teenagers, they would be presented at something called a Cotillion. Only well-to-do girls of color were given elocution lessons. They not only learned appropriate behavior but they also learned how to speak well and in quiet voices. The luncheon would be the biggest event since Ruth invited me as a guest at her elocution class.

"Can I get a new dress?" I asked timidly.

"I don't have time to make you a new dress. You just have to wear one that's nice enough. The dress Hookey bought you for your school program will be good."

Then Grandma added, "Shirley Temple curls are out!"

It was as if she had read my mind.

"Can I wear my hair "out" then?" I asked.

"Out" meant that I would not have the three plaits like I wore every day. "Out" meant I could look older, like Ruth's cousins.

"It gets tangled and you cry too much when I have to comb your hair."

"I won't cry this time, Grandma. I promise."

I was excited about having received the invitation and took this to mean that it was o.k. to visit Ruth. I ran across the street and knocked on the screen door. Mrs. Taylor answered.

"Is Ruth home?"

"No. She's out," Mrs. Taylor said.

"I got an invitation today,"

"Well, the invitation is not for today."

"Yes, Ma'm. I know. I wanted to tell Ruth that I can come. Grandma says it's all right."

"I'll tell her mother," Mrs. Taylor answered.

The day of the luncheon I started preparing right after breakfast. Too excited to eat or to go outside I stayed in where it was cool and played quietly in my room. I had taken my bath the night before so I played in clean underwear awaiting the time to get dressed. When the time finally arrived I was too scared to go, but did not tell Grandma as she brushed my hair.

Ann had been invited too. She was closer in age to Ruth's cousins and Ann's mother, Miss Helene, was a teacher. I decided to see if I could walk with Ann and maybe then, I wouldn't feel so frightened.

I called Ann. "Ann? Ann?"

Mr. Tate looked over from his rocking chair with a scowl. His scowl was worse than the slimy, brown tobacco juice that he spat into the yard.

"What 'cha want with Ann?" he growled.

"I want to walk to Ruth's luncheon with her if she's going."

"You can go on by yourself. Don't need Ann no other time you runnin' back and forth like some wild Indian."

276

Mr. Tate didn't pay any attention to my pale green dress with the white lace around the neck. He didn't notice that my hair was "out" and flowing down my back. He didn't notice my clean, white anklets.

Ann heard me and came out the door grinning.

"Told you I could go," she announced.

At first, Mr. Tate had immediately said "no" to the invitation, but when Miss Helene, Ann's mother, learned about it, she said that of course Ann could go and that it was nice to have been invited. I think Mr. Tate must have really been angry about that. He didn't want Ann to do anything except stay in the yard.

Ann was wearing a beautiful yellow dress with a matching yellow ribbon in her hair. With all the gathers in the dress, she looked like a yellow elephant. As she came down the stone steps I could see that she had on yellow socks and black patent leather shoes. Her shoes had a small heel, like the ones Ruth's cousins wore. I felt "babyish" in what I had on. We walked together in silence. Ann blocked my view of Mrs. Taylor as she opened the door for us.

The living room was full of girls. These were friends of Ruth's from other areas of Cincinnati. Some were the daughters of women with whom Mrs. Hull taught school. Others were school mates of Ruth's, and still others were from girls groups to which Ruth belonged. These were girls Ruth liked a lot. Most of them I did not know. I began to feel more and more ill-at-ease and out of place.

Sitting in two winged back chairs, wearing crisp, white, organdy dresses, Ruth's cousins sat as if they were holding court. I attached myself to the door jamb for support. The giggles were refined, the voices low and intimate. Gone were the days of wearing sun suits and playing War on the living room floor. Now the living room was a queen's reception hall.

Mrs. Hull announced lunch and assigned us seats. The idea of lunch under the gleaming chandelier over a dining room table with its large white linen table cloth and napkins, was something very unexpected for me. We never even noticed the dining room when Ruth and I played together at her house. It was always the darkened, cool room with sunlight shining through a beautiful, small, stained glass side window.

As we took our places, each with silverware and crystal glasses, I suddenly felt that I had forgotten how to eat. It was more than "keep your elbows off the table" and "don't slurp your milk"; it was which one of these forks do I use? There were two forks.

The other question was how do I drink? Could I drink without making any sound at all? Should I hold my breath when I drink and thereby be sure not to make any sound?

Fear dried my mouth and sent my eyes flitting around the table hoping to ferret out answers from somewhere among the girls sitting there with me. They all sat, hands in their laps, very still, at ease and chatting.

Mrs. Hull and Mrs. Taylor had turned themselves into maids. Ruth was transformed into a hostess and sat at the head of the table. The cousins sat smiling demurely on either side of Ruth. I focused my eyes on the cousins, having decided to take my cues from them. They held the answers to "how to eat a luncheon."

Mrs. Hull and Mrs. Taylor served plates with steaming green peas, chicken a la king in patty shells, and hot rolls. I knew I could not handle the patty shells, but the peas kept sliding off my fork into oblivion under the table.

I stared at the cousins. They took three peas on their fork. I took three peas on my fork. They took one tiny piece of creamed chicken. I took a tiny piece of chicken.

They sat stiffly, each with one hand in her lap, and chewed with their mouths closed. I sat stiffly with one hand in my lap and chewed with my mouth closed.

The twitter of giggling started, unnoticed by me, until it grew into a crescendo cascading onto the table making the flower center-piece tremble. Ruth tried to hide her giggle saying, "Sweetpea, what are you doing?"

I did not know that the others had been observing me, but once aware of this, I made the most of it. I exaggerated putting peas on my fork, batted my eyes more demurely than the cousins, pursed my lips and nibbled on the dainty roll like a rabbit with a carrot. The cousins frowned and continued to eat. I continued to imitate them until the table was shaking with laughter.

The guests took Ruth's question to be their cue to laugh openly. The cousins raised their noses in the air, tightened their mouths and sniffed haughtily. From the kitchen, Mrs. Hull heard the commotion and came to see what was happening.

"What's the matter, Ruth? Is everything all right?"

Ruth answered from her chair at the head of the table, "Sweetpea's making fun of Angela and...," she broke into laughter.

It was over for me as quickly as it started. My soul slid out of me and under the table into the dark eternity I had selected for my green peas. My embarrassment was too horrible to hang on to, especially since I thought I was disappointing Mrs. Hull.

I tried to drown my embarrassment with a large gulp of lemonade. I succeeded only in dropping the entire glass in my lap. Lemonade drenched my green dress. Hysterics flew in earnest and rose to the top of the crystal chandelier. Mrs. Hull rushed to help me.

"It's all right, Sweetpea," she said calmly. "Come with me and we'll get you cleaned up. We don't want you to go home sticky from lemonade."

I was a prisoner freed from my plight, but only out momentarily. We still had to eat dessert. Fortunately for me, it was cookies and peach ice cream. When lunch was finally over one of Ruth's best friends, Alberta Ryan, sang while Mrs. Hull accompanied her at the baby grand piano in their large entry hallway.

We sat on the floor in the living room being entertained. Mrs. Hull had given me one of Ruth's dresses while my dress was hung out on the back porch to dry. I sat in the corner near the fireplace wishing that I could disappear up the chimney. My first luncheon was a disaster.

I did not see Ruth's cousins again. They left in the same manner in which they had arrived. A car, driven by one of the Hull's relatives, perhaps the girls' father, pulled into the side yard of Ruth's house one afternoon and by the next morning it was gone and so were the cousins.

I had hoped to redeem myself with Mrs. Hull by completing the play I was writing and taking it to her to read. Unfortunately, on one weekend when I went to visit with my cousins, I took my composition book with me to work on the play. When I looked for it during a lull in our activities, I couldn't find it anywhere in their apartment. It wasn't among my things. I was mystified.

I told Aunt Irene about it. She, too, looked everywhere and could not find it.

When she asked Uncle Francis about it he said that he thought it was some trash and had thrown it away. Aunt Irene was very, very angry with him. I was devastated. I did not try to start over again. I was never able to show Mrs. Hull my play.

25

My Visit to the Country

I don't remember the first time Grandma thought it all right for me to spend two weeks during the summer with my mother. I do remember what it was like to make the trip. The visit began when my mother came from the sub-division, north of Lockland, to get me. She had to transfer twice and take the hour and half ride before arriving at our apartment. My clothes were always packed into a large, brown, Kroger's grocery bag in preparation for my trip.

The bus stop was just a half block from our apartment. It was there we caught the bus and rode it to Sears and Roebuck at the corner of Lincoln and Gilbert. We got off and transferred to the bus that would take us to the Cincinnati Zoo. At the Zoo we transferred to a streetcar that took us to Lockland. This was the longest ride of our trip and my mother did most of the talking. She remained a person with whom I had had so little contact that I did not know her as well as I knew my three aunts, her sisters.

"Sonny, Jimmie and Ronald will be so happy to see you," she said cheerfully. "They just can't wait. Like a bunch of maggots, up and down," she laughed.

It was a loud hearty laugh that embarrassed me. I looked around to see how many of the passengers were looking. I was thinking about what Grandma had said before my mother arrived to pick me up for my trip, with her, to the country.

"Ethel is so loud and country, Out there with those old ignorant people. She acts just like 'em. She always did do what other people did. She never would mind me. I hope she doesn't mess up this nice dress of yours. Never did know how to take care of things."

At the Zoo my mother and I waited on one of the wooden benches that lined the wide promenade leading to the ticket booth and the turnstile to enter the Zoo. I remembered pleasant times inside the Zoo. Every year schools were let out for a city-wide Zoo Day. Ticket prices were reduced and children appeared from all over with relatives and packed lunches. On Zoo Day, Aunt Irene and my cousins met me,

Grandma and Aunt Hookey at the Zoo. Our favorite foods were packed in the lunches. These included bologna sandwiches, deviled eggs, some kind of fruit and cake or cookies.

In summer there was "Opera at the Zoo" and those signs greeted my mother and me as we awaited the streetcar. Our family never went to the opera.

As my mother and I sat on the bench she said, "Mama," she referred to herself, "never wants you to forget that she always loved you and did what she could for you. It's very hard. We don't have much but, I want you to remember that I'm the one who buys your coats and shoes at Christmas."

I listened as she explained these things to me. I felt sorry for my mother, especially when she left our apartment in tears from Grandma's verbal assaults.

Not many people were waiting for the streetcar to Lockland when it arrived. I was earger for the ride that signaled the third lap of our trip. The streetcar was old, but clean. The seats were hard. I sat stiffly next to my mother as she talked to the few strangers that were on board.

"Oh, is that right, honey?"

"Well, what do you make of that?!"

"Well, bless your heart, honey. You'll feel better soon."

Her words were of agreement and gentleness, and if something funny was said, her laughter roared through the car. I cringed, wishing she weren't so loud. But no one was a stranger to my mother. She talked to anybody and everybody. I squirmed on the seat and grew very tired. It had taken an hour, a very long time for me.

"You can put your head on Mama's lap and go to sleep if you want to," Mama said.

I welcomed this suggestion and laid my head on her lap. It was awkward, but better than sitting up. Mama was plump and short with a small protruding belly like Grandma's. She no longer resembled the pictures we had of her as a sixteen year old and nineteen year old, with the short hair cut. She looked so beautiful in those pictures.

282

Mama's hair was long again and braided in the French-braid style. She wore it parted in the middle, braided into two braids and these crossed and pinned into place, in the back at her neck, with very large hair pins. Her face was still pretty but devoid of make up, a requirement of her church, and she wore a brightly colored cotton dress that came down to her ankles. She looked as old as Grandma without gray hair.

Grandma had asked Mama about her dress. "Is it new?" Mama told her no, that it was several weeks old and that she had paid just a few dollars for it at the Dry Goods store. Grandma frowned, saying that she wondered how Mama could afford new dresses all the time when she couldn't get any. Mama just stood with her hands folded across her stomach saying that she didn't get new dresses all the time. She told Grandma that my stepfather didn't make much and that they had enough for food, rent and sometimes for the children to get some of what they needed.

My mother had complimented Grandma on her ability to sew and make clothes for herself and others. Grandma retorted, saying that Mama could've learned to sew if she hadn't been so hard-headed. I was glad we left when we did so that the conversation did not get to the point where my mother's feelings were so hurt that she cried.

Now I laid my head in Mama's lap and tried to nap while the streetcar moved side to side, speeding towards Lockland. I was half asleep when I heard the conductor call out, "Schwartz's Corner." It was here that all the colored people got off. Later, I learned that "schwartz" was the German word for "black." No colored person liked being called "black."

It was dark when we arrived. Schwartz's Corner was lighted by the neon signs in the store windows. We got off in front of Mitman's Dry Goods store, crossed the street and passed the corner Drugstore.

The businesses were owned by Jews and whites, but the people of color from Lockland and the sub-division congregated at Schwartz's Corner to cash and spend their paychecks on Fridays and Saturdays.

Once off the streetcar, Mama and I had to get the bus to the sub-division. We waited for it in a small one-room building. The paint was chipped and faded. Men in their dirty work clothes and heavy boots got on the bus with us as did women coming from shopping or from their work for "private families," white and well-to-do, in the nearby villages of Wyoming and Glendale.

The bus arrived and I was surprised to see how different it was from the public transportation we had taken to get to Lockland. The bus was a small, school bus painted blue. It was very old. We all got on board and started the trip to the sub-division.

The passengers were happy and loud like my mother. They laughed and shouted over the roar of the rickety bus as it left the paved streets of Lockland and entered the pebble and rock strewn, unpaved roads of the sub-division.

"Do you think we'll make it, y'all?"

"This bus gonna' die at the next stop?"

"How long this bus been this decrepit?"

"Ain't it time y'all done got a new bus?" one man said to the driver.

"She sho ain't for this place long!"

"Lawd ha' mercy. This sho is a hard bus to ride."

"Oh Jesus," Mama said, laughing so hard she was crying.

When we reached Van Buren Street where Mama lived, she took the brown paper bag with my clothes and pulled the fraying signal cord. The erratic "buzz" signaled the driver we wanted to get off and we staggered to the front of the bus.

Mama took my hand and helped me down the steep step. We had finally arrived at our destination.

"Take care, Miz Price," the bus driver said.

"I will, honey, and you take care yourself, bless the Lord," Mama answered.

We stood in the dark waiting for the bus to move on. My mother and I took the lonely, very dark walk down the road to her house. I had not known such blackness. My eyes had to adjust. Everywhere was empty black space. There was not one street light. I began to make out flickers from kerosene lamps inside the windows of the little houses. Dogs barked and ran out as we passed. I was frightened.

"Now, stop that barking Blackie," Mama said gently to one of the dogs. "You know it's just me, and this is my baby, Sweetpea, so why are you making so much noise?" She leaned down, speaking to the dog as if it were a person.

"Just stop that fussin' now."

"Praise the Lord, Sister Price," a neighbor hearing my mother's voice called out from somewhere in the dark.

"Praise the Lord, honey," Mama called back.

Mama lived in an upstairs apartment over a small store. The building was made of red brick. It was built and owned by a Mr. Samuels, a local entrepreneur from whom Mama and my stepfather rented their place.

As we mounted the cement steps to the apartment, Mama called out for my brothers.

"Sonnnneeeeee, Jimmmmeeeee, Ronnnnuhld, Sweetpea's here."

The rush of bodies, muffled voices and an open door made way for my entrance. My siblings pushed, shoved and laughed. They were excited to see me even though we were like strangers to one another. I had never seen my baby sister, Lillian. The boys grabbed my bag and pulled at and fingered my belongings.

"What's this, Sweetpea."

"How long you goin' to stay?"

The apartment was not unlike ours in Walnut Hills. It just had more children where ours had more adults.

"Hush up!" Mama said, "Don't act so foolish, now," she scolded. "She just got here. Ronald, leave that alone." She slapped his hand. Ronald, five years old, jerked his hand back, rolled his eyes and laughed.

"You're so devilish," Mama said.

Lillian, who was just two years younger, dark and quiet, stood shyly near the sofa. My stepfather, Neil, was not home. He worked nights as a truck driver for the Darling Company. His run was from Cincinnati to Louisville, Kentucky, carrying horse carcasses and bones back to the company to make glue.

The sub-division sat on a hill overlooking a valley that was part of Lockland. Several industrial plants were located here. Many nights, when the winds shifted, we could smell the noxious odor that came from the Darling Company as the dead carcasses were being burned.

Mama removed the cushions from the sofa and pulled out the bed on which all four of us children would sleep - two at the foot and two at the head. Lillian slept with Mama until very early in the morning when my stepfather came in from work. Then she was transferred to the sofa bed with us.

Mosquitoes were very bad in the summer. Mama went through the apartment with a long-handled Black Flag spray gun, spraying to kill them. We would get under the covers so the spray would not land on us. Mama talked as she sprayed. She stood guard searching with her piercing, black eyes.

"There's that demon," she said, poised to shoot her spray gun.

She pumped away at the handle with such ardor that one would suspect she was after a much larger enemy. She would go after flies with the same ardor during the day.

"I know you're goin' to come out sometime you demons, and when you do, I'll be right here waitin' for you." Mama laughed and we laughed.

"Sweetpea doesn't know what to make of all this," Mama said.

Then, she rocked back and forth on her feet waiting for the next moment when she could launch her attack.

When the room was completely fumigated, Mama placed the Black Flag spray gun on top of the ice box in the kitchen. Only after she was sure that she had gotten every living mosquito, did she go to bed in the next room.

In the early morning and before dawn, I heard my stepfather come in from work. I was awake adjusting to my surroundings. I heard his shoes being dropped to the floor and heard him unzip his jacket. Soon, a half-asleep, Lillian was laid in the bed with us.

We arose early to pillow fights between the boys until Jimmie got hit in the eye and began to cry.

My mother yelled, "Quit that fightin' now. Go back to sleep."

We tried to be quieter but to no avail for by this time we all were thoroughly awake. Since the boys slept in their underwear, they simply pulled on pants and shirts when they got up. I helped Lillian dress.

The apartment had a cement porch off of the living room where we slept. That morning I had a much better view of this part of the sub-division. This section was called the "Upper Sub." Looking over the landscape from the porch, I could see the unpaved streets without street lights. The houses were not large, but small, one-story buildings. Many looked as if they were put together like patch-work quilts. Some were in need of much repair and others were very nice, well-kept structures.

Beyond Jackson Street, which ran in front of the apartment, I could see the last street in the "Upper Sub." This was Congress Street. It was surrounded by acres and acres of thicket and open fields, some of which were converted into gardens. On Congress Street the houses were no more than run-down hovels dotting the horizon.

Even in this section of the sub-division there were attitudes of similar types experienced among people in other areas. Some people in one area considered their area more progressive, or better than another. No one had running water or electricity. People got their water from wells and their light came from kerosene lanterns. The bathroom was an "out-house" in the backyard which was used to empty the "pots" or "buckets" of urine collected during the night, if you had to go to the "toilet." Out-houses smelled worse than the pig sties that were all over because residents raised pigs and chickens. There were many vegetable gardens next to houses.

My mother did not want me playing in the area near Congress Street unless I was with my brothers because it was two streets away, and beyond it were nothing but open fields. Never had I seen so many fields, bushes and flimsy housing structures. This was country and a very different experience from what I had living in the City. I was like the *City Mouse* visiting the *Country Mouse* from that children's story. It was an adventure.

My stepfather left for work at noon. Mama did not get up to prepare breakfast for us. She got up when it was near time for my stepfather to get up. The boys got their own breakfast, usually of dry cereal and milk, but every morning of my visit with my mother, I was treated special.

Mama prepared a large meal, since my stepfather would not eat again until the next morning. He would take a small lunch to have in between. My stepfather was a pleasant, dark-brown-skinned man of medium build and even features. He was well liked by his friends who all called him "Neil."

He knew the Corbin girls when they attended Lockland High School together. He had dated my Aunt Irene and when she rejected him for Francis Green, he married my mother. This pleased Grandma who was so upset with her for getting pregnant without being married. Sonny and Jimmie called my stepfather, "Dadbo."

"Hi Dadbo," they greeted him in the morning.

They teased and had a few moments of horseplay with him; a jab and a run here and a jab and a run there. They laughed and had fun until my stepfather said, "That's enough now. No more rough-housin'."

The large meal that my mother prepared in the morning always included hot biscuits. The meals would vary with some being fried pork chops, fried corn and sliced tomatoes. My mother, stepfather and I all sat down to the table to eat together, but Sonny, Jimmy, Ronald and Lillian stood behind our chairs begging for some of the food we were eating. It was a very small kitchen and a very tight fit.

"You've had your breakfast. Go on away from here, now," Mama would say to them angrily. "Stop beggin'. Let your daddy and sister eat in peace."

288

I felt very uncomfortable about my position, but justified it in my mind because I was the eldest and was just visiting.

My mother was an outstanding cook. My favorite meal was of her fried corn and hot biscuits. These were taken from the oven of the stove that had to be heated with coal and wood. To bake in our oven at home, Grandma only had to turn on the gas and light it with a match. She could get even heat easily. Mama had to be sure that she had enough coal and kindling to keep the fire going.

One morning, I was allowed to eat as many biscuits as I wanted. It turned out to be eight. These were hot with butter and strawberry jam. Never had I been allowed to eat all that I wanted.

"Mama," my stepfather said, "somebody sure loves your biscuits."

"I'm so glad you like them, honey," Mama said.

I felt happy that my mother was pleased that I liked her cooking.

"Sweetpea? Ronald whispered from behind my chair, " Give me one of them biscuits."

Mama didn't hear him.

"Awwww," Jimmy cried. "I'm gonna tell Mama. Mama? Sweetpea gave Ronald a biscuit."

My mother looked at me, then said, "Well, she can give him one if she wants to, but that don't mean you're getting' any."

Jimmy cried in his harsh, husky voice. Mama swatted him with the dish towel. Jimmy cried louder. Ronald giggled and she swatted him. The kitchen was in an uproar. I felt guilty and "special" at the same time.

My stepfather told them to go in the other room. His voice was calm, but he directed them with a quiet command.

"Can't have a minute's peace," Mama fretted. Then, she turned to me and said, "Can I get you some more, honey?"

I left the table stuffed by the number of biscuits I had eaten.

In mid-morning, my brothers and I joined some of the other neighborhood children to go blackberry picking. We all had galvanized pails.

"Is that your sister?" one neighbor girl inquired.

"Unhuh. That's Sweetpea," My brother, Sonny answered.

"She sure has pretty, long hair," the girl said eyeing me suspiciously. "Just like Miz Price." The girl took the liberty to feel my braid. "It's so soft. She looks like your mother," she told my brothers.

It was as if I wasn't there. But that day, she and I became friends as we walked down the hot road in our bare feet. I had never walked outside without shoes before. This was a new and rather difficult experience. Gingerly, I picked my way along the dirt road. The stones and sticks hurt so I went back to the house to get my shoes.

Grandma would never have approved of the scraggily bunch with which I laughed and walked down the unpaved streets. I had heard that going barefoot made your feet big. I thought my feet too big already. I was teased about having "big feet."

With my shoes on, we walked down a narrow path with lots of bushes on either side. On the way we passed Sister Hocker's house. She was a member of my mother's church, a fair-complexioned woman of quiet demeanor. The members of my mother's church called each other "Sisters and Brothers." Mama said that Sister Hocker never raised her voice. She said that she was the sweetest, kindest person in their neighborhood.

The church that my mother attended was held in the rooms over the other apartment building Mr. Samuels had built next to where my mother lived. He had a complex of buildings which formed an enclave around a dirt courtyard. One end was open to the street. We often played in the dust in the courtyard. The boys played marbles and we all played baseball.

As we headed for the fields known by the others to have lots of blackberry bushes, I saw Sister Hocker slopping her hogs in the backyard of their house. The hogs created an atrocious odor, but Sister Hocker never winced.

"Hi Sister Hocker," we called to her.

"Hello there children," she called back. "Where you children headed?"

"Blackberry pickin'," we called back in unison.

"Well that's nice," she smiled and turned back to her hogs.

Being in the country gave me the opportunity to see and be near many things I would never have seen in the city. I could hear the loud squeals of the hogs rooting for the "slop" as that's what their food was called. I learned that slop consisted of food left over from family meals and the unusable leaves of cabbage and other vegetables which people sometimes got from the grocery store owners and their gardens.

My brother, Sonny, headed the line as we had to form a single file as the path narrowed.

"Mama said to watch out for the snakes," he said matter of factly staring down at the path.

"Snakes?!" I shrieked, "Nobody said anything about snakes!"

"Everybody knows you have to watch out for snakes," the neighbor girl laughed.

"They're black snakes. You have to be careful when you stick your hands in the bushes to pick the blackberries. The snakes like blackberries," she said with great authority. Then, she added, "Sonny, I've been pickin' blackberries longer than you and I never have seen any snakes."

"I don't care," Sonny said, "Mama said once they went blackberry pickin' and found this big patch of berries. They reached in and she said there sat this long, black snake peekin' at them."

I envisioned this scene and got more frightened.

"I don't think I want to go blackberry picking," I said timidly.

I looked behind and realized that the pathway was a very long way from where we had begun. It was through the rows and rows of thicket that we had already passed. If I went back, I would have to go alone.

"Nothin's goin' to get you, Sweetpea," Sonny said.

"We been here lots of time," Jimmie said.

I was responsible for Lillian, so I held her hand tight as much to reassure myself as it was protection for her.

Finally we came to a big area surrounded by blackberry bushes. The others dived in and picked vigorously without caution. Each time I picked a berry, I imagined the eyes of snakes peering from the dark thicket. My pail was not as full as theirs when we finished.

As we began our journey back, fingers pricked and bleeding, we could hear Mama's voice. She stood out on the cement porch with her apron still on from breakfast. She cupped her hands around her mouth and yelled, "Sonnnnnneeeeeee. Jimmmeeeeeeeeee, Ron-nnnnnnnullllld." And to this she added, "Sweetpeeeeeeeeeeea."

There we were stumbling down the path single file, tired and quiet, lugging our pails of luscious blackberries. The open space was much like a western prairie that I had seen in cowboy movies. The sky was blue and cloudless. The sun was scorching our heads and arms as we trudged along. Stillness was all around. It was shattered by our mother's voice. Everybody in the area could hear her calling us home.

I believed that if we had walked a hundred miles away, Mama would have stood on that porch and called us, considering no distance too great for her lungs to overcome.

"Mama's calling. We'd better hurry up," Jimmy said uneasily.

When we got home Mama had us empty our pails of blackberries into the kitchen sink where she poured water over them from the larger, kitchen pail. She put them in a strainer to drain. Then, Mama began work on what would be the most delicious dessert that I had ever had.

She got out the flour, lard, water and salt to make a crust that she placed in a large, floured, rectangular pan. Then she filled the crust with blackberries that she covered with lots of sugar, lots of butter, a little flour and nutmeg. Last she rolled out another crust, placed it over the blackberries and, with a fork, poked holes, at intervals, all over the top. When she was finished she placed the pan into the hot oven.

292

That night after supper, we had large helpings of Mama's blackberry cobbler.

That was the most delicious cobbler I had ever eaten. I took pride in the fact that this was made from the blackberries that we had picked that day, and in spite of the fact that there may have been snakes watching.

26

A Brother's Punishment

During my summer visit I noticed that Ronald, the youngest of my brothers, did whatever he saw Sonny, the eldest brother, do. He followed him wherever he went. Jimmy, the next oldest, did not follow after them. He stayed closer to home.

Ronald was tall for his five years and we all thought him cute, but peculiar. Since he was a baby he had a very odd way of putting himself to sleep at night. He placed his pillow against the back of the sofa bed, sat with his back against it and moved back and forth, banging his head as hard as he could against it.

No one could understand why he did that. Mama said that he had been doing this since he was able to sit up as a baby. First, he would move his head from side to side until he went off to sleep. Then, as he learned to sit up, he rocked back and forth hitting his head against the back of whatever structure in which he happened to be sleeping. He never seemed to pay attention to whether that surface was hard or soft.

There was a time when I overheard my mother answering the question, "why does Ronald hit his head like that?" She answered, "he's been doin' that since he was a tiny baby. The doctors say that he had Rickets on the brain. That's why he does that."

I thought Rickets was the disease that made you bow-legged and was associated with bones not developing properly, but I had never heard of Rickets having anything to do with the brain's development. No one ever questioned Mama further and just accepted the explanation as a fact. As a consequence, Ronald's peculiar behavior was just accepted.

One day Mama asked Sonny, "Where's Ronald?"

"I left him playin'. I was gettin' hungry," Sonny said.

Mama did not send us to look for Ronald.

"Jesus," Mama said. "That boy don't mind no better'n a minute. I don't know what I'm goin' to do with him. Now why'd he go off like that? Just wait 'til I get my hands on that demon."

It was after breakfast and my stepfather had left for work. Ronald came home just before lunch time. Mama was very agitated. Ronald knew he was in trouble. Whenever he didn't mind, Mama made him go outside and bring in a switch so she could use it to whip him. Switches were made when a thin branch from a bush or small tree was pulled off and stripped of leaves and smaller branches. When Mama sent Ronald to get a switch, he would start to cry. He cried all the way to getting the switch and all the way back. If the switch was too little, Mama made him throw it away and get another one.

When Ronald finally arrived home, Mama asked, "Where you been, you demon?"

Since Mama had joined the Pentecostal Church, she began to include words from the Bible in her daily conversations. The most common words were demon, devil, saint and phrases like *"Loose here in Jesus' name."*

"We was playin' ball, Mama," Ronald said timidly.

"What'd I tell you?" Mama yelled. Ronald cringed. "I told you that if you weren't with Sonny and Sweetpea that you was to stay in this yard and not go anywhere out of sight!"

My mother answered her own question. Ronald looked puzzled as if this was the first time he had heard this. His eyes got bigger and bigger.

"Don't beat me, Mama," Ronald pleaded. "I forgot." He started to cry.

"Loose h'yah in Jesus' name, you lyin' wonder." My mother raised her hand as she used one of her Bible phrases.

Ronald cringed and covered his head with his arm. But this time Mama didn't hit him, nor did she send him to the yard for a switch. Instead, she dragged him into the kitchen.

Sonny, Jimmy and I followed and stood in the doorway watching. We were in total suspense as Mama took one of the buckets we had used for blackberry picking and filled it with cold water from the pail she kept inside for drinking and cooking. She put the bucket on a chair, grabbed Ronald by the arm and held it behind his back. She took his head, and with her hand, pushed it into the pail of cold water and held it there.

"When're you goin' to mind!?" she shouted as she let Ronald come up for air.

As soon as he had caught his breath, she pushed his head again down into the dark bucket filled with water. Then, up again. Ronald gasped and water ran down his face. Mucous mixed with water ran from his nose and over his mouth. She put his head in the water again and again.

I watched. My body froze with horror. I feared for Ronald's life. I thought he could drown in that pail of water. Finally my mother let his head come up out of the water. She did not hold it down anymore.

"Now get in there and go to bed, you demon. You're not gettin' anything to eat for not mindin' me." Mama's chest heaved as she tried to get her breath.

The violence that shattered the hot summer afternoon turned my imagined quiet prairie scene into fragments of color like pieces of stained glass. I said nothing. I made no outcry. I was reminded of the beating Grandma had given me with Granddaddy's razor strap; but I could not imagine the feeling that must have been like drowning. I had seen my mother angry and seen her whip with the switches, but I had never seen water used as punishment before.

I can't remember what we had for lunch, but I know that whatever it was it sat like a heavy lump in my mouth. I drank the Kool Aid to force it down. I did not want my mother to know how this had disturbed me. I don't remember much of what we did after this. I felt so sorry for my little brother, but there was no way to comfort him or to let him know. All of us were quiet. No one teased Ronald about his new form of punishment.

During the night, the lantern light Mama left burning for my stepfather, cast eerie shadows. I awakened to dogs barking and fighting in the Samuel's courtyard. The sound was more frightening be-

296

cause the fierceness did not stop. My brothers and little sister did not wake up. They all slept undisturbed. I tossed and turned hoping someone would stop the dogs from fighting. Finally it was still and I drifted off to sleep.

The next morning, as I looked out the window to the yard next door, where the commotion had taken place, I saw a red, long haired dog lying dead in the courtyard. Blood smeared the dry dust.

That day Ronald "minded." He never left the yard, but pitched stones and played marbles. We ate the rest of the blackberry cobbler that Mama had made from the blackberries we had picked.

27

Mama's Church

From the time Mama joined the local Pentecostal Church, the talk was joyous and positive as she and her friends spoke of being "saved" and having "received the Holy Ghost in the name of Christ Jesus." Grandma called these people an "ignorant bunch of Holy Rollers."

"It's just like your mama to join some ignorant church like that," she said one day. "Screamin' and yellin'. Jesus wasn't loud and ignorant like that. He didn't run around hollerin' at the top of his lungs. That's so silly."

When she started wearing long dresses and stockings, no matter how hot the weather, Mama told me, "Saints don't like you showin' yourself."

The members of the church were referred to as saints, Sisters and brothers. The older leaders were bishops, elders and mothers. Anyone not a member of the church was a "sinner or heathen" who was "going straight to hell to burn with the devil."

The church was next door on the second floor of Mr. Samuel's building. The Samuels were also members and services were held on Wednesday evenings and Sundays. Mama let us go with her one Wednesday night. This was my first time to attend a Pentecostal Church.

"Now, I don't want you cuttin' up in Church," Mama warned Ronald. "Do you hear me?"

"Yes, Mama," he said.

"Sweetpea, you watch Lillian and if she gets tired take her home and put her to bed."

We climbed the open, wooden staircase to the room where the church services were held.

Mrs. Samuels, an enormous, dark-skinned woman with a gold crown on her front tooth, huffed and puffed up the steps in front of us. I was intrigued with the enormity of her rear end which, when she

298

walked or rather shuffled, rose up pulling her long dress with it. It moved up first on the right side then up on the left. She needed two seats to support her frame, but the church, being a large, plain but clean room, had only low unpainted, wooden benches.

Mrs. Samuels, or "Mother Samuels" as she was called, sat up front while the parishioners, one by one, paid their respects. She sat smiling and nodding like some great, dark queen.

"How do Mother Samuels."

"How do, Sister Hocker."

"How're you, Mother? Bless your heart, honey," Mama purred.

"How do, Sister Price. See you brought the young'uns tonight."

Mother Samuels did not have any children and children kept their distance when she was near.

"Yes, Ma'm, Mother," Mama answered.

"Don't let them make no fuss in the Church, Sister Price."

"Oh, no, Mother. I won't let them do nothin' wrong. Don't worry yourself about that, honey."

I held Lillian's hand tightly and inched onto the last bench, pulling her close beside me. My legs itched from where I had been bitten by some of the mosquitoes that had been missed by my mother's spraying. From where I sat I could see Sister and Elder Hocker who were sitting next to my mother. Elder Hocker was an extremely thin male, pale-skinned and balding. His skin was pulled tightly over his cheekbones and around the neck. He looked more like a skeleten than a human. He had a wisp of a mustache, mixed with gray hair. Both he and Sister Hocker were like the land around their house, dry, hard and open.

Sister Hocker had a softness to her eyes and face and always had a faint smile on her transparent lips. As I watched her, I felt at peace myself, and some of the anxiety I had upon entering the church subsided. Sister Hocker's face was calm and quiet; but this spell was soon broken as Brother Samuels, in his white shirt, dark pants and vest with his gold pocket watch gleaming from its chain, opened the meeting with a song.

Rock of Ages, he sang in a deep, melodious voice which I would never have attributed to this pompous man. *Cleft for me*, he continued.

A thin voice, from the audience joined in, and then another and another until at last my mother's voice, more fervent than the rest, took over the singing. It was a beautiful piece. I was enthralled with the words, especially the word, "cleft" which I continued to turn over and over again in my mind. I had never heard that word before.

Let me hide myself in thee, Brother Samuels intoned. *Let the water and the blood…*

The poetry of the song reminded me of my Uncle Bobby's recitation, of the poem, *Trees*, when one day he took me for a walk at a very early age. It was beautiful and quiet.

Mother Hocker sat with her eyes closed, face lifted up towards the ceiling. Brother Samuels continued singing until a little dark man said, "Amen. Sing it, Brother."

This fed the fervor of the choristers. One lady who was my mother's size, plump but not huge like Mother Samuels, started to shout, "Hallelujah! Praise his Holy Name!"

Then another lady and a man started to shout. Finally my mother could be heard over all the others.

"Yes, Lord! Praise your name, Jesus! Yes, Jeeesus!" Mama shut her eyes and pulled her lips tightly over her teeth saying, "My, My, My."

Tears streamed down her face. She wiped them away with her fingers. I, too, wanted to cry because my mother was crying. The tears welled up in my eyes, but stayed poised on the rims. My nose burned and tingled, but I didn't cry. The tears went away.

Mr. Samuels ended his song to a chorus of "Amen!" and "Bless you Brother!"

"The Lord sho' give you a voice, Brother Samuels."

"Let the Church say "Amen"" a man called out.

All the members said, "Amen."

An Elder got down on one knee. With a hand under the chin of his bowed head, he started to pray. Ronald giggled. Sonny tapped him on the head. Ronald tapped him back. Sonny "frogged" him on the arm, i.e., made a fist with the thumb sticking out so that when he hit him the thumb dug into his arm.

"Owwww!" Ronald yelled.

Mama's head jerked around. She stared directly at Ronald, her eyes black with annoyance. I put my hand on Ronald's arm and whispered, "Ronald, come sit over here, next to me."

"Lord," the man on his knees praying wailed. "We come her'uh tonight, yo' chilrins of sufferin'."

I was interested in how the pronunciation of words varied. It was like a different language. I had heard Mrs. Adams call "children," "chillerings" and now the word was "chilrins."

"Yes, lord. We come befo' yuh tired and weereh, havin' no place to turn."

The congregation interrupted with "Amen!"

The prayer filled the room as the Elder's voice rose, then fell, ebbed and flowed like a great tidal wave of grief. Then, to my surprise, sister Hocker jumped straight up off the bench where she was sitting. She held her arms stiffly at her sides. She did not utter a sound, but just jumped up and down in rapid successions, eyes closed and without expression on her face.

Before any of the members could move, she was in the aisle. They rushed to push the benches away so she wouldn't trip over any of them. Then, just as suddenly as she had jumped up, she sat down.

The congregation quieted as the sermon was given. It was very long. Then, it was time for more singing and the collection plate to be passed. This time, a lady started the singing and accompanied herself with what I later learned was a tambourine. It made a beautiful sound which came from tiny, metal cymbals that danced together as she beat the center and sides of the instrument with the heel of her hand.

My baby sister had fallen asleep. I slowly awakened her as we prepared to leave.

The service was over. Mama's church friends wandered over to greet us and tell us what good "chilrin" we had been.

When we arrived home and were preparing for bed, my mother said, "When the Spirit of the Lord hits you, you feel so happy that it just sweeps you right off your feet. You feel light as a feather and filled with the Holy Ghost."

I felt that the congregation and the sermon focused on troubles, worry, and sorrow as if the weight of the world was brought to church to be lifted.

Later that night, I fell asleep thinking about the word "cleft" and remembered the change that had come over Sister Hocker as she jumped up and down dancing as she shouted.

Each person had a different way of expressing their religious fervor. Mama said they were filled with the "Holy Ghost." I really wondered about this. The only other ghost that I knew about were the ones I had seen in scary movies and I could not conceive of any of them being Holy. The Pentacostal Church's Holy Ghost made people happy.

28

My Visit Ends

My visit with my mother was over. She washed and ironed my clothes getting them ready for my return home. Perspiration poured from her face as she drank lemonade to keep cool. The flat iron had to sit on top of the circular, metal segments of the big iron wood-burning kitchen stove. There was a metal handle that fit into a hole in each section. This allowed her to remove the round piece and put more kindling or coal in to keep the fire going.

She went back and forth keeping the iron hot enough to press my clothes. Mama never drank from a glass. She always saved a large empty Miracle Whip jar into which she poured lemonade or Kool Aid. She kept her drink cool by chipping off pieces of ice from the block kept in the corner ice box.

I had made a few friends. One was Ida Lee, a tall, fair-skinned girl who lived down the street from Mama's apartment. On our other trips to pick blackberries, she began to join us. She was a quiet girl, but we got along very well. I had grown tired of my rambunctious younger brothers. We all knew it was time for me to go when we began fighting.

"Mama, Sweetpea hit me," Ronald cried.

"Mama, Sonny frogged me," I cried back.

"Stop that now!" Mama cried, too. She whined in despair at so much fighting.

The ride back to Walnut Hills from the sub-division was long and tedious but oh, such a welcome trip for me. Once I stepped off the bus at the familiar corner of Lincoln and the Victory Parkway, I ran ahead of my mother. I felt the thrill of having returned to very familiar territory. I was back in the city. I was home.

I arrived in the apartment ahead of my mother. She came in behind me laughing.

"She's faster than a deer. I never could run like that. Lord have mercy."

Granddaddy laughed with her as we hugged. Grandma stood carefully examining me.

"You sure did get black! Whose child are you?" She asked.

My mother quickly began to apologize.

"She's just been out in the sun everyday, playin' and havin' a good time."

Granddaddy laughed harder. "Just like you when you was little. Ain't that right, Eckey?"

"Yes, goodness. You couldn't keep me in the house in good weather."

Mama laughed like Granddaddy, but I knew that Mama did not get black like me. I hoped that I hadn't gotten as black as Mike and Molly Martin.

I gave my mother a big hug before she left. I said, "Thanks for my summer vacation, Mama."

My mother seemed happy to have had me visit as she looked at me with a smile on her face, but she seemed more subdued and more quiet than she had been when we arrived. She returned my hug and said, "Goodbye, Sweetie."

The next morning after breakfast, I ran up front to watch the buses and cars going up and down our paved Lincoln Avenue. I just wanted to see the telephone poles and street lights that would give our street its light at night. I wanted to see the neighbors.

Even old Mr. Tate smiled and asked, "How was your vacation in the country?"

"Fine," I answered, but still, I kept my distance.

I realized that although everything was the same, it seemed different somehow. I felt that the trees and the sky here were different from the sub-division. The morning air was cooler and the sun seemed paler. I couldn't figure it out. It was all the same, but a little different.

304

Outside may have seemed different, but inside the apartment things were the same.

"Look at your knees," Grandma fussed. "all skinned up and full of pus. I knew your mammy wouldn't take care of you."

I worried about the sores on my knees. Grandma took me to General Hospital Clinic right away. "Impetigo," the doctor said. He gave Grandma a particular salve to use everyday. Grandma got busy scrubbing my legs as she cleaned the infected areas. She put peroxide on the sores and after the fizzing stopped, she applied the honey colored salve and placed a large bandage over them.

"I don't want you goin' back to school all scarred up," she said.

29

As Summer Comes to a Close

I did not want my summer to end without spending one last weekend, before the beginning of school, with my cousins.

I was able to walk the long distance to their house all by myself. This made me feel very grown up and a little full of myself. Aunt Irene let us make our own supper on Friday nights when she and Uncle Francis had their nights out. We never varied what we chose to eat. It was always Franco American Spaghetti and Kahn's Franks. Because we had prepared our own meal, it tasted especially delicious.

Even though they had moved to Fredonia Avenue, Uncle Francis still claimed the living room as his place of retreat. His chair sat next to the radio and on Saturday and Sunday nights he expected us to be perfectly quiet while he listened to his favorite programs.

Mitzi and Joan took after Uncle Francis. They all loved really scary movies and radio programs at night. I did not. Uncle Francis still had his *True Detective* magazines in basket on the floor next to his chair, like he did when they lived on Lincoln Avenue.

My cousins and I had lots of fun during the day. In the back yard of their second floor apartment was a very long cement block wall separating their unit from the property behind them. Inside the open space of the blocks wasps were building their nests. We loved making the wasps mad.

Aunt Irene had gotten us lots of balloons to play with. These we filled with water from the kitchen sink and carried them down the outside stairs to the back yard. At the back edge of the building, we waited until the nests seemed quiet. Then, we walked stealthily across the grassy area to the dark, open holes. Then we released the pressure on the tip of the balloons and let the water spray into the nests. We ran like the wind to get away from the enraged wasps flying out of the nests and after us.

We headed for the stairs right behind each other trying to be the first to get into the apartment. This was some of the most fun that we had, until one of us got stung. Mitzi was the one who sustained the most stings. She was the slowest of the three of us. I was the fastest because I was the tallest, skinniest and oldest.

I found Sunday nights to be the worst time of all. Uncle Francis wanted us in bed at dark, because he was turning out all the lights as he prepared to listen to his favorite radio broadcast, *The Hermit's Cave*.

We children had our baths and got in bed. I got far under the covers. Mitzi and Joan were not afraid. When the *Hermit's Cave* came on, a man sounding very old and decrepit had a scary laugh. He said, Hee! *Hee! Hee! Turn out the lights. Turn them out. Turn them all out.*

Then came the sound of a door creaking as it opened. I was terrified long before the story began. I sweated under the covers and held my fingers in my ears to shut out the sound. My cousins laughed at me for being such a "scaredy cat."

Before I was to leave the next day, I was determined to reassert my size, age and authority over my cousins.

Mitzi and I had gotten into a squabble over who could hit the ball the longest in a Hi-Li competition. She missed after hitting the ball twenty-one times. When it was my turn, I snatched the paddle from her and started hitting the ball. When I passed twenty-one, Mitzi got angry. Finally, at thirty-one, I missed.

"See, I told you I could beat you," I announced triumphantly.

"You always cheat," she said accusatorially.

"I did not cheat!" I said.

"You did, too! You didn't count right."

Angry, I threw the paddle accusing Mitzi of cheating because she was mad. The paddle hit the side of the bed and split in half.

"You broke my Hi-Li," Mitzi had wailed.

She lashed out to hit me. I hit her. When she tried to hit me again, I dodged, but not in time to miss her long fingernails that caught me on my right cheek very close to my eye. The fight ended when Mitzi ran into the bathroom and locked the door to get away from me.

When I got home, Aunt Hookey took me to the window so that she could take a closer look at the injury. She put Mercurochrome on it, but a week passed and it had not healed. School was about to begin and Aunt Hookey was concerned. That's when Grandma was given the name of a doctor whose office was at Peebles Corner where I was to go for treatment.

Peebles Corner was a shopping mecca but not as large nor as far away as downtown Cincinnati. My new doctor's name was Dr. Katz. He was the first doctor I had seen who did not have his office at General Hospital.

On that first visit Dr. Katz checked the wound and said, "This will heal, but it might take awhile for any scar to go away."

He gave Grandma a new salve to use which was different from the one she was using for my knees and said he would see us weekly until the wound healed.

Dr. Katz was a gentle man who was friendly as well. He turned to me before we left and said, "The next time you get into a fight with your cousin, make sure she's wearing gloves."

We all laughed as Grandma and I left for home.

PART IV

SOME THINGS ABOUT THE 1940s
Age 7-8

1

The Year of Third Grade

I entered third grade with scarred knees and an infected right cheek. The room assignment system had changed. If a student was placed in the "Y" Group it meant they were more advanced. If the student was placed in the "X" Group it meant that student was working at grade level or just below. This was confusing as it was just the opposite of what we knew from our second grade experience. There was still a "dumb class" for those totally unable to work at grade level.

At first I was confused when I was switched to the "Y" Group, and was quite concerned until I realized that Barbara Reichert and Jon Campbell were in my group. Cornelious Wilson, my Lincoln Avenue playmate, was upset because he was now in the "X" Group.

The boys in the class teased Cornelious, calling him a "Mama's Boy" because his mother still walked him to school. He was among the best dressed of the boys and had the best pencil boxes. His box contained fancy sharpeners, rulers and protractors. He was always well supplied with paper. These added amenities made Cornelious an even greater target for ridicule.

When he and I passed in the hallway, Cornelious gave me faint grins. I knew he was unhappy but this did not last long. By the end of the first marking period he was sent to the "Y" Group. Cornelious was very happy.

I liked Cornelious and that changed to "I love you" in notes we wrote back and forth. But that changed when Cornelious was no longer interested in my tomboy type girl with scarred knees, which I clearly was. He began to like the more "girl" looking girls. The fat legs of the white girls became the rage. Many of them had plump legs with heavy calves like ballet dancers. Girls having the beginning looks of hips also drew the attention of the boys. When these girls wore pleated skirts, the pleats danced when they walked. None of these girls were skinny like me. Eighth grade girls got lots of attention.

In third grade penmanship grew even more important than before. Daily practice of ovals and mountains tediously begun in the second grade, now gave way to writing class assignments in long hand or cursive, as it was called. There were also assignments graded on penmanship alone.

During this time Barbara Reichart was having trouble with her cursive; so I gave her penmanship lessons and extra homework at night to be turned in to me the next day. Barbara paid me five cents a day for helping her. The fact that she was improving in her penmanship increased my confidence in my own penmanship ability. The magical world that appeared to me when I, at age four, and for the first time had stolen a peek at my Aunt Lockey Jane's high school notebook class notes. These were written in long hand and took my breath away. Now I could duplicate those letters. I could make my own magic.

That year a new colored girl came to Hoffman. Her name was Peggy Ann Howard. Peggy Ann's father owned the pool hall on Gilbert Avenue, not far from the Wine Bar where my aunts went on occasion for their entertainment. Peggy Ann's mother and father had her late in life. They had one other child, a daughter, who was married.

Anyone new in the class always received careful scrutiny and was the focus of attention. Peggy Ann was no exception. Her mother and married sister dressed her like a princess and she always had lots of money in her purse and ate in the cafeteria every day. She had her hair straightened and curled each week and she wore barrettes or satin ribbons that matched her dresses.

Peggy Ann had straight up and down legs that were fat, like those of the white girls. Cornelious fell in love with Peggy Ann. That year for Christmas, Peggy Ann received a brown wool coat with a genuine mink collar. No one, white or colored had such an extravagant gift. The girls were all envious. It was not long before Peggy Ann fell in love with Cornelious. I was very disappointed.

2

Great Great Aunt Lucy

The same year that Peggy Ann Howard wore her mink-collared coat to school, Grandma's Aunt Lucy came to visit. She was the sister of Grandma's father and mother of her cousin El. El was short for Ellen. She was really my great, great Aunt Lucy.

When Uncle Bobby had his spells and ran away from home, and before having to be returned to Longview State Hospital, he always went to Cousin El's. It was her son Charles, the undertaker, who always brought him back.

Grandma fussed to Granddaddy one night at supper, "El just wants to get Aunt Lucy out of her hair and put her off on me."

Granddaddy didn't say anything.

A week or so later I was swinging around the telephone pole near Mr. Tate's house, when Charles drove up in his big black car with Aunt Lucy. I ran to greet them.

Charles smiled and gave me a firm hug. Aunt Lucy, who was staring straight ahead, sat waiting in the front seat. She had on a luxurious black hat with a colorful feather curved around near her right ear. A veil softly hung from the crown and covered the upper half of her face leaving only the bottom tip of her nose, her mouth and chin clear.

Cousin Charles, who was always dressed up when I saw him, opened the door for Grandma's Aunt Lucy and with great gentleness, helped her out. He was like a chauffeur opening the door for some grand lady. Aunt Lucy was a fragile, elegantly clothed lady not much taller than me. She was eighty years old.

"Sweetpea, can you help Aunt Lucy down to Cousin Lillian's?" Charles asked.

I carefully supported my great great Aunt Lucy, as we walked towards the cement stairs.

"You're a pretty little thing," she said.

311

Her voice was soft and it quivered. She had perfect diction like a lady. This was the first time that I could remember anyone other than Uncle Bobby calling me "pretty." She smiled at me. I could see that she was wearing jeweled earrings that sparkled in the light as we walked. Aunt Lucy also wore lipstick. Grandma never wore lipstick. I thought Aunt Lucy was a delicate, aging flower. I felt very special as I helped her along the cracking sidewalk and down the stairs. Grandma waited for us at the living room door.

It seemed like an eternity before I finally maneuvered Aunt Lucy into our apartment. She kept talking to me in her soft quiet voice the entire length of our walk. I learned to move slowly. I worried that if Aunt Lucy so much as stepped on the cracked cement, she might break her foot or leg. I easily ran and hopped over this same broken sidewalk every day.

Granddaddy helped Charles bring in Aunt Lucy's trunk and suitcases. It appeared that Aunt Lucy planned to stay a very long time. I had never seen a trunk before. A place was made for her in the living room and her trunk was put in the hallway closet near the bathroom.

"Sweetpea will make the sofa down for you at night, Aunt Lucy," Grandma said. "So you can sleep here in the living room."

"That will suit me just fine, Lillian," Aunt Lucy replied, "But I'm not ready to retire just yet."

Charles didn't take off his coat and hat. He said that he had to get back to Lexington. I was glad when he left, for I could then help Aunt Lucy all by myself.

I helped her take off her things and put them away. She patted and folded each piece carefully and tenderly before placing them in her trunk. She wrapped her luxurious hat in tissue paper and had it placed on the closet shelf. She said she had a house dress in her trunk. I got this out for her.

"This helps me keep my nice dresses nice," she smiled.

"Grandma makes me take off my good school clothes and change into everyday clothes after school," I informed Aunt Lucy.

312

As Aunt Lucy took her house dress from me, I saw that under the gloves she had on in the car, she had red polish on her fingernails. Several rings glistened on the fingers of her left and right hands. I was unaccustomed to such elegance in dress and manners.

Every day when I came in from school, Aunt Lucy waited for me in a crisp, clean, house dress. Then she sat in the rocking chair by the pot-bellied stove to keep warm, a woolen shawl draped around her narrow shoulders. She kept her eye on the door as if she was looking for company. Aunt Lucy always talked with me about my day at school.

After supper Aunt Lucy helped me with the dishes. When we did the dishes, I carried the tea kettle from the stove to the sink and poured the boiling water into the dishpan. Aunt Lucy washed the dishes and I dried them.

She never wanted to add any cold water. Instead, she let the bar of Ivory Soap float in the steaming dishwater while she daintily took the tip end of the dish rag and dipped it up and down to make suds. The soap didn't last as long because it melted in such hot water. Grandma didn't like this. She said Aunt Lucy was "wastin' soap."

The plate and saucers lay on the bottom of the dishpan, soaking in the hot, sudsy water while Aunt Lucy kept dipping. As the dish rag got hotter, Aunt Lucy pursed her lips, inhaled and exhaled breaths of air in such quick succession that she made shrill, whistling sounds. This also irritated Grandma.

"Aunt Lucy," she exclaimed from her bedroom, "Why don't you put some cold water in the dishpan? You'll burn yourself and it wastes the soap."

Aunt Lucy gave her standard reply, "No, Lillian, you do your sewing and I'll do these dishes. Cold water will not kill the germs."

Aunt Lucy kept dipping the dish rag while the dishes rested in the boiling water. Her hands never touched the bottom of the pan; were never immersed in the water. I waited patiently for each for plate, cup, and saucer. Knives, forks, and spoons came out last as Aunt Lucy emptied the water into the sink.

After the dishes were completed Aunt Lucy joined Granddaddy in the living room until bedtime. Grandma didn't smile much while Aunt Lucy was with us. As Aunt Lucy's stay stretched into spring, Grandma began to openly and vociferously air her complaints. She complained that Aunt Lucy took too long putting her hair up at night.

"Why do you have to do all that primping?" Grandma asked. "You're not goin' nowhere."

"Oh, Lillian, someone might come in. I want to look presentable."

Grandma wore her hair the same way every day. Each morning she parted her hair in the middle, brushed then rolled each long section, twisted it around; and again rolled it up into a giant ball which she pinned to her head with a large, tortoise shell hair pin. Then she repeated the ritual on the other side. At night, she removed the pins, oiled and brushed her hair then made two plaits that hung down her back.

Grandma thought Aunt Lucy's preparations showed too much vanity. Soon she added new complaints.

"I don't have time to fix breakfast exactly like you'd like it. I have my work to do. This ain't El's house. I don't have nobody around here helpin' me," Grandma fumed.

One night, in front of Aunt Lucy, she told Granddaddy, "She wants to be treated like a queen. Her hair has to be fixed just so and her nails done. And she's getting' so finicky about her food."

At those times Aunt Lucy sat quietly in the rocking chair in my room while I did my homework. I felt sorry for Aunt Lucy. She never said a word. She never raised her voice. She never defended herself against any of the harsh things Grandma continued to say about her.

The time arrived when Aunt Lucy got ready to return to Lexington. Grandma helped her pack. Aunt Lucy had not worn any of her special dresses while she lived with us. She did wear one when she left.

I had tears in my eyes when Cousin Charles came to get Aunt Lucy. She kissed me lightly on the cheek and patted my shoulder with

314

her delicate, aging hands. As I helped her out the door, she held tightly to my hand. When Aunt Lucy let go, I looked into my palm. There was a gold ring with a tiny red stone. It was a real ruby. She smiled at me and said, "Don't tell anybody."

Aunt Lucy was gone. At school I showed off the real, ruby ring that she had given me. It was just as nice if not better than Peggy Ann Howard's mink, collared coat.

One day at school, while washing my hands after having used the lavatory, I removed the ruby ring from my little finger where I wore it. In my rush to get back to class, I left the ring on the basin. Horrified at the discovery and knowing that there was no one in the restroom when I was there, I told my teacher. She allowed me to go back to get it. When I got there it was gone. It was the saddest that I had felt in a long time. I was devastated.

Later I got up the courage to tell Grandma about Aunt Lucy having given me the ring and that I had lost it. I had tears in my eyes as I told her.

Grandma said, "Aunt Lucy didn't have no business givin' you nothin' that nice anyway. You don't know how to take care of good things."

3

Some Wounds Heal

The infection on my knees from summer in the country healed shortly after I entered third grade. The infection on my face caused by a fingernail scratch, from the fight with my Cousin Mitzi, took much longer. Grandma continued to take me to Dr. Katz's office every Monday after school.

Sometimes we walked to Chapel Street and Victory Parkway where we caught the streetcar to Peebles Corner. Dr. Katz's office was on the second floor of a building across the street from the Lindner Ice Cream store. Dr. Katz had given Grandma a supply of white cream to use on my injured cheek. This came in a round, metal container.

Finally, Dr. Katz said, "This has healed nicely. The infection is all gone."

He held my face under an examining light. He had a slight smile on his face this time.

"It's a good thing you didn't catch those nails in your eye. They came very close, but all is well now. It still might take awhile for the scar to go away, but as for now you've made your last visit."

Then Dr. Katz reached into a big jar he kept near his desk and removed a lollypop and handed it to me. "This is for being such a good patient." He smiled. "And don't forget what I told you when you first came to see me. Next time you get into a fight with your cousin, make sure she's wearing gloves."

As Grandma and I walked from Dr. Katz's office, Grandma said, "It's a shame your face will be scarred like that."

This final visit to Dr. Katz came on my eighth birthday and I was much more interested in that than the scar on my face.

"We need to hurry back so we can finish your birthday cake," Grandma said.

We both walked hurriedly to catch the streetcar home. We did not take time to look in the store windows or go to Woolworth's, as we usually did.

Finally, we got off the streetcar and started walking the two blocks home. As we walked, Grandma looked at me with a grin on her face. This seemed odd to me as Grandma did not smile very often.

"I'm not supposed to tell you," she said, "but when we get home there's goin' to be a surprise party for you. Ruth, Joanne and some of your other girlfriends are goin' to be there," she said.

I was speechless and immediately full of excitement. It was to be my first, real birthday party where my friends were invited. At other times it would be my cousins and Aunt Irene or Aunt Hookey, Aunt Lockey Jane and Grandma and Granddaddy.

"A Party for me!? Oh, Goody!"

"Now, you act surprised because I wasn't supposed to tell you," Grandma announced.

"I won't tell," I said.

When we opened the door, my friends were there waiting for me in the living room.

"Surprise! Surprise!" Everybody shouted.

I pretended to be surprised. Aunt Hookey, who had made all of the arrangements and had the idea to make it a surprise party, had gotten my friends from school to keep the secret for the entire day. They had. No one knew that it was Grandma who gave the secret away and that I was pretending to be surprised.

The party was still a lot of fun even though Grandma had forewarned me.

It was not long after my eighth birthday when Grandma had new names that she added to the list of the ones that she called me when she was angry with me. In addition to my being a "little black bastard," the new words were that I was an "ungrateful wimp" and "a parasite sucking the life's blood out of her."

I thought about "Dracula" movies. I could see Dracula's long fangs imbedded in a victim's throat. I knew that Dracula drained the "living" of their blood. I wondered if Dracula was a parasite.

One night after work, as Granddaddy sat at the kitchen table rubbing lemon peelings over his hands to remove the stains that were deep in cuts and grooves from his tinsmith work, I asked, "Granddaddy, what's a parasite?"

Before he could answer, Grandma said, "It's what you are. It's a thing that attaches itself to something and feeds off of it."

I was horrified at what I took to be Grandma's description of me. I could not conceive of being a parasite.

"Your grandmammy's right," Granddaddy chuckled. "And she ought to know."

Granddaddy threw the dirty lemon peelings in the trash and headed for the living room and his evening paper.

"What do you mean, 'and I ought to know'?"

Grandma followed him, hands on her hips, glowering at Granddaddy.

"Just teasin' you, old gal." Granddaddy laughed in earnest this time.

"Well, you just better be," Grandma said. "After all the work I do around here with no thanks and no help." She looked at me.

Granddaddy got up and hugged Grandma, but Grandma poked her mouth out and complained more.

After getting this explanation of a "parasite," I made some significant decisions for myself. From the time I could remember, whenever Grandma called me those bad names I would always cry. Now I decided that I would not cry anymore, no matter what she said and no matter how angry she got. I was never going to let her hurt me with those bad words again!

I held back every tear until I got to the point when I didn't have to hold them back anymore. I just wasn't bothered by Grandma and what she said. I also decided that when school was out and it was vacation time, I was going to take a vacation from all school work and from my household chores, like washing dishes and sweeping the floors.

These decisions marked the beginning of a full scale war between me and Grandma. Her assaults met my strong resistance. The hostility in me took the form of "sassing" or "mouthing back" as Grandma called it.

When Granddaddy came home from work he asked me, "What you been doin' all day?"

Before I could answer, "Playing," Grandma said, "Mouthin' back at me word for word, the little smart alecky thing. She's goin' to be just like her old hard-headed Mammy."

Grandma threatened to hit me in the mouth if I didn't stop sassing back. She never did. She said that she was going to knock me in the corner, but she never did. When her only friend Laura Haskins, who lived in Lockland, visited us, Grandma complained to her how bad I had become and how I sassed her like I was grown after all the good she did for me.

Mrs. Haskins looked at me in disbelief. Before, she gave me dolls and nice gifts at Christmas, but the Christmas when I was eight and had made my decisions, she did not give me any gifts. After turning Mrs. Haskins against me, Grandma got mad at her for not continuing to be nice to me. Mrs. Haskins thought she was being supportive of her friend. Children were never to be "impudent" as she called it.

Because she couldn't make me cry anymore, Grandma said I was mean and cruel like Aunt Hookey. I pretended that I didn't care.

Aunt Hookey told Grandma, "I don't know what's come over her. She needs to be popped on her behind. You'd pop us on our behinds when we were little, but you let her get away with murder."

Aunt Hookey had never heard any of the names that Grandma called me when no one was around. She never knew how those words had hurt me even when I didn't know what they meant.

Aunt Hookey did not know that I had decided that Grandma would never be able to make me cry ever again.

4

War

Sunday, December 7, 1941, I was bored. Grandma and Grand-daddy were subdued and calm after their normal Saturday lunch which always made them quiet on Sunday. I had finished reading the *Katzen-jammer Kids*, *Blondie* and *Lil' Abner* in the Sunday comics. I could not play with Ruth because it was Sunday.

Ann, who had turned fourteen, said that she was too grown up to play with little kids. She meant she had her "period." Ann now wore light, pink lipstick. Granddaddy said that the lipstick made her mouth look like a baboon's behind. This reminded me of how Aunt Irene and Aunt Hookey laughed at the baboons' behinds when, on our school's Zoo Day, we stopped by their area at the Cincinnati Zoo.

With nowhere to go and nothing to do, I decided to visit the Bells. The steps had finally been repaired so I could take them up to the next floor and from there take the second flight of stairs to the Bells apartment.

Mrs. Bell was in the kitchen preparing dinner.

"Hello, Sweetpea," she said cheerfully.

I noticed that she was in her work uniform.

"There's nobody home but me. You can come in if you want to."

I watched Mrs. Bell as she pulled a plump, brown, chicken from the oven. She dipped into the drippings with a large metal spoon and poured this over the chicken.

"Where's Christine?" I inquired.

"She took the baby out to get some air. She'll be back soon."

Just before Christine was to graduate from Withrow High School she got pregnant and had a baby boy. She endured a lot of hostility and negative comments about having a baby without being married. Mrs. Bell was not mean to Christine like Grandma was to my mother.

"Where's Frank?" I asked.

"Only the Good Lord knows where that Frank is. I don't think he even came home last night."

Mrs. Bell finished basting the chicken, slid it back into the oven and closed the oven door. She turned the knob to regulate the oven's heat then sighed. "There, that'll be done before I leave for work."

I could not remember a time when I saw Mrs. Bell sitting down. Whenever she was at home, she was either cleaning, washing, ironing or cooking. When she went out, it was when she was on her way to work or on her way to shop.

Mrs. Bell talked very fast as she worked, so I had learned to listen carefully.

"Have you eaten lunch yet?"

"Yes, M'am."

"I have some little cakes. Would you like some? I brought them home last night from the party Mayo's did."

I was hoping Mrs. Bell had some of her little Petit Fours. That was one of the main reasons I liked going to the Bell's apartment.

"Here, take one of these. You can have more, but I don't want you to eat so many you'll spoil your dinner. Mrs. Corbin might blame me."

Mrs. Bell took a box from the top of her ice box. Inside were the beautiful petit fours, the little cakes with tiny, colorful flowers on top. The icing covered the entire square. It was very hard for me to choose. I very carefully removed one with white icing and a tiny red, icing flower and a small, green leaf on top.

"Grandma was taking a nap when I left, Mrs. Bell, so I don't think we'll be eating dinner for a long time."

"Oh, well then, why don't you take two? If you promise me that you'll be very careful, you can eat in the living room. You can't stay long though because I have to leave for work in a little while. But if Christine gets back before I have to leave, you can stay as long as you want."

Mrs. Bell gave me a large paper napkin. I walked slowly through their bedroom and into the living room. This was my favorite place since they had moved from the front apartment where Frank could jump over the porch railing to the yard below.

I liked sitting on the sofa near the window which looked down into the back yard. It was the only place that I could look down and see how the back yard looked from above. I was as high up as some of the top branches of the cottonwood tree. I could also see over the hedge-covered fence that separated our back yard from the yards of the houses behind us. These houses faced Chapel Street where we walked to get the streetcar.

This time, I didn't look down into the back yards of our neighbors. I was too busy relishing each bite of my petit fours. Mrs. Bell had turned on the radio to keep her company while she worked. That was the only sound as the sun streamed in from the window behind the sofa and the one near the arm of the sofa. Mrs. Bell's apartment had so much more light than we had in our apartment. That was another reason I liked going up there.

I was taking the last bite of the last petit four when the radio music stopped. An announcer's voice came in the middle of one of the songs. He said, "We interrupt this broadcast to bring you a special news report from the nation's capital."

I paid little attention. Sunday was like that. It was a quiet, slow day when people who had attended church had dinner and sat quietly listening to their radios or taking naps after a busy week. The interruption by the announcer seemed of little consequence to me as I wiped my hands on my napkin and decided that I would re-examine the scene from the window.

As I surveyed the section of the yard that displayed a particularly tangled group of vines and shrubs, the voice of our President, Franklin Delano Roosevelt, came through the radio.

"This day is a day that will live in infamy. This morning, the Japanese bombed Pearl Harbor. The Nation is at war."

I was stunned. War! At first, I thought that it wasn't really serious, but then sitting alone in the Bell's living room, I became very frightened. I moved off the sofa and without saying a word to Mrs. Bell, I ran down the back stairs as fast as I could to the safety of my own apartment.

What did this mean? Was there going to be fighting close by? Would we be killed? These were very scary questions indeed. At eight years of age, I knew no answers. I knew only that suddenly I was very, very scared.

Frank Bell was drafted into the Army and I learned a new word, "drafted." Walter Bell was already in the Navy when the War came. We were afraid that Walter would be killed. People in the Helena Apartments and the neighborhood talked about the war breaking out like it was the measles or the chickenpox.

Granddaddy sat glued to the radio at night to hear who was winning. He buried his nose in his evening paper to find out the latest information. It was about the Yanks, the Krauts (what people called the Germans), the Japs (what people called the Japanese) and another word that was unfamiliar and one I can't remember.

Granddaddy had never been to war. Grandma said that he was a "pantywaist."

"I ain't no 'pantywaist' neither, Sister," he told her. "I was too young for the first world war and I'm too old for this one. Had too many young'uns anyway."

He paused for a minute. Grandma made no reply. He continued making his defense, "Uncle Sam don't want no old codger like me. Uncle Sam needs young men."

Hoffman School and my class took on an entirely different atmosphere. "War" was on everybody's mind. We learned what to do in an air raid. The Woodburn Avenue Fire department siren signaled an air raid drill. We quietly but quickly lined up in double file, held hands and were ushered out of our classrooms to the cafeteria below. Curtains were drawn over the windows. Our teachers smiled to reassure us, but their lips were firmly held together and their eyes constantly darted over the area. They counted us to be sure we were all safely in line. Air Raid Wardens had decided that the cafeteria was the best place to shelter us, but warned us away from the windows.

The boys in our class went to war with crayons, chalk and pencils. Walls, windows, paper and any other solid surface became a battleground. Drawings resembling toothpicks with wings became airplanes dropping bombs on German ships at sea. Those same toothpicks became German planes being shot down by American planes. The iron cross was prominent on the tail of the plane going down.

Our comic book heroes and heroines took on the Axis. Plastic Man's arms stretched around the globe with his hands appearing on the opposite side, clutching terrified Japanese sailors and upending Japanese submarines.

Each Friday we bought Defense Stamps for ten cents each. These we put in a Stamp Book which, when completely filled, could be traded in for a twenty-five dollar war bond. For this, we only needed $18.75.

As the boys at school imitated fighting men, the girls imitated Veronica Lake. She had become a movie sensation with her shoulder-length, blonde hair which she wore seductively over one eye as she lured her Japanese captors to their death at the hands of Yank prisoners of War.

We brushed our hair to resemble this style. In the movie Veronica Lake sat in a chair, crossed her legs and slowly pulled her skirt up, little by little, until one of the Japanese guards noticed what she was doing. Once she had gotten the guard's attention, she quickly jerked her skirt down. Then, just as she had raised her skirt a considerable height, she jerked it down again. She repeated this scene until her captor was so overcome with lust that he left his post to go after her. It was at this point where she was being kissed by her captor that the leading man, who had been hiding behind a door, stepped out and killed the Japanese soldier.

This movie scene so fascinated us that we repeated it for weeks afterwards. I was playing after school at my friend Jo-Anne Jones' house. I played the part of Veronica Lake for the umpteenth time. I was wearing a cotton dress that Grandma had made. I carefully inched it up my, seductively, crossed legs and yanked it down over my knees when Jo-Ann, playing the part of the Japanese soldier, looked my way. When the climactic moment arrived, I yanked my dress so hard that it split, exposing a very bare and spindly knee cap. My friend Jo-Ann collapsed on the floor in laughter. For days afterward and much to my embarrassment, Jo-Ann repeated the story to our friends.

"Sweetpea's knees are so bony they poked right through and tore her dress."

The Veronica Lake scene became comic from then on. The War lost its most patriotic sex symbol and all because of my boney knees.

I tried to save face by informing my friends that the dress was an old one and that the material was wearing through. But I could never live down Jo-Ann's story no matter how hard I tried.

Walking the Victory Parkway on our way to school or other streets on our way to the movies, we began to notice tiny flags with a star in the center hanging inside the windows. People we did not know on Chapel Street had a flag in their window. We learned that they had a son who had been killed in the War. I worried about Walter and Frank Bell. They were the only people I, personally, knew who were in the war.

5

C.J. Parrish

When World War II started, Aunt Hookey finally got a job. She began working at the Wright's Airplane Factory near Lockland. I learned that she made sand cores for airplane engines. Her earnings from shift work were very good, the best money she had ever made. She paid Grandma generously for food and rent. Grandma was happy with all the money she was getting. Aunt Hookey bought me additonal winter clothing for school and I was allowed to eat lunch in the cafeteria every day.

Aunt Irene let my Cousin Mitzie have a "Vee" hairdo when she went to get her hair straightened. Grandma said the "Vee" made Mitzi look too grown up. Aunt Irene wore her hair in a Pompadour. This was a hairdo with the front section of hair, rolled and piled high then anchored with large, hairpins so that it stood up.

There was a new family that moved into the Helena Apartments. C. J. Parrish, his wife Juanita and their two young children, Michael four and Carolyn, a baby took an upstairs apartment near the Bells.

C. J. also worked at Wrights. He did not go to war like Frank and Walter Bell. I thought it was because he had "young'uns" like Granddaddy had that kept him out of the war. C.J. was short for Charles J. Parrish. We didn't know his middle name.

The Parrishes moved from Glendale, Ohio, a town close to Lockland and Wyoming. Grandma considered Glendale "country" and said that C.J. was a "country boy." C.J. made fast friends with my grandparents and spent a lot of time when he wasn't working visiting with them.

When C.J. moved, it was a stroll, a smooth and easy gait. He was "pigeon toed."

My aunts said this added to his attractiveness. He was very gregarious and always full of cheerful conversation. His entrance into our apartment changed our negative, often solemn, environment into anticipation of something adventuresome. I liked it when C.J. came.

Many times he brought son Michael with whom I would play despite the fact he was younger and a boy. Juanita, C.J.'s wife and their baby daughter seldom left their apartment, so we did not get to know them very well. Grandma and Granddaddy liked C.J. He called them "Mom" and "Pop."

Like my grandfather, C.J. was a large man. He was in his early twenties, tall with strong muscular arms and broad shoulders. He had a beautiful, reddish-brown coloring set off by gleaming, even white teeth and a finely sculpted head. He wore his hair cut very close to the scalp. He had high cheek bones and a smile that at once was disarming and captivating. C.J. appeared to know that he was very handsome. My aunts had their description of C.J. Like Aunt Crystal's boyfriend, Andrew Fant, C.J. was "sharp."

He loved to hunt. One day during hunting season he came to our apartment, gun in one hand, bloody newspaper with a dead rabbit inside, in the other. C.J. wore his tan hunter's cap, ear flaps waving as he walked into the kitchen where he found Grandma and Granddaddy. His hunting jacket had his license pinned to the back. This gave him permission to kill wild things.

"Hi Mom," he said flashing his great smile. "Hi Pop. I brought you a rabbit I caught today."

Grandma and Granddaddy loved fried rabbit. It was a treat for them. They gathered happily around the kitchen table where C.J. had tossed the newspaper with the rabbit. Grandma unwrapped the dead prey.

C. J. had not only shot and killed the rabbit that he brought Grandma and Granddaddy, but he had skinned and gutted the poor thing as well. There were no rabbit's feet that people could keep for good luck.

I found the sight of the skinned, reddish-gray rabbit, disgusting and disturbing. I thought of Peter Rabbit and the rabbit stories that I loved. To me, C.J. was worse than Mr. McGregor. I wondered why he liked killing. I wondered how any of them could eat the poor rabbits.

Fall was like that. It brought out the hunt and kill urge in a lot of the men we knew. Only Uncle Francis and Granddaddy did not go hunting.

328

"When you goin' huntin' with me, Pop?" C.J. asked Grand-daddy giving him his familiar slap on the back.

"Next time you go, I'm goin' with you," Granddaddy replied, choking on his cigarette smoke from the back slapping.

"You believe that lie, C.J?" Grandma asked. "He's been tellin' it for years."

I watched as Grandma spread the newspaper, on which the bloody rabbit was lying, and with a huge butcher knife, split the skinned rabbit down the middle, cut off the legs and put the rabbit parts in her blue, speckled granite pan. She took it to the kitchen sink and ran enough cold water to cover the rabbit parts. Then, she uncere-moniously sprinkled salt over it and let it float in the water.

Granddaddy watched then responded, "Oh you don't know what you're talkin' about. I am too goin' huntin'. Just you wait," Granddaddy responded.

I stood by the sink looking at the dead rabbit parts floating around in the salt water while C.J. and my grandparents laughed and talked.

Grandma turned the rabbit into a browned, gravied delicacy served with mashed potatoes and biscuits. I did not eat any of it. Grandma dismissed me as 'finicky.'

"She didn't use to eat chicken either," she said as if to apolo-gize to C.J.

My not eating rabbit did not affect their appetites in the least.

"I'm goin' fishin' and huntin' next year," Granddaddy contin-ued in his effort to convince C.J. of his sincerity.

C. J. left after sharing the meal. He took his gun and hunting jacket with him, satisfied that he had pleased my grandparents.

Another day, four year old Michael came to play. He had a deep husky voice for his age. It made us laugh just listening to him. He had, like his father, adopted our apartment as his second home. Mi-chael had a habit of breaking wind at will, laughing at each expulsion. This irritated Grandma. She yelled from her seat at the sewing machine, "Michael Parrish. Stop that pootin' in my house. Where're your manners, boy?"

Michael laughed and again broke wind. At that, Grandma pushed her chair away from her sewing machine, slammed her scissors down on the wooden, machine housing and went after Michael. He was too fast. He dashed out the door and up the back stairs before she could catch him.

Grandma had the last word. "Don't come back down here anymore, you nasty little thing," she shouted.

All you could hear was Michael's steps on the stairs and that husky laugh of his.

PHOTOGRAPH OF AUTHOR WITH COUSINS AND OTHER CHILDREN
WHEN THE PARRISHES LIVED IN THE HELENA APARTMENTS

L to R, Bottom Row: Michael Parrish 4, unknown holding C. J. Parrish's hunting dog. Cousin Joan Green, directly behind her, Cousin Mitzi Green. Back Row: Unknown, Author, Lula "Sweetpea," age 8 and Bessie, apartment neighbor. Photograph was taken in the backyard of the Helena Apartments, 1941

AUNT HOOKEY 1940s

C.J.'s visits became more frequent. He and my Aunt Hookey spent more time talking with each other. My aunt became less irritated with my grandmother and their constant arguing subsided. I thought my aunt was tired from her job which did not allow her a lot of time, and because she at last had enough money to have what she needed to help her parents.

The time came when Grandma grew suspicious of my Aunt and C.J.'s relationship She began to protest C.J.'s visits to our apartment.

"He's a married man and you have no business spending so much time with him."

"I'm not thinking about C.J. Parrish, Mama," Aunt Hookey assured Grandma.

Then Grandma turned her words on C.J., "C.J., we love you like a son, but if you're comin' here just to see Hookey, then I don't want you to come here anymore."

"I come to see my sweet Mom and Pop. You know that!" C.J. said hugging Grandma.

"Well, I'm tellin' you. It ain't right and I don't want no one thinkin' that I condone you comin' here to see Hookey. You're a married man with a wife and two little children; and that just ain't right. I'll have no part of it."

For awhile, C.J. brought Michael and Carolyn each time he came. But other people on Lincoln Avenue were beginning to notice. Gossip started that Aunt Hookey was trying to take C.J. away from his wife.

My friend, Ruth, who lived across the street, was not allowed to visit me. Her grandmother, Mrs. Taylor, spent hours on the front porch watching the comings and goings of people, especially those living in the Helena Apartments. She particularly seemed to be watching the Parrishes and the Corbin girls.

There was no mistake that Mrs. Taylor thought that the people living in the Helena Apartments were very common people, not in the same class as her family. She was always reluctant to let Ruth come over to play with me and insisted that we stay up front where she could watch us from across the street. Grandma never minded my going to Ruth's house to play. She said that I just wasn't to go too often and wear out my welcome.

Now, with the gossip about Aunt Hookey and C. J., my relationship with Ruth became strained because of Mrs. Taylor.

Aunt Hookey went out as usual one night. She was wearing a beautiful bright red dress. She and Aunt Lockey Jane walked down Lincoln Avenue to the corner of Ashland. There, they separated.

Aunt Hookey slipped into the back seat of a car driven by a friend of C.J.'s. The friend drove back up Lincoln and as they neared our apartment building she was seen sliding down to the floor as C.J. emerged from the apartment, dressed to go out on the town. He quickly got in the front seat with his friend and they drove off.

His wife, Carolyn, who was looking out of their upstairs front window, caught a glimpse of the figure, dressed in red that she had just seen walking down the street.

Mrs. Taylor started the neighborhood buzzing. Grandma was in agony and crying each morning.

"Everybody on the street is actin' like I'm runnin' a bad house," she moaned.

332

"I wasn't brought up to live like this. What have I ever done to deserve such a life? I think it's just terrible."

Even when there was no one home but me, and as she sat at the kitchen table drinking her coffee, Grandma would talk aloud and cry. When Aunt Hookey was there, she never missed an opportunity to make her point.

"Hookey, C.J. just can't come in here anymore. Do you hear me?" she shouted.

Aunt Hookey hummed and pretended to ignore her.

"You can try to ignore me all you want, but I mean it!" Grandma said.

I loved my aunt, but now she seemed more hardened and removed than ever.

"I don't give a damn about what that nosy Mrs. Taylor says, Mama. She doesn't run my life," Aunt Hookey shouted back.

Granddaddy agreed with Aunt Hookey, "You're right, honey. Don't pay your mammy no mind. She always worries about what other people think."

"I know you don't care, you old fool! What did you ever care about? You're not the one working for people around here. You're not the one who has to walk the street to get the groceries," Grandma cried.

She was pleading with them to ease the pain she was experiencing, but Granddaddy and Aunt Hookey ignored her.

"You don't know what you're talkin' about, Sister. I know lots of people around here. A lot more'n you think."

"Name one outside of Margaret, Mae Georgia and Doodlum!"

"Well, there's Mr. Tate and Papa Green," Granddaddy said timidly.

"Mr. Tate! Papa Green?" Grandma screamed at him. "When do you ever see them? You sure don't go to church......Papa Green! Mr. Tate!"

333

Grandma shook her head and continued to fuss.

Mrs. Taylor circulated a petition to run Aunt Hookey off of Lincoln Avenue.

Grandma was the first person to sign it.

Granddaddy said, "Piss on 'em!"

———————————

C. J. and Juanita separated and moved from the Helena Apartments. They later divorced. Aunt Hookey stayed, continuing her relationship with C.J. He gave Aunt Hookey a beautiful black and white Springer Spaniel as a present. She loved having this dog. She named him Tippie.

One day, while I was at school, Tippie got out of the apartment, ran up front and right into the traffic on our busy street. He was hit by a car and killed. My aunt was inconsolable.

C.J. wanted to replace Tippie, but my aunt said she didn't want any more dogs. She went back to feeding the gray squirrels in the backyard.

It took weeks before Ruth and I could play together. I was angry at Mrs. Taylor, her grandmother, for trying to hurt my Aunt Hookey. It was a conflicting situation for me with Grandma on one side and Granddaddy on the other. But I loved my Aunt Hookey even though she was a little mean, and I liked C.J. because he was so nice and happy.

6

Changes, War and Bubble Gum

C. J. gave Aunt Hookey a very expensive gold watch for Christmas. One weekend morning as she opened the door to the pot-bellied stove. I was still in bed and watched her as she went to throw in the trash she wanted to burn. Aunt Hookey had not fastened the watch band on her arm. She had a cigarette hanging from the right side of her mouth and she was squinting because the smoke was drifting into her eyes. As she tossed in the bag of trash, the watch slipped off and went into the fire with the trash.

Aunt Hookey found the remains of the watch when she cleaned out the stove's ashes after they cooled. C. J. took this pretty hard as he had paid a lot of money for the watch.

Aunt Hookey pretended that it wasn't so bad. It was just a watch.

We were fully into the depths of World War II. Fear and uncertainty were the emotions everyone felt, adults and children alike. Food rationing and rationing books and stamps made us more aware of the precarious nature of our existence.

At school we had trouble getting bubble gum, but some of the kids had a special way to get the prized commodity. When word got around about who had bubble gum, that person was surrounded by a crush of school mates. Bubble gum was very expensive when you got it from these classmates. We had heard of the "Black Market" because of the shortages due to the war, but "Black Market" bubble gum seemed outrageous to us, which not many could afford.

Grandma sent me to Rosen's with the rationing book whenever she needed sugar and certain meats. I tried to get bubble gum but to no avail and for me I could not understand what bubble gum had to do with the war.

That spring Aunt Hookey decided to make a big garden in the backyard. Others were doing the same thing. These were called Victory Gardens. Before the war Aunt Hookey was the one who made small gardens of string beans and tomatoes in the back yard. With the

Victory Garden she added seeds to grow lettuce and onions. She really liked having a garden even though there were days when working the night shift made her tired when she went out to do the weeding.

For most of those early days of the war Uncle Bobby remained in the hospital and was home for only very short stays. When he had to be returned to the hospital we continued our visits, Grandma on Wednesdays and Granddaddy and me on Sundays. I was glad Uncle Bobby didn't have to go to war and that he was safe in the Longview State Hospital.

7

Red Flyer Wagon

There it was under the small Christmas tree in the corner of the living room, red and gleaming like a fire engine. The handle was black enameled metal. The wheels were black rubber. It was a red Flyer wagon.

I never dreamed I would get a wagon, even though I had put it on the list I sent to Santa Claus at the North Pole. I ran over to the wagon, lifted my cotton flannel night gown, got in and pushed off. I held the handle securely and turned it to maneuver it, as I had seen the boys do, around the legs of the sofa. It was more difficult than I had imagined, especially because there was so little space. I bumped into the side of the doorway as I tried to get it from the living room into my bedroom where there was a little space in front of the pot-bellied stove.

I continued to move about the apartment bumping into walls and door jambs. All that Christmas Day, except when I was gorging myself on the candies inside my Christmas stocking, the red Flyer wagon held my attention.

Granddaddy said, "Ain't never seen her stick with nothin' more'n five minutes."

Grandma said, "Stop bumpin' into the walls. You'll scar the paint."

That same Christmas, Santa Claus left me a large red hardbound *Christmas Book* with a picture of Santa Claus on the cover. Inside it had lots of stories, songs and games. It was the thickest book I had ever seen. It became my favorite. By now, though, I was beginning to suspect that Santa Claus was really Grandma or Aunt Hookey; but a part of me wanted to hang on to the belief that there really was a Santa Claus. I knew that Mama bought my new shoes and coats sometimes at Christmas.

I felt that it was Aunt Hookey who had bought me the *Christmas Book* and that Grandma and Granddaddy had bought me the red Flyer wagon. I immersed myself, in my special book, working the puzzles and reading the stories. The *Night Before Christmas* I read repeatedly, but was stumped by the word "luster."

"The moon on the crest of the new fallen snow gave a..., " I read aloud.

Frustrated, I started again and when I came to the word, I ran to the kitchen and asked Grandma. She told me the word was luster. In the *Christmas Book,* luster was spelled *lustre*. I was using the phonetics that I had learned in school to figure out the pronunciation. The "re" instead of "er" confused me.

For the first time I had mazes to work. I loved them and I worked and re-worked them until I made a hole in the pages. I sang *The First Noel* and *O Little Town of Bethlehem*. I had learned these at school and was transported to the magical black starlit Christmas Eve that was celebrated in a far off country where there was no snow. With the *Christmas Book,* given me by Aunt Hookey, I relived Christmas for many days long after the holiday was over.

The Flyer wagon stayed inside. At night when I went to bed, it was stored in the hallway and was the first thing I saw each morning. I could not wait until the weather was warm enough to go outside. I would be able to drag my wagon up front where the sidewalk was smooth, and I could scoot down Lincoln Avenue, free as the wind.

I was the only little girl on our street that had a red Flyer wagon.

PART V

A TIME FOR LEAVING
Age 7-8

1

To Make Uncle Bobby Well

Grandma didn't leave the apartment at night. She rarely left it during the day. She went out only to keep appointments to cut slipcovers, to do the weekly shopping, to take me to the clinic for checkups, and to the Longview State Hospital to visit Uncle Bobby. She did not go out on social calls. On this night, she did leave the house.

I was leaning over my third grade arithmetic homework as I sat on the side of our bed. The light from our silken-shade floor lamp illuminated the pages beside me. Earlier, right after Grandma left, Aunt Hookey saw that I was having difficulty and pulled up the only chair, for which there was space in our bedroom, and proceeded to help me.

We could hear Granddaddy in the kitchen washing the supper dishes. Seeing that I was following her last set of instructions and was working at the problem, Aunt Hookey left her chair, turned at the foot of the bed and went to the doorway we used to get to the kitchen. The other doorways in our bedroom were one from the outside near the pot-bellied stove standing in the corner, and one to the living room, also next to the pot-bellied stove.

The only thing against the wall between the doorway to the living room and the doorway to the kitchen was the wooden dresser that held mine and my aunts clothing and towels. I loved the large tortoise-shell mirror that was attached to the dresser. During the day you could see the window near the bed with its reflection of the backstairs and backyard where I could take a short-cut to the Bells' apartment and where I played.

It was a narrow walking space between the foot of our bed and the dresser. Aunt Hookey stopped when she got to the doorway where she could talk to Granddaddy and keep an eye on me, as I did homework, at the same time.

"Where's Mama?" She called out to Granddaddy.

Granddaddy answered, "Out! She went to see some woman she heard your Aunt Margaret talkin' about."

"What for?" Aunt Hookey continued questioning.

"Well, somebody told Margaret that they knew this woman who was a healer and Margaret told your mama. She said the woman might be able to help Robert - maybe get over his spells."

At the mention of my uncle's name, I stopped to listen. Granddaddy left the kitchen, walked across the space that separated our bedroom and the living room from Grandma and Granddaddy's bedroom and kitchen, and settled in his comfortable chair in the living room.

Aunt Hookey walked back and stood, this time, in the doorway to the living room, still keeping her eye on me.

"Now why would Mama be listening to ignorant talk like that for?" She asked.

"Well, you know your Mammy. Once she gets something in her head you can't knock it out with a ton of bricks. I tried to stop her," Granddaddy chuckled.

"How'd she get there this time of night?"

"Your Aunt Margaret took her. Your Mammy talked her into it. Talked her into giving her the twenty-five dollars to pay for it, too, girl."

"Twenty-five dollars?" Aunt Hookey exclaimed. "Mama ought to be ashamed of herself."

"Well, she wasn't goin' to get no twenty-five dollars from me. I might as well walk out in the street and throw my money down the sewer. Where she gets these crazy notions beats me." I heard the paper rustle as Granddaddy reached for it.

340

It was dark outside. I grew concerned for Grandma. Everything Aunt Hookey and Granddaddy were talking about was so mysterious. Then, the front door, the one in the living room, opened just as Aunt Hookey returned to help me with my homework. Grandma came in out of breath.

"Well, what'd she tell you for twenty-five dollars?" Granddaddy asked.

"Just wait a minute and let me get in the house," Grandma said as she took off her coat and removed the pearl tipped hat, pin holding her brown felt hat on her head.

Aunt Hookey got up again and went to the doorway. She was impatient.

"Mama, can't nobody do nothin' for Robert that the doctors haven't already tried. He's sick. Been sick all his life and you just have to accept that," she said with finality.

I looked past Aunt Hookey so I could see Grandma. She jabbed the hat pin into the felt hat running it through a section several inches long. I heard the hanger scrape the rod as she hung up her fraying brown coat in the living room closet and heard the soft sound of her hat as it landed on the shelf where she had tossed it. Grandma took a seat on the mohair sofa facing Granddaddy and Aunt Hookey.

"You don't know what you're talkin' about, Hookey," she said irritation sounding in her voice. "You and your daddy're like two peas in a pod."

"Me and Daddy don't have a damn thing to do with it, Mama. What'd this lady or whoever or whatever she is, say?"

Grandma looked off into space with a smile on her face. I thought she was going to start humming like she usually did to cut Aunt Hookey off. Instead she started telling what happened.

"First she wanted to know about Robert," Grandma said. "How he was - how he acted."

I sat very still so that I would not miss a word. Grandma seemed so happy and self-assured in the face of Aunt Hookey and Granddaddy's skepticism. I was filled with anticipation and impatient to hear the miracle cure that Grandma had found. Aunt Hookey rested against the door jamb, one hand on her hip.

Grandma continued, "I told her that Robert had been sick since he was eighteen. How as a baby he had been so pretty and sweet and that as he grew up he was the nicest child I had. I told her that he never ever gave me a minute's trouble. How mannerly and good he was to everybody. Then one day, when he was eighteen, right before we moved here, he, for no reason went over to the window and put his fist right through the glass. Wham!" Grandma made the motion with her fist, imitating my uncle breaking the window.

"Then," she continued, "how I ran to the living room to see what had happened; and there he stood, hand all bloody just standing there lickin'the blood off, and I said, 'Robert, what happened, son? What's wrong? How'd you do that?' And how he just looked at me, his eyes strange, staring, and he said, 'Nothin', Mama'."

I sat entranced. I had never heard this story about my uncle before. I envisioned the picture that Grandma was describing. I felt the horror. My stomach burned at the thought of my uncle cutting his hand that way and then licking the blood. I looked at the window in my room, as if to give some reality to what I was hearing. I wondered if my uncle had cut his tongue while licking the blood away, or cut his mouth or stomach. I felt the fear of that even though I was not there. I held my breath.

"Then I told her," Grandma continued, "we had to put him in the State Mental Hospital…put him in Longview. I told her that since then he had been released every year for a short time, and that there were times when he got better and was like his old self. But each time, after a few months, he started locking himself in the bathroom and running the water. Just run the water for hours. And I'd tell him to come out."

I remembered those times. I listened to be sure that Grandma told every detail.

"And," She went on, "that I called him to unlock the door. 'Unlock the door, Robert'. Finally he would and his hair and shirt would be sopping wet, but he didn't pay any attention and tried to leave the house like that, even when the weather was icy cold outside. You

342

know how he mixed all those things, in the medicine cabinet, together in the sink? Camphorated Oil, Castor Oil, my toilet water…all mixed together?"

I knew that Uncle Bobby added orange and lemon peelings, too, but Grandma didn't say anything about that.

"Mama, what did the woman say? We know all that mess you're talkin' about," Aunt Hookey interrupted.

"I'm tryin' to tell you, but you just keep cuttin' me off," Grandma said.

"Well, it just takes you so long to say things. Don't nobody want to go back over all that past confusion," Aunt Hookey said.

"I told her that when he started doing this, then he would run away from home." Grandma rushed her story. "He always ran away to my Aunt El's and Cousin Charles down in Lexington."

Grandma's Aunt El and her son Charles were well-to-do funeral directors in Lexington, Kentucky. Whenever Uncle Bobby ran away Grandma got a call, from Charles, that came on a neighbor's telephone, telling her that Robert was there with them and that they would let him stay the night, and that Charles would bring him home the next day.

These were the only times we got to see Grandma's cousin, Charles. When he came he wore a dark suit, white shirt, tie and a hat that was rounded on top. I thought him very handsome and distinguished. Grandma would act a little embarrassed that my uncle had gone to their home.

"Then," Grandma continued, "I told the healer lady that Robert would have to be committed to Longview again, that the same thing happened over and over again, year after year.

"The lady was real nice. She studied what I said for a long time. She shut her eyes as if she was prayin'. Then, she looked right at me and told me that it sounded like Robert's problem began with water - since he ran the water in the bathroom for so long.

"She told me to get a bucket and on a night when the moon is full take it down to the Ohio River. She told me to dip the bucket into the water and throw three buckets of water to the east and three buckets of water to the west; then throw one bucket of water over my left shoulder and that Robert would be cured of his spells." Grandma sat back on the large, mohair sofa cushion pleased.

I was so excited and relieved. It was so simple a thing. I wondered why the doctors had not thought of this before. I wanted my uncle to be well, to be able to stay home with us instead of in that awful, dreary hospital with all the scary people. Home again so that he could take me to the park for walks and play with me like he used to. Oh, to have him home again. I was happy.

My grandfather was incredulous.

"You paid twenty-five dollars for some jack-legged healer to tell you that! I'd've told you that for twenty-five cents, Sister," he laughed. Then picked up his newspaper and started reading again.

"What're you talkin' about?" Grandma raised her voice. "Somebody has to try to do something to help Robert. You never would," she shouted at him through his paper.

"I sure ain't goin' to do nothin' dumb like goin' down to the Ohio River dippin' water!" He said.

My Aunt Hookey shook her head. "Mama, you just wasted your money."

Grandma got mad, yanked herself to her feet and stormed from the living room, arguing as she went. "Well, if you won't go with me," she said, ignoring Aunt Hookey, "then, I'll get somebody else to take me. You all are so ignorant and backwards. I've never seen a more ignorant bunch in my life. You don't ever try nothin' and ever do nothin'. I'm the only one around here who does anything."

The tears began and Grandma's nose started to run. She retreated to the confines of her bedroom and continued attacking Granddaddy and Aunt Hookey.

"Old ignorant niggers!" she called them. "Then when I try to do somethin' you always make me out to be the bad guy." She blew her nose loudly.

344

"Nobody's makin' you the bad guy, Sister," Granddaddy called out to her. "You make yourself the bad guy."

Aunt Hookey turned and returned to her chair near me. Grandma continued crying. Granddaddy laughed. I could hear him flipping his paper, this time to give emphasis to what he was saying.

"Three buckets of water to the east! Three buckets of water to the west! If that ain't the biggest pile of shit I ever heard of."

I sat stunned. I was on Grandma's side, fighting with her inside myself. But at least she can try it, I said to myself. *Just try it*!

Grandma never went down to the Ohio River at night when the moon was full. I carried the picture of her in my head. She, a lonely figure in her brown coat and felt hat with the pearl-tipped hat pin holding it on her silver hair; there on the banks of the Ohio River dipping the muddy river water, three buckets to the east, three buckets to the west and one bucket over her left shoulder to save her only son, to save my Uncle Bobby.

2

The Operation

Uncle Bobby did not get better. Late one Wednesday afternoon, Grandma came home from one of her regular Wednesday visits to the hospital with a long white piece of paper. The banana pudding she had made for my uncle, she put back in the refrigerator. Tonight, it would be our dessert and not Uncle Bobby's.

When Grandma planned her Wednesday visits to Uncle Bobby, she made banana pudding the night before. It was his favorite dessert. If she had not prepared it for her Wednesday visits then she made sure that she prepared it on Saturday so that Granddaddy and I could take it when we visited Uncle Bobby on Sunday. We all knew that Uncle Bobby expected to have banana pudding every week.

"Robert's been fightin' again," she told Granddaddy as she slowly dished up our supper. We sat waiting at the table, listening to Grandma. She sighed. Granddaddy was silent.

"The orderly said he beat another patient so bad that they had to take him to the infirmary."

Still Granddaddy said nothing. I stared in silence at the plate of stew she had handed me.

"They wouldn't let me see Robert today. They said he was too disturbed. If they'd told me ahead of time, I could've saved myself the trip.

"They want us to sign a paper so that they can do an operation to keep Robert from being so violent. Here it is."

Grandma placed the paper in front of Granddaddy near his plate. The moist steam from the beef stew bathed his face. I looked up at the paper Grandma was showing Granddaddy.

"I ain't signin nothin', Sister. If they want it signed, you sign it!" Granddaddy refused to look at the paper.

Grandma kept talking. Granddaddy took a spoonful of the beef stew, a large chunk of buttered cornbread, and started to eat.

"You could at least read it - see what it says," Grandma said.

"You already told me. They want to give him an operation. I ain't signin' it, I said!"

Granddaddy stopped chewing. There was a set to his jaw, one we had learned not to ignore or misunderstand.

"You're as stubborn as an old mule," Grandma said, exasperated. Granddaddy said nothing. Just chewed.

"The doctor told me that it would be a very simple operation," Grandma began, this time with a cautious tone to her voice. "They take a long needle and go up through Robert's eye, and clip off a piece of something called the frontal lobe of his brain."

Grandma tilted her head under the kitchen light hanging over the table, ran her index finger up along the top inside corner of her eye and made two, quick jabs with it as if the finger was the surgeon's needle entering my uncle's skull.

My stomach started to burn as I watched her. The beef stew stuck in my throat and would not go down. I drank my milk to help it.

"Don't drink while you're eatin'," Granddaddy scolded.

"The operation would only take a few minutes. The doctor said that when Robert recovered, he wouldn't be violent anymore. He'd just have real dark circles under his eyes for awhile."

Grandma stopped talking and sat down to eat.

I had never seen Uncle Bobby violent. When he was home, he never hit anybody. He never got mad at anybody. He was always so nice. He smiled and spoke quietly to people. He always spoke to the old people on Lincoln Avenue, even old, tobacco- spitting Mr. Tate and the ladies at the Home for Aged Colored Women. What did they mean that my uncle was violent?

When we went to visit Uncle Bobby on Sundays, he'd call the patients over: 'Come over here, Benny. I want you to see my little niece, Sweetpea. Ain't she pretty?' He never knew how scared I was of Benny and all the other patients on the ward. But, I smiled, shook my pigtails and swung my feet which could not reach the floor from the bench where I sat next to my uncle. Grandma said that it was Benny whom Uncle Bobby had almost killed.

"How long will it take him to be alright?" Granddaddy asked.

"The doctor said not long."

"Well, maybe it'll be better for Robert. He won't be gettin' into trouble on the ward, givin' Bert trouble."

Bert was the orderly on the ward eighteen, the ward for violent patients. He was large, muscular and menacing. Granddaddy always grinned and laughed whenever he saw Bert. '*Hi Bert. How're you today, Bert? Nice day out, Bert. Hee Hee Hee!*' I wondered what Granddaddy found so funny. It was scary on ward eighteen. Bert was white, grim-faced and twice the size of Uncle Bobby. I didn't laugh for Bert like Granddaddy.

The long white paper giving approval for my uncle's operation was still lying next to the dish of cornbread as if it had been an unwelcomed guest who pulled up a chair and had decided to stay for supper. Granddaddy cut himself more cornbread. Crumbs fell on the fine print. Grandma picked up the paper and wiped it clean, on her apron.

"Well, I guess like everything else, I'll have to sign for this, too," she said.

"That's right, Sister. You're the one who wants to be the big shot in the family, just like your old, big shot Daddy." Granddaddy let out a wry laugh.

"Big Shot? Since when did I get to be the big shot? Doin' all the dirty work maybe 'cause you won't never do none of it. But, I sure wouldn't call that being a big shot. Huh!" Grandma said, staring down at the paper. The bold, black letters across the top spelled "P-e-r-m-i-s-s-i-o-n t-o P-e-r-f-o-r-m P-a-r-t-i-a-l L-o-b-o-t-o-m-y."

Grandma got up from the table to dish up what was to have been Uncle Bobby's dessert. For the banana pudding she used the best dairy cream, perfectly whipped and sweetened. Once the vanilla wafers had been crisp, the bananas light and firm, thanks to the recipe on the back of the Vanilla Wafer's box; but now, the wafers were soggy in the perfectly whipped cream and the bananas had turned black around the edges.

Grandma served dessert, Granddaddy's portion first, mine second. She did not eat any. She said that she did not feel like it.

We ate in silence, a silence that held questions that no one knew how to formulate; questions that held images of Uncle Bobby's brain being clipped like a piece of Grandma's sewing, a silence that held the image of my uncle who, the doctor said, would never be violent again.

3

Aftermath

After Grandma had signed for my uncle's operation, she nor Granddaddy had visited him. It was a chilly Sunday morning in April, a week after Easter, when Granddaddy and I were preparing for our first visit to Longview State Hospital to see Uncle Bobby.

The week before, on Easter Sunday, Grandma had transformed my normal three plaits into a head of glistening Shirley Temple curls by taking a parted section of my freshly washed hair, oiling the scalp and strands with Vaseline Petroleum Jelly, brushing each section around her finger, then letting the curl ease gently off her fingertip. My new outfit this particular Easter consisted of a new pale lavender coat bought by my mother, a pink dress, with pearl buttons down the front, black patent leather shoes, new white socks and a little girl's pocket-book, bought by Aunt Hookey.

But now, a week later, the curls were already beginning to get tangles as Grandma struggled to comb my hair. I sat, impatiently on the kitchen floor in front of the open oven door. I always stood or sat here to keep warm when getting ready for school or hospital visits in cold weather. Grandma held my shoulders firmly between her knees as she sat in the chair next to the kitchen table.

"Sit still," Grandma said as she wrestled with the week-old curls.

"It hurts, Grandma."

"Well, you're the one who wanted these curls."

She was right. I wanted the curls so they could bounce up and down and be swung back and forth like Shirley Temple's. The curls were fine the first few days as I preened before the mirror, glad not to have to see the same three plaits that were my trademark. But once the curls had been made, and after a week of my playing during the day and sleeping with them at night, dust and dirt in the air caused the curls to get tangled. I hated it when the time came to comb out the curls. So, I squirmed and grimaced on the floor between Grandma's

350

knees while she brushed and combed, then brushed the hair around her fingers one more time.

"This is the last day for these curls," she announced. "All this scroochin' and hollerin' is makin' me a nervous wreck. Tomorrow, it's back to the plaits and no amount of cryin' is makin' me change my mind. Do you hear!?"

"You about ready to go, Miss Prissy?" Granddaddy called from the living room.

"Never thought I'd see the day when the tomboy did so much primpin'. If we don't leave soon, we'll miss the bus."

I knew Uncle Bobby would be very upset if we were late. He'd stand by the door waiting and waiting as he did every Sunday. I didn't want him to be disappointed.

"You know how Robert is. He'll be lookin' for us," Granddaddy continued.

Grandma drew her chair back from the open oven door. She relaxed her knees from around my shoulders and said, "There. I'm all done. Now be careful puttin' your dress on so you don't muss up your hair."

She cleaned the comb of the strands of hair that held the naps and dust at the end. It was the naps that hurt. She gathered up the brush, Vaseline, naps and comb, stood up and shook any remaining particles out of her apron and onto the floor.

I dashed into the bedroom. "I'll be ready in a minute, Granddaddy," I called, hurriedly pulling on my pink dress.

When I finished, I hurried into the living room. Granddaddy handed me my coat.

"Got anything in that pocketbook?" He teased, taking it out of my hands.

"No" I shook my head.

"What good's a pocketbook gonna do ya if it don't have nothin' in it?" he asked.

"She wouldn't keep nothin' in it no way," Grandma said. "It would be spent soon's she had a chance to get to Rosen's."

On Easter Sunday, the week before, I had had ten cents. Five cents went into the Sunday school collection plate at First Baptist Church and on Monday morning, five cents went into my mouth in the form of wartime black market bubble gum. It was one delicious piece bought from a white school mate whose uncle owned a corner store near our school.

Granddaddy shook my pocketbook. "Sure is empty," he laughed.

Then, he reached into the pocket of his best, Sunday pants, retrieved a quarter and dropped it into my new Easter pocketbook. He closed it, shook it again and said, "Sounds like it's in business," he winked.

A whole quarter. I was thrilled. Grandma handed Granddaddy the banana pudding. It had been wrapped in a large, brown grocery bag.

"Tell Robert I'll be out to see him Wednesday," she said.

Before we made it to the top of the cement steps leading up front, I became acutely aware of the cold air on my legs but I would never go back to trade my white anklets for the long, brown, ribbed cotton stockings that Grandma made me wear to school all winter.

The sun had a cool glare as it often did in winter and early spring. In order to dare to wear lighter clothing, I rushed spring, in my head, into a warm flower-filled season.

I hovered close to Granddaddy as we walked to the corner to catch the bus. I felt shielded from the cold by his six foot height and beer belly, and by the fact that he had the good sense to wear a winter overcoat.

The soles of my new shoes had not been broken in yet, so my feet kept slipping as I walked fast to keep up with Granddaddy's long strides. One time, I almost went down in the middle of Lincoln Avenue as we tried to beat the light.

"Whoops," Granddaddy said, grabbing my arm, narrowly escaping dumping the banana pudding. "Careful there somebody'll think you've been drinkin'," he laughed at his own joke.

As we waited for the bus, he kept one hand in his pocket and held the pudding with the other. He didn't have gloves. I danced first on one foot then on the other. I pulled one leg up, as far as I possibly could, under my thin coat. The chill now permeated it and began to pierce my pink dress and flannel underslip, the only thing keeping me the least bit warm.

We waited for the bus in the section of Lincoln Avenue where the housing was more varied than in our section. This was the last block before Woodburn Avenue where Lincoln Avenue ended. The housing in this block was comprised of large, single family, two and three story houses. Because of the steeper incline of this section of Lincoln Avenue, the houses were built on the slope of the hill. To accommodate this change in topography, there were often two tiers of steps that helped people negotiate the distance between the sidewalk near the street and the front porch and doorways of their homes on the top of the hill.

I had been able to go into one of these large homes many times. My classmate, Jo-Ann Jones who had moved to our area from downtown Cincinnati lived in one. I thought it was a mansion the rooms were so large with wide staircases to the upper floors. I thought the people living in this section were "rich colored people."

The lawns of these houses were always well kept and in the spring, beautiful tulips and daffodils filled the lower areas where a break in the steps appeared. The flowers were now in bloom.

Except for a few cars, this Sunday Lincoln Avenue was deserted. Although it was not too early to catch the bus to Longview, it was too early for church. I was very happy to see the bus. I darted down the aisle, relieved to get in out of the cold. I rushed to the seat where Granddaddy and I were to sit and slid near the window to look out.

Granddaddy fished in his pocket for the money for our bus fare. The bus driver started off, throwing him against the coin box. The bus, like the street, was empty except for the two of us.

"Two Sunday passes, please," he told the driver handing him a wrinkled dollar bill.

On Sunday Granddaddy bought each of us a Sunday Pass. We could, if we wanted to, as we did in summer, ride all day anywhere on any bus line without having to pay an additional fare. For this, Granddaddy paid fifty cents.

"Here's your pass. Don't lose it," he instructed me, "and don't forget to show it to the other bus driver when we transfer."

When we neared the corner of Gilbert and Lincoln, Granddaddy said, "Pull the cord."

I did. And the loud hollow buzz resounded through the bus. We got off at the corner in front of Sears Roebuck Department Store just at the time when the chill was beginning to leave me. Here we waited for the bus to Bond Hill, the one that took us directly to the Longview State Hospital. We had no more transfers. But while standing near the walls of Sears, the wind swept between the building and other buildings across the street. This tunnel of air was even colder than what we had been experiencing. My nose started to run. I opened my pocketbook to get the new, stiff, rumpled handkerchief, but changed my mind and wiped my nose on the back of my hand.

"Here! Here!" Granddaddy scolded. "Don't wipe your snotty nose on the back of your hand. Use your handkerchief."

"It hurts."

"Aw, hold this."

He handed me his Sunday pass, lifted his overcoat and got his handkerchief out of his pants' pocket.

"Now, blow!" he said.

I blew a little bit and wiped my nose with his handkerchief. It was so big it covered my entire face, but it was softer than my stiff, new handkerchief.

I ran up and down in front of the Sears windows, stopping only where there were manikins of children displaying toys or clothing. This is how I killed time and distracted myself from thinking about the cold.

"Bus's comin'," Granddaddy called as I raced back.

It was not long before we would see Uncle Bobby. He would be surprised. He would like my new shoes, coat and dress; and he would say "look at those curls." He would laugh. Granddaddy had teased me, saying that the Shirley Temple curls looked like "rat turds," but I didn't pay Granddaddy's teasing any attention. We rode in silence.

I looked out the window as we passed through Bond Hill. This was a section outside of downtown Cincinnati that was inhabited by very wealthy Jewish people. There was a large, country club where only Jewish people could belong. The country club had a large green lawn that was part of the golf course. In the summer we could see Jewish men in their golf clothes, walking the course.

I thought that Sunday school had given me a lot of information about the Jewish people and Moses and the Ten Commandments. I felt that I knew why Mrs. Rosen always pumped me for information when I went to her store. I thought it was because I learned all about her in Sunday school, but she didn't know anything about the people on Lincoln Avenue. I thought it only right that I tell her about Uncle Bobby's being in Longview getting his brain clipped. Grandma got mad at me and said it wasn't any of Mrs. Rosen's business, and that Mrs. Rosen was just too 'nosey.'

I enjoyed riding through Bond Hill absorbing the magnificence of the homes. At one time Aunt Hookey had worked for a Jewish family, the Freulands. She said they were very nice people, but they didn't pay enough. They wanted her to work long hours and do everything from cooking, cleaning, washing and baby sitting. She liked them, but quit as soon as the Wright's war plant opened.

On the Bond Hill bus, we were joined by a lot more people going to Longview like us.

"More whites than colored," Granddaddy said.

The closer we got to our destination the more excited I became. As we alighted from the bus, Granddaddy said, "We don't have to cross the street this time. Robert's on Ward Seven now. That's on this side."

"This side" was surrounded by the same low chain link fence, and resembled the Bond Hill Country Club in comparison to the medieval hospital look on the Ward Eighteen side. The buildings on this side were one story and modern. The road curved around past a building with tall Ionic Columns. This building had an auditorium that held programs for patients. Beyond was a grassy area which had at its far end Ward Seven. It was so clean and calming in the newness of its outward appearance.

"That's a nice building," I told Granddaddy.

"Ummmmhuh," he replied absentmindedly.

"Are they going to let Uncle Bobby live there now?"

"Don't know. Have to wait and see," Granddaddy said.

There was a tense look on his face.

"Are we going to take him to the Commissary today?"

My uncle loved going to the Commissary. He loved getting ice cream and soda pop. His favorite candy was called Charms. This was a very hard candy with different flavors in a package. They were like Life Savers, only they were square and not round.

"We'll have to wait and see," Granddaddy said. "Don't ask so many questions."

We walked the rest of the way in silence. The metal door to the Ward Seven building was salmon-colored. This in itself signified a different building. Ward Eighteen's doors were all a brown painted metal. Granddaddy rang the buzzer. I held onto his coat. I looked up staring, at the small, glass window, reinforced with wire. I knew that an orderly would soon appear and stare, eye to eye with Granddaddy. The eyes appeared. The orderly waited.

"We're here to see Robert Corbin," Granddaddy said.

The unsmiling orderly nodded. After a series of clicks and scrapings, he opened the heavy door. The antiseptic smell of the ward greeted us first. We walked down a very short corridor. It was clean, bright, but barren. I expected to see Uncle Bobby waiting for us as we went through the double doors of the visitor's lounge.

"Wait here, I'll get him up for you. He sleeps a lot lately," the orderly said.

My apprehension returned as it did when we went into Ward Eighteen. I scanned the room looking at the unfamiliar faces of the patients. Men were slumped in chairs, staring straight ahead. Some on benches were talking to their visitors, others only being talked to.

When Granddaddy had brought me to Longview on my first visit, he told me not to stare at people. He said that it was impolite. On Ward Eighteen I was too scared to stare at anyone. But I thought this was a very different place, so I felt more comfortable looking around. Still, I didn't stare, but just quickly looked around.

Then I spied Uncle Bobby. The orderly was holding him by the elbow and guiding him towards us. What I saw shocked me. I saw a ghost of my uncle. The "ghost" had jet black hair, softly waved, like his. There were brilliant, blue-black rings encircling what had once been sparkling, intelligent eyes. Now Uncle Bobby's eyes were vacant orbs staring into nothingness. These seemed to follow the slow scuffing of first one of his feet, then the other. I did not move my eyes. I stared in unashamed disbelief at Uncle Bobby. He was a Zombie in blue jeans and an undershirt with *Property of Longview State Hospital,* stenciled across the front.

"He's coming along fine," the orderly informed Granddaddy when they had completed the journey to us. "It will take a while longer, but he's coming along just fine."

"Thank you," Granddaddy replied.

"Robert," the orderly called as if talking to someone at the end of a long tunnel, "your people are here to see you."

We waited for what seemed like an eternity. Then, my uncle's words came out, one by one, like his footsteps.

"Yyyyyyyyyyeeeeeesssssss."

"Hello, Son," Granddaddy said nervously. "We brought you some banana pudding."

The "Zombie" tried to formulate the words with his lips. The effort was too great. He gave up.

"It's your favorite," Granddaddy encouraged. He waited. "Here's, Sweetpea, too."

"Sweeee," the Zombie attempted to say my name. It was too difficult.

I stepped into full view from behind Granddaddy's coat where I had partially retreated. My uncle's ghost stared at me. I took hold of his hand. It was cold and lifeless.

"Hi, Uncle Bobby." I forced a smile.

The orderly helped Uncle Bobby sit down on the hard, wooden bench. Granddaddy sat on one side of my uncle and I sat on the other. He stared straight ahead.

"If the package is for Robert, I can take care of it for him," the orderly volunteered.

Without looking up, Granddaddy handed him the bag with the banana pudding.

We did not stay long. Granddaddy talked in a falsetto voice to my uncle. I tried hard to think of some things to say, but Uncle Bobby made no further effort to talk.

I sat silently staring at the dust particles dancing in the sun's rays as they streamed through the barred windows of the visitor's lounge. Granddaddy went over to speak with the orderly, whose arms were folded as he stood near the double doors to the room. I couldn't hear what they said, but soon the orderly came over to take my uncle back to his room.

"Goodbye, Uncle Bobby," I said. It was a whisper. I released his lifeless hand. I kissed him on the forehead and felt the hardness of his skull against my mouth.

"Goodbye, Son," Granddaddy said. "We'll be back next Sunday. Mama's comin' to see you on Wednesday."

The orderly helped my uncle get up from his seat on the bench. He ushered him through the doors to the visitor's lounge. The doors closed behind my uncle. He had gone, just as he had come, slowly, silently with the blue-black circles around his eyes and the white Longview State Hospital undershirt and blue jeans.

The salmon-colored, metal door closed behind me and Granddaddy. The sound of the lock scraped against the door and sealed us off from the world inside Ward Seven. I looked back, but the small glass in the door no longer held the eyes of the orderly. Uncle Bobby's eyes did not follow us like they did when we left Ward Eighteen.

Granddaddy and I walked back to the bus stop. I could see the old Ward Eighteen in the distance. It stood like a fortress splitting the sky. The aging red-brick building forced the eyes up, up, up, until they rested on the top of the roof that covered the floor where my uncle had been kept when he had been violent. Ward Eighteen, the Ward that resembled Frankenstein's mansion. Ward Eighteen with the iron stairs that resounded under each step I made with my patent leather Sunday shoes. But no lightening flashed around the roof of Ward Eighteen. This was not the darkest of nights. It was Sunday and the sun was bright.

I looked at Ward Eighteen knowing that this was not in a movie. This was the Longview State Hospital. This was where my uncle had lived and was now living only on a different Ward. Ward Seven was where the "Zombies" lived. Zombies were the living dead.

The long white sheet of paper that Grandma had to sign to help my uncle, the paper that spelled, "Partial Lobotomy," that held words that nobody in our family had ever heard before and had no idea what they meant; I realized what it really meant when I visited Uncle Bobby that Sunday. I saw what had happened to him. I still did not understand.

On Monday morning I got back the three plaits I had before Easter and the brown, ribbed, long cotton stockings that protected me from the cold. After school, I ran like the wind from my apartment building to Rosen's Store. I spent my twenty-five cents that Granddaddy had given me on Sunday. Mrs. Rosen smiled and leaned on the glass- topped candy case. I handed her my quarter and picked up my bag of candy.

"How was your Uncle Bobby yesterday?" she asked.

"Fine," I said.

I grabbed my bag of candy and hurried out the door. The bell jingled behind me. I could feel Mrs. Rosen's eyes on my back.

When the next Sunday came, I told Granddaddy and Grandma that I didn't want to go to the hospital. Granddaddy went alone, returning with the news of Uncle Bobby's improvement.

One Sunday when Granddaddy went to visit Uncle Bobby, the orderly on Ward Seven told him that Uncle Bobby had been transferred to Ward Eighteen. He had beaten up a new patient and had to be sent there.

We did not know how it had happened but it was evident from my uncle's violent behavior that the partial lobotomy had not worked.

4

A Time for Leaving

Aunt Hookey and C.J. Parrish decided to live together. They were both working the night shift at Wright's Plant and said that it would be much more convenient if they moved to a government project newly constructed in the sub-division. It was called the Valley Homes. They were just ten minutes away from work instead of being forty-five minutes away.

The Valley Homes were new barrack-style units spread over many acres, of once open land in the sub-division. It was very near to where my mother lived.

I was very saddened by my aunt's leaving. Grandma was concerned as well because this meant she would not have the additional income and help around the apartment. She said this many times while Aunt Hookey prepared to leave.

When school let out for the summer, my year in third grade was over. I dashed home with my report card and school papers. Third grade became a very important grade for me because I became more determined to be a teacher when I grew up; especially now that I had had such success helping my classmate, Barbara Reichart, improve her penmanship and the excellent grades I had made that year.

The best papers and my report card I took home for Granddaddy to put in his tin box. I got all As and Bs except for the one C in arithmetic from the second marking period.

Grandma looked up from her sewing as I ran in waving my report card. She glanced at it for a moment.

"That's good," she said, then returned to her sewing.

She didn't say anything else after that. It didn't matter. I gobbled down a bologna sandwich and dashed outside to explode from the new-felt freedom.

"School's out. School's out. The teacher's letting the monkeys out," Cornelious and I yelled at each other over the sound of the traffic. Hoffman School was out a full day ahead of Douglas School. My friend, Ruth, attended the all-colored Douglas School and her mother taught there. When Ruth came down the street and saw us playing, she got mad and crossed over to the opposite side.

That night, as Granddaddy and I sat at the supper table with Grandma, she said, "Sweetpea, it's time for you to go live with your mother."

"For my summer visit?" I asked spreading Oleo on my soft, slice of Taystee Bread.

"No. This time you'll have to stay with her for good." Grandma did not look at me as she talked.

"But why?" I asked stunned. "Why do I have to stay?"

No one answered for a moment. Granddaddy kept eating as if he had not heard me. I panicked. I wanted to run from the table, to go outside and play. I couldn't move. The bread was a soggy lump in my mouth. I swallowed hard, forcing it down.

"I just can't take care of you anymore. I'm getting too old," Grandma said. "Besides, children should be with their own mothers."

I stared at her fighting back tears. Visiting my mother in the country for a month in the summer was one thing, but living there forever and ever was something I could not grasp. I didn't want to stay in the country where there was no running water or electricity.

I searched Grandma's face for some sign of this "getting too old." She looked the same to me. Before Aunt Hookey moved away, she talked about Grandma fussing all the time and having hot flashes. I thought that Grandma fussed all the time anyway. Nothing had changed. About the hot flashes, I looked for signs of her sweating and fanning like the women at First Baptist Church in the summer. There were no signs.

I wanted to keep asking, "Why, Grandma? Why?", but the words wouldn't come.

I do not remember Grandma packing my clothes. I do not re-member my mother coming to get me. I do not remember the bus and

streetcar rides that took me to live with my mother. I did not understand why Grandma had sent me away.

PART VI

My Year in the Sub-Division
and
My Return Home

1

That Summer

It was the summer of 1942 when I was sent to live with my mother. She and the the rest of the family had moved into a single-family rental dwelling on Jackson Street in the sub-division. This was fifteen miles from my Walnut Hills, Ohio home where I had lived with my grandparents, aunts and uncle. It was the first time I had ever lived in a single-family house like that of my close friends, Ruth Hull and Jo-Ann Jones.

The house was a gray wooden structure with three tiny rooms and a front porch. The yard was not fenced-in and it had patches of dry grass and worn paths from the front to the back. The back door led from the kitchen to the out-house which was in a line with all the other out-houses on our side of Jackson Street. These reeked of the same odors that I remembered from my visit the summer before.

Within a few weeks, the fact that I thought I would never again be able to get away from the primitive aspects of the country enveloped me in an invisible blanket of sadness. This feeling I never wanted to reveal to my mother for fear she would be saddened by my unhappiness. Nothing could assuage my grief. I felt that I was in a deep, dark hole. Many times I wanted to cry, but dared not. The tears pooled inside my mind like a storm cloud threatening to burst, but never did. I missed Grandma and Granddaddy. I missed Aunt Lockey Jane, Aunt Irene and my cousins. I missed busy Lincoln Avenue. I was homesick.

My brothers, Sonny, Jimmy, Ronald, my little sister, Lillian Beatrice, who was named after Grandma, Mama and my stepfather were so happy to have me with them. I continued to call my stepfather, Daddy, as I had begun years before. I continued to appreciate the fact that, to them, I was special as my seat at the table with Mama and Daddy for the morning meal was an accepted occurrence. Eating my mother's cooking gave me a comforting feeling that helped soothe my longing for my old home. Sonny, Jimmy and Ronald saw me as the "big sister." I could not be a baby and reveal my true feelings. Gradually I began to accept reality.

Jackson Street was unpaved and had more traffic than the street where my mother lived before when she rented from Mr. Samuels. The rickety bus I had ridden with my mother when we had arrived, made daily runs carrying passengers to and from destinations within the subdivision and to the business district of Lockland. Another means of transportation was one taxi owned by an entrepreneur who did all of the driving.

Across the street was a large empty lot where we gathered to play softball with other children who came from distances as far away as the lower-sub. Weeds grew tall around the perimeter and it had a footpath made when people took this as their shortcut to Jackson Street from the street that ran perpendicular to it.

Being able to play so close to home was a great advantage and I remember having fun learning to play softball. Ida Lee was the only carry-over of good friends from the previous summer. My relationship with some of the girls my age was not as comfortable. The girls focused on my hair and made daily references to it as my "pretty hair," or eyed me up and down with suspicion. Ida Lee and I played jacks on our family's front porch in addition to playing softball together.

Mama's best friend on Jackson Street was Mrs. Rose Green. She, her husband and eight children lived in a larger house across the street. It was next to the vacant lot where we played ball. The Green's house had many cement steps that led to their porch which had no railing around it. I was amazed at how high their house was from the ground below and I thought it a miracle that no one ever fell off their porch.

Mrs. Green never left her yard during the week. Mr. Green left for work early each day and evidently had rules that no one was to leave their yard. Their oldest son was the one who enforced this rule with the younger Green children. It seemed odd to me that Mrs. Green wasn't allowed to go anywhere except when Mr. Green accompanied her. As time passed, I came to realize that this was the case with many of the women in the area. Some families had wire fences around their yards and the women were not allowed to venture beyond them. A few women even seemed afraid to talk with their neighbors.

I was struck by this tacit obedience to the husbands. Women in my family would not have paid any attention to such dictates.

Where most everybody on Lincoln Avenue was light-skinned, in the sub-division, most were dark-skinned. All those living near Mama were poor, like those of us who lived in the Helena Apartments. This "poor" seemed different somehow. I thought it was because these people were the "country" poor and lacked the amenities of poor people living in the city.

Mama and Mrs. Green visited by standing on their front porches and shouting at each other across the street.

"Rose, how're you doin' today, honey?" I could hear Mama say.

"I'm just fine, Ethel. How're you?"

Mrs. Green was a very pleasant gentle lady. She had a quiet voice unlike Mama's which could be heard from a long distance away. Mrs. Green came outside to sit on her porch when all of her work was done and her meals prepared for the day. Their shouting their daily greetings and conversations were interrupted only when the bus rumbled past, momentarily blocking their view of each other and drowning out the sound of their voices.

It was very interesting to me to see how well-behaved the Green children were. Their oldest son seemed more like an old man than a teenager. He had a beautiful girlfriend who came by to visit with him on occasion. She had gorgeous, long brown hair and was as beautiful as Aunt Lockey Jane. She had a very fair complexion and light-brown eyes. The two young people always sat outside on the porch. We children would watch and giggle as we observed the courtship of the two. They also had to stay in the yard.

366

The more I observed Mrs. Green, the more she reminded me of Mrs. Robinson, our neighbor living in the Helena Apartments. She was, next to the Bells, my favorite neighbor and I often was allowed to sit with her on her front porch and have lemonade.

Mrs. Green, was short, plump and soft-spoken just like Mrs. Robinson.

Summer was hot and slow in the sub-division. There was more ease playing outside where there was a large field in which to play. I missed having drawing paper and coloring books, but the more I played outside and learned new games, the more I began to adapt to my new home.

2

Night and Day

Grandma had always talked about Mama never staying in the yard when she was a child. She constantly said that she was hard-headed, never would mind her and never did her jobs in the house well, always escaping to play ball.

As an adult Mama spent afternoons working for Mr.Lyle, who owned the grocery store on the corner. The store could be seen from our house and sat directly across the street from our playing field.

At night Mama left us alone while she went to church prayer meetings held in someone's home. Nothing was more scary than night in the sub-division which had no street lights. Every home was lit with oil lanterns. When I lived with Grandma, I was never left alone at night. Grandma made sure that I was safely in bed before dark.

As had been the case before when I was visiting, I was in charge of my little sister, but now as the eldest, I was in charge of all my siblings. As Mama left for her prayer meetings, I received the same instructions each night.

"Sweetpea, you all stay in the yard. Don't let Sonny and Ronald go away from this house, you here?"

"All right Mama," I replied. We never had to worry about Jimmy disobeying.

"And don't let nobody else come here, either."

I don't think Mama needed to worry. None of us liked the dark. I did not let my brothers and sister know how scared I was, after all I was the oldest and I was in charge of them. I did a good job of pretending to be brave.

When Mama returned, we would all be asleep on the let-out sofa-bed in the living room. I would sometimes awaken to her getting the Black Flag spray gun and spraying the rooms for mosquitoes. She always talked to them as she pumped the handle, "I'm goin' to get you demons." When she finished, she turned in for the night and went to bed.

Neil, my stepfather, was home only to sleep, eat and go to work at Darling's, the factory that made glue from the carcases of dead horses. The noxious odor from the Darling Plant competed with the smells from the out-houses on certain days when the wind was blowing in just the right direction. On the weekends, my stepfather sometimes did not come home until dawn. My mother would be very upset with him. She no longer physically fought with men as she had done before she was "saved," now she whined and cried. I awakened at one of these times to my mother's trembling voice.

"You can't gamble all your money away. How'm I goin' to pay for groceries?

"A whole pay check gone!"

My stepfather was a quiet, gentle man. I was surprised that there was so much tension between he and my mother because at the breakfast table and during the time he prepared for work, there were never any unpleasant words between them.

Gambling seemed to be my stepfather's vice of choice. I don't know if it was card-playing or what, but he continued at it. My mother complained, with tears in her eyes, about the poverty and the uncertainty. We children heard it at night if awakened. My stepfather was not a member of the church like Mama, so he continued with what Mama said were "worldly ways." There was one thing my stepfather did not do. He did not argue back at Mama like Granddaddy did with Grandma. He was passive but unchanging in his habit.

I took my stepfather's gambling to be the reason Mama took the job at Lyle's Store – to have money for food.

3

Mama's Second Job

Before Mama left for her job at Lyle's, she washed clothes and did her housework. Mama's wash day was different from Grandma's wash day. Grandma had a washing machine that washed our dirty clothes. Mama had a galvanized tub, a washboard and bar of Tag soap.

I was fascinated by this difference and paid more attention as she went about her work. I liked watching as she got out the washboard. It had metal ridges held together by wooden legs and a wooden top that had a place for your hand to steady the board. Mama had to fill the tub with hot water she had heated on the wood-burning kitchen stove and put the clothes in to soak. After awhile, she stood over the tub, took one piece of dirty clothing and placed it on the washboard. Next, she took the bar of Tag soap. Tag was a caramel-colored bar with a slightly pungent odor that was twice as big as a bar of Ivory Soap.

Then Mama rubbed some Tag on the article of clothing, and bending over the washboard, pressed the piece up and down on the board. You could hear the sound the material made as it was pushed and pulled over the ridges. Except when at my mother's house, the only time I had seen a washboard was in a Spike Jones movie. The washboard was a musical instrument. Mama's washboard made some of the same sounds but without the whistles and the horns. How Mama made the music didn't seem like much fun. It looked like hard work.

Mama then put each scrubbed piece of clothing into a tub of rinse water. She wrung each piece out by hand, put it in another tub, and when every piece was washed and wrung out, she took the loaded tub out the back door and into the back yard where she had strung several clotheslines from the edge of the out-house to the house. The house and out-house had nails hammered into them to secure the clothes lines.

Some families had clotheslines made of a heavy wire. Mama's was like a small rope.

When Mama finished pinning her wash to the line, she said, "Now, I don't want you all playing out here gettin' my clothes dirty. You play in the field or front yard.

I'll take the clothes down when I get home."

She had a serious look on her face and we knew better than to cross her.

Then she put on a nice house dress and left for her second job at Lyle's Store.

Many times I would take my baby sister, Lillian, and stop at the store to watch Mama. I learned a lot about the Lyles and what Mama did while she was there.

Mama was Mr. Lyle's only helper. She cleaned the store, waited on customers and learned to butcher the meat. She cut the loin parts of pork into chops and she ground cubes of beef into hamburger. Her meat grinder looked exactly like the one Grandma used at home to grind meat, only bigger.

At other times, I took my sister, Lillian, by the hand and we walked to Lyle's store to cash in an empty Pepsi Cola bottle. I would collect the two cents deposit and buy candy for me and my sister. Then we hung around the store watching my mother as she cleaned the meat cases and washed off the counters.

I was fascinated by my mother's ability to do so much. Grandma always said she didn't like to work - only play ball, but Mr. Lyle gave her a lot to do at his store.

Mr. Lyle was a prominent and well-respected businessman in the colored community of the sub-division and in Lockland where he served on the Board of the Y.M.C.A. As children, my mother and other relatives played and attended dances at the Y.

Mr. Lyle's store took up one half of the red-brick building, his residence was attached to the other half. Inside steps led from the residence to the store. He was a slightly built brown-skinned man, who was nearly bald. He wore gold-rimmed glasses and walked with a very bad limp.

His wife, whose name I can't remember, was very fair-complexioned and plump. I learned from my mother that she had graduated from college and belonged to a prominent club for colored women. She did not associate with any of the women who lived close to the store; but she did like my mother and the two of them laughed and talked together a lot when my mother was working in the store.

Like many colored men of importance, Mr. Lyle had a beautiful car which he kept looking like new. It was a large car; I think it was a Cadillac or Buick, which he drove to his meetings in Lockland or elsewhere. He took Mrs. Lyle to her women's club meetings in their car. She was dressed in her finest clothes and did not look like the same person who laughed with Mama in the store.

The Lyles had no children of their own, but had adopted a fair-skinned sickly child who they called, "Juney," short for Junior. Juney was about three years old and loved my mother. He spent most of his time following her around the store as she worked. The Lyles said that Juney acted like my mother was his mother and Mama carried him on her hip or let him follow behind her as she did her work.

Mr. Lyle's customers liked my mother, too. Everyone called her Miz Price, Ethel or Sister Price. No one called her Eckey. I did not know one person who did not like my mother. She would talk to people about being "saved" and they did not disagree with her. Not many did what she said, but they enjoyed talking with her. She listened to their problems and at times shared her own, which always ended with, "But God takes care of everything." The customers would nod their heads and leave the store with smiles on their faces.

I would have liked to have worked in the store with my mother. It seemed like such an interesting place to be with all the different people coming in buying things like canned goods, fresh vegetables and meat that Mama had cut.

I missed being able to look at books and especially work in my coloring books, or just drawing on plain pieces of paper which I always had when I lived with Grandma. The only book Mama kept in the house was her *Bible*. She studied this when she wasn't working. The only book Grandma kept in the apartment was the *Daily Word*. I think Mama had memorized the *Bible* because there didn't seem to be any situation or problem that arose, that she could not quote a verse and tell the person the Book, the chapter and verse number where it could be found in the *Bible.*

Grandma always said that my mother wasn't very smart in school, but during this time as I observed her at work, I saw that she could handle Mr. Lyle's cash register calculating the prices for the meat that she weighed on the scales, and taking in the money from customers. Mr. Lyle didn't seem to have any complaints about my mother's work. My mother had complaints about Mr. Lyle, which she told him about. She was always respectful to Mr. Lyle but that respect did not keep her from telling him the truth as she saw it. One day while I was there at the store, Mama was very upset.

"Mr. Lyle, you're chargin' much too much for the pork chops. Now these aren't the freshest any more and you should reduce the price so they can sell."

"Now Ethel, I just can't afford to do that. They'll sell eventually."

"It's not right to try sellin' bad meat."

"Well, you just wash the chops off in a little salt water and they'll be fine. Make sure you keep the doors shut tight on those refrigerated cases so things don't spoil."

"Mr. Lyle, I'm not goin' to sell bad meat and that's that!"

"Oh, Ethel, you sure are a stubborn woman. Alright then, have it your way."

After hearing this exchange, I knew that Grandma was right about one thing. She always said that my mother was hard-headed and stubborn. Mr. Lyle found that out. Mama was hard-headed and she was stubborn.

There was no doubt that Mr. and Mrs. Lyle liked my mother. She was such a good worker that he just gave in. I think that my mother's being such a pretty woman who was so kind and good with customers, also had a lot to do with her success as a grocery store clerk and neighbor.

4

One Night's Occurrence

As the eldest, the responsibility I was given for watching over the others was at times difficult. Mama was the only one who could control Sonny and Ronald. Jimmy, who bore the scars of his being scalded with hot water when he was a toddler, was a quiet more serious child. He was no trouble, but the other boys were always going places when Mama expected them to stay around the house. Responsibility became tedious. At home with Grandma and my aunts, I was always the one being taken care of. Living with my mother reversed that.

One evening Mama had gone to her prayer meeting. A group of us were playing softball in the vacant lot. In the group were Ida Lee and several girls from other streets nearby. I had to take an out-house break and asked Ida Lee if she would watch my sister, Lillian, while I was gone.

When I finished, I realized that it was getting too dark to play so I stood in front of the house and called for Ida Lee to send Lillian across the street while I waited for her. Ida Lee and several of the girls went into a huddle. They were whispering to each other but not sending Lillian to me.

"You'll have to come and get her," Ida Lee said when she got out of the huddle.

I had a sense that something was not quite right, but didn't know what. I hesitated for a minute, and then being a little suspicious, started across the street. The girls just stood looking at me. When I took Lillian's hand and turned my back to return to our house, the girls ganged up on me and started pulling my hair and beating me in the back. I was hanging on to Lillian and did not want to let go. Sonny, Ronald and Jimmy came to my aid and I was able to get away with Lillian in tow.

I don't remember if I was hurt enough to cry, but I do know that the attack really upset me. It showed me that Ida Lee was not a good friend. She had turned on me and joined the pack, if indeed she

374

hadn't been the leader. I knew it was all about "hair." My so-called pretty hair that was like my mother's had gotten me in trouble.

I watched as the girls did not disperse but simply stood there staring across the street at me. I had the idea that if I talked to Ida Lee and the girls and told them how what they had done made me feel, maybe it could all be straightened out and we could be friends.

I called across the street, "Ida Lee, can you all come over here. I have something to tell you."

After some hesitation, the girls slowly came over and stood in front of our porch.

I was not on the same level as the girls. I stood on the porch like some orator getting ready to make an important speech. I addressed Ida Lee. She was the only one I knew.

I said, "Ida Lee, I really like you and we have had so much fun together. It really hurt me that you would turn on me for no reason."

I don't remember the rest of my speech. I do remember that all of the culprits, including Ida Lee, just stood there staring up at me like I was crazy.

Later, with Lillian and my brothers, I went looking for Mama. It was very dark and we weren't sure whose house she had gone to for the prayer meeting, but one of my brothers thought she said she would be at Sister Hocker's house, so we went searching. We were scared because it was pitch black, but the smell of the pig sty in the Hocker's yard let us know that we were close.

The prayer group was meeting by lantern light and we could hear someone praying as we approached. I went up to the screen door and tapped loud enough to be heard. A gentleman came to the door.

"Can I talk to my mother, please?"

She came to the door. At first she seemed annoyed that she was being disturbed. "What are you all doin' here? You're supposed to be in bed."

When I told Mama the story she was very angry at what had happened. She excused herself from the prayer meeting and walked home with us. The next day she had a long talk with Ida Lee's mother. Ida Lee had to come to our house and apologize to me for what she and the other girls had done.

This was the only incidence of violence that I had personally experienced while living in the sub-division. Ida Lee and I, as well as a few of the other girls who had been involved, got along fine the rest of the summer.

One night when it was very dark and the lightening bugs, as we called them, were out, Ida Lee, my brothers and I got some of Mama's empty Miracle Whip jars and lids, and proceeded to gather as many bugs as we could catch as we stumbled around the open field. When we finished, Ida Lee and I sat on the steps to our house and proceeded to pinch off the part of the bug that was lit up. From these we made rings for our fingers.

5

Speaking in Tongues

As summer drew to a close and the beginning of a new school year was approaching, my mother seemed very tense. She complained that she didn't have enough money to get the four of us ready for school. Lillian was not in school yet. My mother's tension rubbed off on us and my brothers and I started getting into unnecessary squabbles. This added fuel to my mother edginess.

I began to have the same breakfast of cold cereal like Cornflakes and Puffed Rice, as the others. These were quick and easy to pour into bowls and add the milk and sugar. At times there was a race for the milk.

"Don't take all the cereal. Save some for me," Sonny told Ronald.

"I ain't takin' all the cereal! Here!" Ronald shoved the Puffed Rice at Sonny.

I grabbed the cereal box out of Sonny's hand before he could pour it into his bowl. He grabbed it back and the struggle was on.

"Give that back," Sonny said.

"I'll give it back when I'm finished," I told him.

As I poured the cereal into my bowl Sonny punched me on the arm and cereal flew out of the box and onto the table.

"See what you made me do?" I was so angry; I put the box down and punched him in the arm.

"Mama! Sweetpea punched me."

"You all stop that fightin' in there do you here?" Mama shouted from her bed where she had been sleeping.

This was becoming the morning ritual. No longer was I special. I was just one of the "young'uns" as we were called. I did not like being lumped together with my brothers who Grandma would have

377

called a bunch of wild Indians like she called me when I got out of hand. Two of my brothers, Sonny and Ronald, always seemed out of hand. Ronald would not have been had he not always followed behind Sonny. Little Jimmy was totally different, rarely going too far from home.

My stepfather's gambling increased my mother's stress and no matter how much she protested, he did not stop his habit of gambling. He continued to lose money. The closer we got to the beginning of school, the more my mother worried.

One evening after she came home from her job at Lyle's, Mama changed clothes and went to the kitchen to prepare our supper. I followed her and sat at the table to watch and just be near her. I always liked sitting at the kitchen table and watching Aunt Irene when she cooked at our apartment in Walnut Hills. Mama's kitchen was a place to have some peace away from my rambunctious siblings. It was hot and quiet in the kitchen with Mama. She began to assemble her cooking utensils, but as she went over to the stove to make the fire, she suddenly stopped what she was doing. I wondered what was happening. She closed her eyes and put her right hand in the air and let her head drop to her chest.

She did not move. She stood still for a moment and then she raised her head and started to pray. Her voice trembled and I thought she was going to cry, but she didn't. In the midst of her praying a complete change came over my mother.

She started saying, "Yes, Lord. You know, Lord. Bless Your Holy Name, Lord. My, my, my. Thank you, Jesus. Mmmmmm, yes Lord. Thank you, Jesus. Mmmmmmm."

I felt like I was in Mama's church.

My mother's face seemed to glow. With her eyes still closed, she had a smile on her face and kept her face towards the ceiling. Then my mother went into a place I had not known before because I had never seen this happen. She began to speak in a foreign language. She had not finished high school so I knew that she had not studied a language like French or German. Her hands trembled in the air above her head. Her body moved to the rhythm of her chant. I watched with the same fascination I had when I visited Mama's church and seen the ladies "shout." But this wasn't shouting. My mother spoke a new language. I sat stark still. My brothers and sister were playing on the porch and did not seem interested. I dared not move. The words of the language rolled off Mama's tongue like lyrics of a beautiful song that no one understood but her.

Her speaking in this language went on for several minutes. This concerned me.

I grew apprehensive thinking that something might be very wrong with my mother. I didn't know what to do. I continued to sit very still. Then, Mama stopped speaking the foreign language. She quieted down and finally was standing still. Her hands were no longer trembling. She took them out of the air. She stood with a calm look on her face - a look of total peace.

Then my mother quietly and without any frenzy or tension in her voice said, "Yes, Lord. Thank you, Jesus. Yes, Jesus. Thank you, Lord."

She opened her eyes and was more at peace than I had seen her in days. There was no more strain on her face or tightness in her body. There was no rushing to finish the task at hand – just a calm steady movement as she put a black iron-cast skillet on the stove, then added a pat of lard that sizzled from the heat. Last the meat she planned to cook for our supper was added. She did not talk. She just started to sing one of the songs they sang in church. She didn't stop singing until she was finished with our supper. I was entranced. I did not move for a long time. I kept thinking about what I had just witnessed. I was no longer apprehensive now that Mama had returned to herself.

Mama later explained to me that she had been "speaking in Tongues," and that only those who were "saved," who knew Jesus Christ and the Holy Ghost, could speak in Tongues.

I thought that Mama was telling me that there was a secret language that she spoke to God at certain times. The language of speaking in Tongues, I thought, meant that when a saved person is really scared and in trouble they speak in Tongues so that only God could know what they were saying and would know what was scaring them.

When I got scared of monsters, I hid under the covers and sweated. Mama spoke in Tongues and started singing. Mama was happy.

6

School Registration and A Miracle for Mama

Mr. Lyle paid my mother her wages at the end of each week. She was paid in cash but it often was not as much as she had expected. When money ran out, Mama got the food we needed from Mr. Lyle "on time." This meant that he let her have the food, the cost of which was deducted from what he would owe her in wages. The fact that she had already purchased the food, and her pay reflected that, made Mama feel that she was working for nothing. Mama said that she could never get ahead. We never went without being fed, but there was not enough for some other important things like new clothes for school.

A few weeks before school was to start Mama took me to South Woodlawn School and registered me for the Fourth Grade. The red-brick school building was very large with an open grassy area in front. Cement paths from opposite sides and the street led into the main entrance of the building. A large flagpole flying the American flag was off to the side in one of the grassy areas. It was a very pleasant looking school building. It wasn't Hoffman, but it looked fine to me. I was very anxious to get back to books and learning new things.

One Saturday night, or rather, early Sunday morning, my stepfather came home from gambling with his friends. When he got up the next morning he told Mama that he had won a lot of money. I don't know how much it was, but Mama said, "Thank you, Lord. Now I can get the children's shoes and clothes for school. Thank you, Jesus."

I remembered Mama praying and speaking in Tongues. I thought her foreign language between her and the Lord had gotten through and that her prayers had been answered when my stepfather won that money just before we were to go to school.

We were really happy. Having the money meant that Mama could take us to Sears and Roebuck's to do the shopping. This was the Sears near Grandma and Granddaddy. I secretly hoped that we would be able to see them.

Shopping at Sears with my brothers and trying to keep tabs on my sister was an ordeal. Mama was yelling at the boys the entire time.

I was so embarrassed I didn't want to be seen with them. The boys were excited about the bright lights, all the clothing and toys, but of everything they had seen, it was the escalator that most impressed them. They just kept wanting to ride up and down and do nothing else. Mama stood at the top of the escalator calling out as if she was in pain, "Sonny, Jimmy, Ronald, come on now!"

Neither the escalator nor Sears was new to me. I had been there many times with Grandma. I made it through the shopping, and our exhausted mother rushed us to the bus and the trip back. We did not stop to see Grandma and Granddaddy. I had not heard from Aunt Hookey, who always bought school clothes for me. I thought they had all forgotten me. I was devastated.

7

The South Woodlawn School Year Begins

To get to South Woodlawn School, we walked with other children to the end of Jackson Street and took a well-worn dirt path down a very steep hill that ended on the flat land of the lower-sub, and next to the school's side entrance.

At South Woodlawn School, I entered the classroom of Miss Young, a fragile looking light-complexioned lady who wore her hair straightened and slightly curled. She wore very little make-up – just a hint of lipstick. Children who had attended South Woodlawn knew of her reputation as a very stern teacher who expected much from her students. She was respected and feared.

Other members of my stepfather's family, the Prices, lived in the lower-sub-division and I met some of my older half-cousins when I entered school. Sarah and James, Jr. were two who I remembered. They were just a little older than me and I socialized with them at recess or after lunch.

On October fifth, I turned nine. I don't remember that birthday, but by then I had settled into South Woodlawn School's routine. I liked school very much and I soon learned that there were children in my class who were smarter than me in math, like Barbara Reichart and Jon Campbell had been at Hoffman. I remember having to learn times tables and how Sandford Vinegar and Theophilus Smith were the smartest in math. Aunt Hookey was not there to help me with math so I was on my own.

Boys and girls came from other than rural areas of the sub-division. Several others lived near an Episcopal Church at the far end of Matthews Drive. It was an area we passed on the sub-division bus, but never ventured to on foot. This area had small single-family brick homes where many professional colored people lived. They also had electric lights and running water. Because it was called St. Simons, I thought it was a Catholic Church. I had not heard of the Episcopal Church before living in the sub-division. I also mistook it as Catholic because its minister was called a priest. I thought only Catholics had priests.

St. Simons had a private school to which a few of the children attended, but most of the children from this "wealthier" section of the sub-division attended South Woodlawn School.

The sub-division also had a Catholic Church where only colored people attended. It was smaller than any Catholic Church I had ever seen. At home in Walnut Hills, we had a gigantic stone Catholic Church called St. Francis DeSales. Its clock that was in a huge tower sounded out the time of day, every hour, quarter and half- hour on the hour. Sometimes I wished the clock didn't tell time, because it was so loud. With the sub-division's colored, Catholic Church, one wondered if any people attended as whenever we passed on the bus, no one was ever seen, not even a priest.

Theophilus Smith was the smartest girl in our class and she came from this "wealthier" section of the sub-division. She was a quiet girl and much like my friend, Ruth Hull, whose mother and father were teachers. I think they said thatTheophilus' father was an attorney. She had an air of gentility about her.

There was something missing from the sub-division and my new school. At home and at school when I lived in Walnut Hills, World War II was ever present. My grandfather read about it in his newspaper. He listened to its progress on the radio and our school focused on War Stamps while the children drew war planes and pictures. The Nazis and the Japs were everywhere in our minds. But this was not the case in the sub-division and my new school. It was as if the war did not exist. There were no Nazis or "Krauts" as Granddaddy used to call the Germans. There were no Japs. There were no newspapers or radios around me in the sub-division. There were no movie theaters to see war pictures. World War II only existed at the Wright's Plant where people worked to make things for the war; and even that was only important because people were able to make more money for necessities.

South Woodlawn School seemed to me like a "Peace Zone." I could tell that my teacher, Miss Young, liked me. Her voice was always gentle and encouraging when she called on me in class. I wanted to do well in school. Each morning we went row by row and recited the times tables. I did fine until we got to nine times. I had not done well practicing at home. It got dark early as winter approached and doing school work by a kerosene lantern light was very difficult, especially when contending with brothers and a sister who also got in the way and were now becoming exceedingly irritating.

The day that I faltered with the nine times tables was an embarrassment. Miss Young thought I should do better and she chastised me for not knowing my numbers. I did not want that to happen again, so I did finally do better.

8

Winter Arrives

I had never in my nine years experienced a winter like this winter in the sub-division. I don't remember sledding and playing in the snow. The sub-division snow seemed menacing. My feet and hands without, at times, having galoshes and mittens, made me more aware of what snow could really be like.

Mama had to be sure there was enough coal to burn in the kitchen stove. This was the main source of heat. She was the one who went out in the cold and as she had done all the other times, she cut the kindling wood to start the fire. She had to have enough money for the coal. I don't remember how the wood for the kindling, or the coal were delivered. I only remembered the big trucks that delivered our coal and me and Granddaddy rolling it down the hill into the windows of the basement of the Helena Apartments.

Mama was the person I saw doing all the hard work inside and outside the house. I don't remember her giving us jobs to do. Because he left so early each day, my stepfather never did any of the hard chores like Mama. The fact that we children all slept together was a plus in the winter. We huddled together and our combined body heat kept us very warm.

From the time of my first summer visit, we children had always slept together. I remember how odd it seemed that Ronald had to sit up and bump his head against the back of the sofa-bed in order to put himself to sleep at night. I remember how Mama had said that he had Rickets of the Brain. As he got older, nothing changed. At night, Ronald still had to hit his head against the back of the sofa to put himself to sleep. It didn't keep any of the rest of us from going off to sleep.

I felt a warmth and tenderness towards my little brother and had so since I witnessed his head being put in a bucket of cold water as punishment. He was a cute little boy, curious and always getting into trouble. He never seemed to understand why. I felt sorry for Ronald like I felt sorry for my mother. I saw both of them as victims. There was Grandma's harshness to Mama and Mama's harshness towards Ronald. The only difference was that many times Mama could be very nice to Ronald. There was never a time when Grandma was nice to Mama.

9

An Infamous Day at School

My mother never got up with us in the mornings to get us off to school like Grandma did with me. We awakened to cold rooms and a cold cereal for breakfast. No more hot oatmeal or cream of wheat like I had been accustomed to. That would have required a lot of work laying the fire and getting it hot enough to boil water. I did not think about this. I longed for the hot cereal Grandma always prepared for me.

One morning one of the schoolmates we walked with to school knocked on our door. She missed us meeting her outside. All of us had overslept and we were going to be late for school. The schoolmate did not wait as we scurried to get ourselves dressed. I shivered in the cold kitchen as I rushed to wash my face in the shallow pan of cold water. We hurried down the path that was frozen hard from the cold and made a dash for our classrooms.

There was a bell ringing protocol at South Woodlawn very similar to Hoffman School's. Many children arrived at school early so they could play before classes began. South Woodlawn's first bell meant we had to head for our classrooms. The second bell meant the classroom door would be closed and everyone was settled in their seats prepared for roll-call.

I entered the room just after the first bell had rung. I was out of breath, hair uncombed and disheveled looking. Miss Young called me over just as I was about to sit down. When I faced her, she was very critical of my appearance. She said that I had not washed up in preparation for school.

"Lula, you have soot all over your face. Surely you don't think this an acceptable way to come to school," she said.

I could not believe what she was saying. Yes, I had hurriedly washed up in cold water, but I couldn't understand how I had gotten soot on my face. We only had one mirror at home and that was in Mama's and my stepfather's room. We could not disturb them in the morning, so I couldn't look at myself in the mirror before leaving home.

As I was standing before Miss Young, my cousin Sarah entered our classroom to see what was happening. She heard Miss Young talking about my dirty face and uncombed hair. I was horrified by what happened next.

Sarah told Miss Young, in front of my classmates, "Miss Young, she was never allowed to go to school like this when she was with her grandmother."

I felt betrayed by Sarah. I felt humiliated by Sarah and Miss Young. I went over to the window near Miss Young's desk, turned my back to everyone and with my hands covering my face, I cried for the first time since I had moved to the sub-division.

The tears flowed. My nose ran. What made it worse was that I didn't have anything to wipe my nose or the tears. What Sarah said struck at something deep inside. School had always been my safe haven from being home with Grandma. Here in the sub-division living with Mama and siblings – going to school cold, living in the cold and always in the shadow of my mother's uncertainty about everything – my life, and on this day, school had disintegrated into physical and emotional chaos. There was no safe haven, not even at school.

That moment standing by the window humiliated and feeling forsaken and truly sorry for myself, I let the tears flow to wash away the grief that I had held in for months.

Something must have struck Miss Young, too, for her voice turned gentle as she told Sarah to take me to the restroom so that I could wash my face and be ready for class. Sarah was no longer critical but very gentle with me. Through my sobs, I knew that I no longer trusted her, even though I knew that she was right. Grandma would have never allowed me to leave the house in my current condition.

The only redeeming event that day was the morning snack time. Each morning at 10 a.m., we had a windmill or ginger cookie and a carton of milk – you could choose chocolate or regular. South Woodlawn School was different from Hoffman in this regard. The snack time made up for many of us not having breakfast. This was a saving grace.

I could not shake the events of the day. It had brought me face to face - made me aware of how homesick I truly felt and how hard I had tried to forget, but really had not.

A few days later I decided to stop by Aunt Hookey's apartment in the Valley Homes. I can't remember how I learned exactly where she lived, but I knew she lived in the complex of new apartments built in barrack-style to house families and workers of Wright's, the war plant.

I did not tell Mama nor my brothers that I was going there. I just got away from my brothers after school and slipped off by myself to see my aunt. Her apartment was just a few minutes walk from school along a paved sidewalk and paved street. When I arrived, I knocked on her door. The glass top of the door was covered with a shade. No one answered. I knocked again.

I waited, and in a few minutes Aunt Hookey came to the door. She did not open it all the way. She only opened it slightly. I was so happy to see her, having not seen her in four or five months, an eternity to me.

"Hi Baby," she said smiling. "How are you?"

"Fine," I said.

I was so hoping she would ask me in. She didn't. Only a part of her face was visible as she kept her body inside and the door only open a crack, to keep out the cold air.

"We work at night, baby, and we have to sleep in the day. C.J. is asleep and we can't wake him up just yet. You'll have to come see me another time."

I could not tell or show her my disappointment. I stood outside with a smile on my face and said, "O.K."

I turned to leave knowing that my Aunt Hookey was watching me go.

Winter was passing and spring and Easter were approaching. Before Easter, Aunt Hookey came to see me. I had not seen her except for the one time when she couldn't let me in. I was wonderfully surprised. There had been no warning. She came with a large dress box in

390

hand. Inside she had brought a new plaid pinafore dress for me, a white eyelet blouse and white socks. This was to be my Easter outfit. My aunt did not bring anything for Sonny, Jimmy, Ronald or Lillian.

I was so happy to see my aunt and to have the new clothes; but again duality overshadowed the occasion – happy for me, guilty, sorry, and sad that my siblings got nothing.

10

South Woodlawn School Year Ends
I Decide to End My Year in the Sub-Division

I don't remember much about the end of the school year except that I learned that this all-colored school was a very good school. I had had one of my best teachers in Miss Young. I thought she was a cross between Miss Nose, my stern, no nonsense first grade teacher and Miss Denman, my beautiful fairy princess, kindergarten teacher at Hoffman. This cross between meant that she wasn't as stern as Miss Nose and not as pretty as Miss Denman. I loved Miss Young and I learned a lot from her. I had a good report card at the end of the fourth grade school year and was happy that school was out.

I don't know when I got the idea to make this next step, but I did not tell my mother. I didn't want her to know that I did not want to stay with her any longer. I knew if she knew what I was doing, it would upset her. I knew she would feel Grandma would blame her all over again. I know that she was happy having me with her.

I secretly took an empty Pepsi-Cola bottle to Lyle's Grocery Store when my mother wasn't there. I took the two-cents deposit that I got and bought a First Class stamp. This time, I did not buy candy.

I got paper and an envelope from somewhere and wrote a letter to my grandmother.

> *Dear Grandma*
>
> *Can I please come back home. I promise not to sass you back and I promise to do the dishes without being told.*
>
> *Please, please let me come back home.*
>
> *Sweetpea*

I put this letter in the mail and waited.

My grandmother did respond. She let me come back to my home, the Helena Apartments, the Bells and the Robinsons, Walnut

392

Hills and my beloved Hoffman School, mean old Mr. Tate, Granddaddy, his newspaper and radio, and most of all, electric lights and inside toilet.

I learned a lot. I learned that my beautiful mother was kind to her neighbors, and so many people loved her. I learned that she did not avoid her responsibilities, she worked very, very hard. I learned that she had a beautiful singing voice that was beginning to turn raspy from her loud singing and shouting during church. I learned that she may not have been smart in school, but that she had memorized every verse in the Bible and could recite any one of them at any moment, relating the verse to the immediate situation. I learned that she spoke in "tongues." I learned that she did the best she could and I learned, as I had always felt, she did not deserve to be so mistreated by my biological father Mike Martin and my grandmother.

She was harsh with her children as her mother had been harsh, and continued to be harsh, with her.

I hated it that I would also be one to hurt her by leaving, but I wanted to save myself, not so much from her, but from a few of her ways, and mainly the conditions. I wanted to return to what I knew, even though what I knew was Grandma's complaining, depression and unhappiness, and Granddaddy's fanciful promises to himself and others that he never kept.

Finally, I also learned that Grandma had been wrong about another thing. A colored school could be as good as my white school. I learned that at South Woodlawn.

I cannot remember returning home. I can't remember Mama's preparation or the ride on the rickety bus, streetcar and the Lincoln Avenue bus. I can't remember entering the Helena Apartment nor being greeted by Grandma and Granddaddy. Just as I had forgotten how I got to the sub-division when Grandma sent me away; so too have I forgotten how I returned when she said I could come back.

THE END

EPILOGUE

The writing of these autobiographical sketches, which were parts of memories from childhood, made it possible for me to see my earlier life with greater clarity and appreciation.

For many years I escaped the existential pain and the trauma I experienced seeing my beloved Uncle Bobby recovering from a partial lobotomy. I was only six years old, but was allowed to visit him on many occasions at the Longview State Mental Hospital. In doing this writing, there was no escape. I realized how deeply I was effected by this as a child. Without this writing, it would have remained hidden from me.

In the examination that came I could see the care that I had been given. I learned to be grateful. No matter when, in one's life, we are able to learn gratitude, it is never too late to say, "Thank You."

At many speaking engagements, I have encouraged people to write their own stories. As difficult as it may be or as unworthy as one may think, the writer, as I did in my case, will always be rewarded with a gift that would have remained unopened had the effort not been made, the path not taken.

I cannot tell others what their gift will be. I know that mine was grace.

To achieve a state of grace, I had to work through many old hurts in order to find the love and care that existed in my growing years. It is never too late to grasp a sense of humility. What I discovered was not what I thought I would find when I began this work.

As I was writing one night twenty-eight years ago, I had a dream. I was standing before the house of a friend whose name was Grace. There were no door knobs or bells to ring. There was no way for me to get in.

As I stood there, a voice said, "To enter the House of Grace, you first must rub the symbol above the door." I looked up and saw the symbol. It was an "A" with an "O" connected to it in the lower right corner. It was the symbol for Alpha and Omega, the beginning and the end—the symbol of wholeness.

I rubbed the symbol. The door opened. Inside Grace's house was a beauty and stillness I had never seen or felt before. There were wonderful paintings and other works of art. There was no one there but me.

I interpreted this dream to mean that in order to discover what is truly inside yourself, you have to go inward alone. I found beautiful creations and peace existing within me, where before, from the outside, I thought was only chaos, uncertainty, and insecurity. In doing this Creative Writing, I found the essence of Amazing Grace.

ABOUT THE AUTHOR

Lula Cooper was born in Cincinnati, Ohio on October 5, 1933. She attended Cincinnati and Lockland, Ohio Public Schools.

Lula was given a scholarship to Knoxville College, a Presbyterian Mission School, in Knoxville, Tennessee where she was on the Dean's List for the three years she was in attendance. As a member of the College Choir, Chorus and touring Octet, she travelled west giving concerts to raise money for the college in the spring and summer of 1954.

Lula left college to marry John R. (Dick) Cooper, a graduate of Yale University who received his Ph.D. in Organic Chemistry from the University of Cincinnati. She worked as a secretary at the Wyoming Y.M.C.A. where she organized and supervised programs for teenage girls while he completed his degree.

The Coopers had their first child, Alicia, in 1956 and moved to Wilmington, Delaware where her husband was hired, as one of the first two African-American Ph. D. chemists, by the DuPont Company. President Eisenhower's Executive Order to hire African-Americans with technical backgrounds or lose their government contracts made this job opening possible.

With the lack of housing and public accommodation in Delaware, the Civil Rights Movement of the 1960's dominated the Coopers' lives, and in November of 1963, with three girls, Alicia, Ellen, Lynn and a baby boy, John, Jr., Lula's work with local Civil Rights leaders led to the passage of a State Public Accommodations Bill. Dick's efforts, in addition to his work with DuPont, led to the integration of housing under his chairmanship of the Fair Housing Council and Secretary-Treasurer of the Runnymede Corporation. Runnymede built the first integrated housing development in Delaware.

Lula became the first African-American woman appointed to the State Board of Education. Other gubernatorial appointments were to the State Civil Rights Commission and State Day Care Advisory Board. In her professional life, she was the first African-American Center Director of the Wilmington Y.W.C.A. when the Y.W.C.A. integrated its inner city branches, and directed the largest Head Start/Day

Care Program in New Castle County and was the Center Director for the first grass-roots day care program, West Center City Day Care, in inner-city Wilmington.

Throughout her life, Lula has been involved in Art and Writing. Her oil paintings were exhibited throughout Wilmington along with her pottery and later, wire and beaded jewelry shown at the Susan Isaacs Gallery in Wilmington. A local art teacher and newspaper journalist, in an article about Lula, called her a "Renaissance Woman." Lula published, and read publicly, a book of poetry, <u>A Murmur of Essence</u>. Her poetry was included in the Delaware First State Poetry Anthology.

Because of her work in the Arts, Lula was appointed, by President Richard Nixon, to become one of two Delaware representatives to the John F. Kennedy Center for the Performing Arts Advisory Committee in Washington, D. C. in 1971.

Lula considers her most prized award to be a Wilmington, Delaware group's presentation, to her, of The Martin Luther King Award for Community Service.

Lula resides in Prescott, Arizona with her husband John "Dick" Cooper where the two have continued work for the public good. Lula's artistic endeavors in jewelry and children's creations continue.

THE AUTHOR 2009

Lula Cooper

THE AUTHOR AT THE WHITE HOUSE 1971 REPRESENTING DELAWARE ON THE JOHN F. KENNEDY ADVISORY COMMITTEE

L to R: Charles Parks, First Lady Patricia Nixon, Lula P. Cooper